THE CAREER PRESCRIPTION

HOW TO STOP SABOTAGING YOUR CAREER AND PUT IT ON A WINNING TRACK

JILL A. SEARING
ANNE B. LOVETT, Ed.D.

PRENTICE HALL
Englewood Cliffs, New Jersey 07632

Prentice-Hall International (UK) Limited, *London*
Prentice-Hall of Australia Pty. Limited, *Sydney*
Prentice-Hall Canada, Inc., *Toronto*
Prentice-Hall Hispanoamericana, S.A., *Mexico*
Prentice-Hall of India Private Limited, *New Delhi*
Prentice-Hall of Japan, Inc., *Tokyo*
Simon & Schuster Asia Pte. Ltd., *Singapore*
Editora Prentice-Hall do Brasil, Ltda., *Rio de Janeiro*

© 1995
Jill A. Searing
Anne B. Lovett

10 9 8 7 6 5 4 3 2 1

Library of Congress Cataloging-in-Publication Data

Searing, Jill A.
  The career prescription : how to stop sabotaging your career and
put it on a winning track / Jill A. Searing and Anne B. Lovett.
    p.   cm.
  Includes index.

  ISBN 0-13-303322-8
  1. Vocational guidance.   2. Career development.   3. Managing your
boss.   I. Lovett, Anne B.   II.   Title.
HF5381.S448   1995
650.1—dc20   94-41289
                                                                  CIP

ISBN 0-13-303322-8

PRENTICE HALL
Career & Personal Development
Englewood Cliffs, NJ 07632

Simon & Schuster, A Paramount Communications Company

Printed in the United States of America

ACKNOWLEDGMENTS

We knew we were lucky to get Ellen Schneid Coleman as our editor. Just how fortunate we were was even more fully realized as we moved into the final phase of the manuscript, when we could only see the mountains which seemed unpassable. Then Ellen would appear. Her continual encouragement, enthusiasm, and direction brought us forward. The mountains did not go away, but Ellen guided us through the passes and we were able to make our thoughts and concepts a reality.

The other travelling companion, with us from the beginning, is Beth Searing, who typed the manuscript. Beth lived and typed her way through every revision, wacky ideas and all, with patience and professionalism. We haunted her weekends, her evenings, and even her precious vacation time. She stayed with us every step of the way.

Throughout the entire project, others came forward to listen to our ideas and provide their own, to read the early manuscripts and, most importantly, to urge us on. Most of them would discount their role, but friendship and support have a cumulative effect. Their presence and help was inspirational to us. This list includes our professional colleagues, our friends and, of course, our families. We are grateful to them all.

Last, we want to acknowledge that anonymous group of people who shared their stories with us. It was their lives that inspired this book and it is to them that this book is dedicated.

CONTENTS

Chapter Two   Playing the Game: Keeping Your Career on Course   37

Chapter Three   Healing Careers in Crisis: What to Do If Your Career Goes Off Course   85

Chapter Four   Managing Your Boss: A Delicate Balance   127

Chapter Five   Avoiding the Land Mines: The Traps That Can Explode Your Career   167

Chapter Six Corporate Street Smarts: How to Get Where You Want to Go 201

Chapter Seven Master Your Career: How to Make the Prescription Work for You 241

Appendix 251

Index 259

INTRODUCTION

Two people are competing in a boat race. Both have first-class boats to skipper, but one knows only the basics of sailing while the other is a master sailor, with vast experience in all types of weather conditions and competitive situations. Who will win? It is the master sailor, of course, who will take the race. The master has finely honed skills. He knows how to adjust his sails to take advantage of the changing winds, he has encountered and conquered crises, and he knows the tactics of the race. This level of skill not only positions the master sailor to be part of a world-class team, but even to lead that team to victory.

When it comes to your career, *you* need to be the one with master skills. These skills are the ones that will ensure your survival and success in today's competitive, hard-driving business climate. These are the skills of smart players in the corporations who understand how organizations work and who use that knowledge to their advantage. These are the skills of that practiced, savvy group of players who are given increasing levels of responsibility and challenge and who get ahead. These are the types of skills you will learn from this book.

At the most basic levels, career success is the result of applying your talent, skills, personality, and drive to making your organization successful. But there are other factors at work that can influence your career progress. Once you understand these factors and how they play out in organizations, you will have the corporate savvy needed to compete today. Your entry skills are like those of the sailor with only the basic skills, the ones that help them push off the dock and move out into the water. But if you want to win the race, to be the one who stands out ahead of the rest of the pack, you need to understand and master the dynamics and nuances of the competitive arena.

This book is designed to help you learn what types of behaviors can maximize your career potential. It is based on material from our own experiences and from the experiences of other professionals in our field. We talked to employees who have been through the fire and to managers who had to confront these issues firsthand. These discussions included people from all types of companies—large and small, successful and struggling. We talked to people in different industries, from profit and non-profit environments, and from various professions and levels within their organizations.

From our discussions, we identified those issues that could make or break careers. We determined what behaviors would help people get ahead and which ones could derail them. We learned that certain self-sabotaging behaviors could result in people being pigeonholed, plateaued, or put on a shelf in some obscure corner of the corporation. In some cases, the sabotage was so glaring and destructive that it resulted in people being offered outplacement, better known as going gently into the unemployment line. We also observed that many of the people were repeat offenders; they did not appear to learn from their own mistakes. For them, the result was often career destruction—a kind of corporate kamikaze.

We have focused on the self-sabotaging behaviors because those are the behaviors that people can change. In these turbulent times, there are many factors affecting our lives that we cannot control— the globalization of business, the competition from abroad, our own unpredictable U.S. economy, and the struggle to develop the kind of modern management practices and processes demanded by the technological and economic revolution.

If that is not enough, there is the greater competition within our workplaces for an even smaller number of jobs. It is already tough outside; it is getting even tougher inside. You need every advantage you can beg or borrow if you are to survive and succeed. You need to know which behaviors have the potential to bring you down and which ones can save you. You need to know how to extricate yourself from difficult situations. You need master skills. This book will teach you those skills and give you that critical edge.

HOW TO USE *THE CAREER PRESCRIPTION*

We have written this book to help you achieve career success. The definition of "career success" needs to be your own: what do you really want from your career? How high do you want to go? Are you content to develop at your current level or do you want to reach the top? You make that decision. Regardless of your aspirations, however, this book will help you develop the kind of savvy that will help you reach your goal.

This book will also help you as you move through the different stages of your career. Your skill needs will vary as you take on new roles, move into new organizations, or as your company changes around you. This year, you may be starting out in a new job; six months from now, you may get a new boss whose style perplexes and frustrates you. Next year, your issues may be completely different. This is a handbook that should sit on your desk or at your bedside to consult as you negotiate your way though the whitewater that characterizes the environment of today's organizations.

You can use *The Career Prescription* to examine your career as a whole or to deal with a specific problem. To fully understand the types of behaviors that will lead to success or failure, read the book through in its entirety. As you do this, keep track of which chapters hit you—the Aha! that signals you have stumbled into an area that describes your own issues. Imagine yourself in the situations we have described. Have you been in a similar circumstance? How did you—or would you—respond? Do any of your behaviors or attitudes mirror those in the story? What would your boss say about you in a parallel scenario? By identifying what you need to learn, you are on the way to developing a plan to make yourself a master player.

Each chapter is comprised of stories that describe problems people encounter at work. Next is a diagnosis of the key factors and areas for consideration. These include critical points that you need to understand about implications for now and later, about the way that managers may think or respond, and the dynamics of each scenario. The Rx that follows will help you undertake ways to address each issue, to redefine it, or to take other actions to solve the problem.

Throughout *The Career Prescription*, you will find charts and quizzes to help you self-diagnose. These will help you analyze your current situation, the environment you work in (or should), and your own developmental needs. Keep a pen and paper handy as you read this book so that you can put together a list of the key areas you want to address. Then use the last chapter, Master Your Career, to help you assess yourself and plan your strategy for developing your skills. You may need only slight adjustments in your attitude, demeanor, or approach. Or you may require a long-term plan for developing your organizational savvy. Either way, you will now have the keys to your future. You will be able to meet the challenges of the workplace of the '90s. You will become a master at the skills for success.

NOTE FROM THE AUTHORS

These are stories that represent real issues, but not real people. To protect the privacy of the people whose experiences these stories represent, we have depicted the key dynamics of the issues, but developed fictional stories around them.

Chapter 1 GETTING YOUR TICKET PUNCHED

Starting Off Right

SCOPING OUT THE ENVIRONMENT:
What to Look for Before You Take the Job

Walking into a new workplace is like walking into a stranger's house. You don't know its occupants, you don't know how they live or relate to one another, you don't know how they operate or what's important to them. This was Tracey's situation when she changed jobs.

For the past five years, Tracey has been a supervisor in a small firm. During that time, she has been relatively happy with her job, especially in the first three years. But now there are problems. Business is not good, the management team doesn't seem to be able to develop a strategy for increasing sales, and the company has begun to lay off selected people. Although Tracey has survived the first wave of pink slips, she has begun to look actively outside the company for other employment opportunities. Her first interviews did not pan out, so she was thrilled when an executive recruiter helped her line up an interview for what sounded like a dream job in a dream company. It was for a midlevel managerial position in a division of a conglomerate with great diversity of enterprises and a good financial history. She would have a staff of five people and would be reporting to a director. The executive recruiter told her that a personnel representative would meet her at nine o'clock on the day of the interviews, which would culminate in a two-hour session with the department director.

Tracey was a bit surprised when she arrived for the interviews. Outside, the building was quite modern and well kept. The grounds were landscaped and the front entrance was banked with newly planted spring flowers. Inside, however, was a different scene. Plastic chairs lined the wall of the waiting area and the floor was covered with indoor/outdoor carpeting. The receptionist sat behind a smudged glass window, her desk piled high with memos and papers. The personnel rep met her as planned, and he seemed friendly enough. In fact, Tracey was a bit disarmed by his demeanor. He was very casually dressed and very informal. He invited her into his office, which was furnished as shabbily as the lobby. Like the receptionist's work area, his office was filled with boxes, his desk piled high with manila folders and thick reports. The desk itself was banged-up metal—his chair looked as if it had been around the world and back.

He told Tracey that this was a great opportunity for her—the previous manager had been promoted and now headed a different unit in the corporation, the staff was hard working, and the department was well considered. Tracey liked what she heard.

Because she had to wait to see the department director, the personnel rep suggested they get a cup of coffee in the cafeteria while waiting. As she sipped her coffee, Tracey observed the people who were obviously on their morning break and talking together. They seemed casual and relaxed, and the cafeteria emptied out gradually. Shortly thereafter, the director, Joe, came to get her for the interview.

Tracey liked Joe right away—he seemed open and spoke bluntly about the management challenges in the unit as well as about some of the people problems. To Tracey, his openness in sharing information with her made her feel as if she had finally made it to a higher level in the corporate hierarchy. She felt she had good experience as a supervisor and could handle the problems with the staff.

Moreover, the work was in an area about which she felt very confident.

She did feel a nagging concern, however, and tried to put her finger on it. This office environment was very different from what she was used to. In spite of the financial troubles, the office she was presently working in was well equipped and aesthetically appealing. Although the people in her company were friendly, they were formal in how they dressed and in the way they talked to one another. "Was that it?" she kept asking herself. Or was there something else? And what did it mean?

Although she had misgivings about the prospective job and its culture, she was even more nervous about what was going to happen to her if she stayed with her current company. So, when the offer came through for the managerial spot (the money wasn't quite what she wanted, but . . .), she took the job. It held the promise of great things to come.

Two months into the new company, Tracey knew unequivocally she had made a big mistake. The level of computer automation in the new company was on a par with the condition of the furniture in the lobby. The "people problems" with staff were critical: three of the five had serious technical performance issues, and the other two had attitudes that bordered on belligerent insubordination. Her director was still a great guy, but she never saw him—he was working on an assignment out of state and was sorry, yes, but Tracey would have to find the way herself in these difficult days.

It also bothered her that the office culture was not at all like the more formal environment she was used to. In this company, the employees complained about everything and everyone. People yelled at each other in meetings using language she found distasteful. Work standards were sloppy and deadlines were routinely ignored. She began to feel that she had taken a big step backward and began to hate where she now worked—(in her words) "in a dump."

Luck was with Tracey, though. Another company she had interviewed with earlier had come back to her about a job opening. She discussed very frankly with them why she would leave this new job after only a short time. They thought her reasons credible; they wanted her skills, and so she made the move, but only after a much more scrupulous analysis of this company's environment.

In the first months in her new job, she reveled every night that she had been able to get out of the "hell hole" so quickly.

Diagnosis _____

Tracey jumped too soon in taking a job with the new company. She ignored telltale (and, in this case, "warning") signs of its culture. She knew that "something didn't quite fit," but she didn't allow herself to examine her own feelings.

The ability to "scope out" a new environment is critical to your success in a company.

You may think that career success depends primarily on the correct application of your technical skills and knowledge. In reality, career success is also directly related to your ability to fit into an organization. Of course, if you can't do the job (performance reasons), you'll never make it. But many people's careers today are stymied or derailed because of their inability to fit with the culture and style of their company. That's why it is critical to your success that you evaluate the culture and environment and decide if it's a match with you—your likes, your preferences, and so on.

Once you've been hired, you must continually read the signs in your organization and adapt yourself to fitting in. Without this ability both to read the signals ahead of time and to assimilate yourself into the culture, your career options and satisfaction in any organization will be limited. Company cultures vary greatly, and some are more successful than others. But, for you, the secret is to find a compatible culture—one where you feel comfortable and fit in.

Rx _____

The best time to find out about a company culture is *before* you accept a job. Here's how:

While Visiting the Company: Take careful notes of the interactions among employees:

> As you sit in the reception area, observe the employees coming and going into the building; check out their attitudes and personal conversations. Look at how they dress and at how they treat the receptionist or security guards.
>
> See how the receptionist treats employees versus how he/she treats visitors.
>
> Observe employees at all levels—the cafeteria staff, maintenance, administrative, executive personnel. How energized are they? With

whom do they interact? How guarded are they? Do people look at you or avoid you? Are they gathering in some friendly clusters, or do they tend to ignore one another? Do the people look harried and worried, or do they seem relaxed and confident?

Remember, the people who are interviewing you or speaking with you formally during interviews are on their good behavior, even as you are. Watching the informal behavior will give you clues as to what the real world of this company is all about.

Look around at the physical environment. Is it stiff and cold? What type of furniture is in the reception room? Are there awards on the wall? Does the company display its products or is it hard to figure out what the company does? Does the reception area impress you? How are the work areas arranged? Are they large open places where employees can mingle easily, or are they tight little cubicles that inhibit communications? Are the executive perks highly visible? Are support people housed in decent, well-equipped spaces or as a second-class-citizen types of arrangements?

During Interviews: Ask "culture" questions of the people you meet. If you are able to ask the same questions of people, look for trends in the responses. For example,

How long have you been here? (This enables you to determine rates of turnover.) What do you like best and least about the company?

How would you describe the culture of the company? What is it like to work here?

What does it take to get ahead here? (This enables you to determine the role of politics in determining promotions.)

What type, if any, of team projects would I be working on? (Is this a culture of individuals or do people work together on things?)

Do Your Homework: Read everything you can that has been written about the company in business publications *(Business Week, Fortune,* etc.).

Ask questions of (past or present) employees of the company. You may need to temper your assessment of their comments, that is, "consider the source"—but, by going beyond the public relations puffery and finding out the inside story from others, you can develop a more accurate picture of what the company is *really* like. If you know or used an executive search firm or employment agency, ask them what they see as the company's strengths and weaknesses.

Know Yourself: Generally, the larger the organization, the more structured and hierarchical it will be. Smaller companies can often be poised for quicker action through less formality and policies (note, however, that family-run companies are often extremely paternalistic and autocratic). You can evaluate the possibilities about how you'll fit in by looking at the organization structure (how many levels between you and the top) and asking questions about the approval cycle (how many layers and how long) and characteristics of successful people ("she is a real team player," "he's decisive, then acts," etc.).

There are different sets of rewards and payoffs for all different types of organizations. A big fish in a small pond or a small fish in a big pond may earn different levels of compensation, have more or fewer opportunities for advancement, and have varying degrees of "job security." Given today's vulnerable economic environment, you must assess trade-offs. But do be true to yourself—you'll be most successful and happy in a company that fits with you.

ADAPTING TO THE CULTURE ONCE YOU'VE ARRIVED

Now that you're on board, you need to continually read the new environment. There are cues from the moment you go into the company, the department, or your specific work unit. You have to be aware of everything. Observe how people interact with each other, their bosses, the janitor. Ask questions to help you determine what kind of place it is. Do people stay alone in their offices or go out for drinks together after work? How does the department work? Is it memo-crazy or are informal notes de rigueur? Are people using electronic mail in lieu of face-to-face discussions? Are there team projects, or task forces, or do staff specialists dictate the processes? Is there a baseball team? bowling? Who participates?

Look at bulletin boards, read the company newsletter, ask questions of peers and people who have worked there in the past—what's important to be successful in your department? Then once you've been in the department, test your assumptions.

As a newcomer who doesn't yet understand how the system works, even seemingly minor incidents can trip you up. "Jennifer Tucker, I'd like to introduce Mark Smith, the General Manager." After the introduction, in an attempt to appear to be part of the team,

Jennifer responds, "Hello, Mark, it's a pleasure to meet you." The only problem is that everyone refers to old man Smith by "Mr. Smith" and Jennifer has just made a serious blunder.

John is meeting his lunch group in his new company in the cafeteria and is the first to go through the cashier line. He sees an empty table in the left corner and grabs it for the gang. As Carl, his lunch buddy, comes through the line, Carl looks over at the table and cringes because he knows the table John has chosen is the one where the senior executives always eat.

The unwritten rules run the gamut of possibilities: Who speaks first at a meeting? How much dissent and disagreement is tolerated? Who sits where at staff meetings? How early are you really supposed to leave? 5:00 P.M., 5:05 P.M., 6:30 P.M.? Many of the informal structural underpinnings are very subtle but well cast. They will vary by organization and often even within the organization. How can you learn them? By osmosis, by hooking up with "players" who can clue you in, by watching carefully, by asking questions and being aware of the company mores and operating principles that are never found in the Employee Handbook. Have your antenna up and working 24 hours a day when you enter a new environment—and learn the unwritten rules. Remember, you are the one who needs to adapt to the environment to become successful since the reverse never happens.

WHERE DO YOU FIT IN?

Different cultures value different skills, personalities, and attributes. Your career success will be greatly enhanced if you can find the organization that fits you. Here are some broad characteristics of the types of organizations that exist, which can help you assess companies and yourself. When they mesh—that is, fit—your success and theirs will be greatly enhanced.

Pick Your Poison: Types of Corporate Cultures

Take No Prisoners Culture

This is a *high-risk* culture that provides *high payoffs* quickly. The games can be rough, but very rewarding.

Characteristics

This is a young organization.
The focus is on speed, not endurance.
Not taking an action can be as critical as taking action.
Financial rewards come early.
The pressure is intense; the pace is frenetic.
Burnout often occurs before middle age.
You'll need a tough attitude to live with high risk.
Competition exists within the company as well as externally.
Little or no value is placed on long-term employment or loyalty.
There is little or no cooperation among colleagues.
Turnover is high.

Examples: Wall Street trading firms, companies in the TV industry, advertising, movie production industries.

Best Fit for Individuals Who: Like immediate feedback, have high tolerance for risk, and are highly individualistic, entrepreneurial, and aggressive.

Unenlightened Monarchy Cultures

Characterized by private ownership or domination by powerful boss and a hand-picked board of directors who will do as they are told (or promise to sleep through board meetings), this culture is *high risk* for individual employees. There is *quick feedback* if the king gets cross, but financial rewards are high, and career opportunities are good to excellent.

Characteristics

Fear is rampant.
Expediency is more valued than observing rules and principles.
Outstanding performance is outstandingly rewarded.
Being the boss's favorite is good; being the boss's relative is better.
Business strategies can be wildly off target or divinely correct.
Arrogance and ignorance are the norm.
Personnel policies are exercised capriciously.
Compensation is linked directly to bottom-line results (when it's good, it's very good; when it's bad, it borders on cruel and unusual punishment).
Lots of energy is spent on jockeying for king's attention.

Disproportionate amounts of time are spent on deciphering the king's latest word, glance, action, that is, "what kind of a mood is he in this morning."

Examples: Family-owned businesses, communications conglomerates.

Best Fit for Individuals Who: Are comfortable taking orders, skilled in developing relationships with powerful people, motivated by high stakes and high rewards, and comfortable in many roles, ranging from "errand boy" to sitting very near the throne.

Father Knows Best and Father's Very Rich Culture

This culture is characterized by big-stake decisions, when years may pass before the company knows which decisions have paid off This is a *high-risk/slow-feedback* environment.

Characteristics

Up-front investments are enormous, with high stakes and long-term feedback.
Progress is slow—months and years elapse.
Primary ritual *is* the business meeting.
Decisions come from the top (once all the inputs are in).
Focus is on the future and the importance of investing in it.
Employees are in for the long term.
There is a deep respect for authority and technical competence.
Employees are highly dependent on one another and share hard-won knowledge.
People treat one another with courtesy; politeness and civility mark relationships.
Employees generate a lot of paperwork.

Examples: Oil, drug, chemical industries, and telecommunications and computer firms.

Best Fit for Individuals Who: Have patience, intelligence, like ritual, are team oriented, can accept administration and bureaucracy.

Saturday Night Live Culture

Fun and action are the rule. Employees take *few risks* and have *quick feedback.*

Characteristics

Hyperactivity is abundant.

Persistence is valued and pays off.

System is full of checks and balances to keep the risk factor low (and, therefore, manageable).

Company demands a high level of activity and initiative.

Employees work as a team—there are few stars.

Company revels in contests, meetings, promotions, conventions.

Employees get a lot of work done and get quick tangible feedback on their efforts.

Volume can displace quality in rush to sell more and more product/ services.

Company can get fooled by today's successes and not develop strategy for the lean times.

Employees more committed to "the action" than to the company.

Culture tends to attract young people who want to prove their worth.

Examples: Food and cosmetic industries, some start-up computer firms, most retail operations.

Best Fit for Individuals Who: Love the team environment, are motivated by "fun" and action, have short attention spans, like immediate feedback, like variety and need excitement to make them enjoy work.

Ticky-Tacky Little Boxes Culture

In this world of *little or no feedback,* employees find it hard to measure what they do; instead they concentrate on how it's done.

Employees are *not expected to take risks* and are rarely evaluated on or rewarded for going out on a limb. Greatest danger lies in the drift toward bureaucracy.

Characteristics

No one action or decision will make or break the company or anyone in it.

Employees rarely get any feedback on how and if they are contributing to the organization.

Memos and reports disappear into a void.

Finger-pointing rages erupt when things go wrong.

Numerous task forces write voluminous reports that get carefully filed, never to be read, let alone acted upon.

Employees tend to develop a "cover your behind" mentality.

How neatly and completely employees do things is often more important than what they do.

Organization is highly susceptible to political whim.

Hierarchies are tightly organized.

Examples: Insurance industries, government, utilities

Best Fit for Individuals Who: Don't need individual recognition, value stability and security, value the process of getting work done instead of the results themselves, like to play political games.

Seat-of-Your-Pants Culture

In these organizations, no one appears to know what to do, but everyone is very busy. Fighting fires replaces long-term strategy. Employees are expected to take risks and solve problems. Greatest danger is that no one appears to be planning for the future—all energy is expended on crisis of the day.

Characteristics

Everyone is empowered to do everything, but no one is responsible for anything.

Competition lurks around every corner; everyone reacts to changes the competitor makes.

Short-term decision mentality results in short-term effects.

Rewards go to employees who "saved the company."

There is lots of activity, but results may not show.

Profit margins are low.

Employees work hard and play hard.

Rapid changes occur frequently to adjust to external activities.

Examples: Often small companies, computer/telecommunications environments, start-up organizations.

Best Fit for Individuals Who: Love activity, can tolerate chronic change, are tactical, enjoy variety, and are able to make quick decisions without a lot of information.

PASSING THE PRESSURE TEST:
The Interview

Even though the interview process appears somewhat like a medieval torture device dreamed up by dedicated sadists, the truth of the matter is that nearly everyone must go through the interview process to nail the new job. Sometimes, employees even have to be interviewed to be considered for a position in another part of the company. No matter how great you feel about yourself, you are still bound to be nervous or apprehensive about the process. For some, the interview process can be so unnerving that candidates lose out to someone else who may be no more—or even less—qualified, but who is more skilled at the interview.

Consider Sarah's interviews for a slot in the relocation department of a large company. Sarah had a background in real estate and banking that positioned her well for helping transferred employees handle their problems related to housing and mortgages. But she also knew that the company was interviewing at least three other people for the same position.

The first interview went like clockwork. She was asked fairly standard questions and given a chance to talk about her experiences. She also made it through the second round, which included talking with people with whom she would be working. However, this company had a long tradition of making all new employees go through what they proudly called the stress test. The personnel rep told Sarah that this was her last hurdle and that she should be prepared for some rough questions. Sarah was told to expect to speak with people outside the department as well as some from within whose task it was to see how she did under pressure. Since there was no way to prepare for this session, the personnel rep told Sarah to relax and "just be yourself."

Sarah had heard from someone who worked for the company that this phase of the interview process was the most difficult thing he had ever experienced in his life. So the advice to "relax and be yourself" did not give Sarah a lot of comfort as she waited to be interviewed.

However, she stayed cool. When she walked into the room, she noted that she knew two of the people from the earlier interview. That gave her some hope that there would be some mercy on their part since they had both indicated that they liked what they heard when they met with her earlier.

After introductions, Sarah was asked to go over her background and experience. She told her story quickly, emphasizing how her experience matched the company's needs. No one challenged her, so Sarah began to feel more confident about her ability to carry it all off. Then suddenly it started as if from a script. "Tell us what you know about our company in terms of its strengths and weaknesses." Sarah stopped. While she had done her homework, it was not that detailed. She looked at the person who asked the question for a long moment, then she answered. "I chose this company for its long history in this community as a good place to work. Furthermore, the service it provides makes it an outstanding organization. Additionally, if the yearly report is to believed, it's doing very well financially. As for its weak·nesses, I would expect it to have the same type of problems many organizations do when they are working hard at changing how they work while trying to increase market share." Dead silence.

People smiled and another person popped a question. This time it had to do with a hypothetical situation involving an irate employee and her role as the supervisor. Again, Sarah carried the day. Next she was challenged to explain how she, a newcomer, could hit the deck running, given the fact that she didn't have any experience actually working in relocation. Sarah didn't like the belligerent tone of the inquisitor's voice, but she remained composed. She drew on her knowledge of the problems of people who had been transferred and suggested the areas to which she would be paying special attention as a result of those types of predictable problems. Again, a long silence. Then she was asked to leave the room to prepare for a presentation. The personnel rep handed her a written assignment that asked her to prepare a presentation for senior management on a radical policy change in the relocation department. Sarah shook her head. This one looked impossible. What did she know about policy? Who were "senior management"? What were the other issues that were sure to be impacting on this policy that she was not aware of?

Finally, Sarah decided that this exercise was designed to see if she was willing to go out on a limb, make a fool of herself, and get shot down by the stress team. She felt angry, but that anger quickly turned to resolve. She thought, "I'm not going to lose out on this job because I can't play the fool, if that's what this is about." She quickly outlined her case and was ready 10 minutes later when they asked her to come back into the room. Sarah's attitude was: if you are going to make a mistake, make it a big one. At least she would demonstrate that she could handle the stress. And so she did. Her presentation was so outlandish that the group started to laugh. Sarah stayed in role and even played around with the group trying to get them to respond to her wild suggestions. Finally, the personnel rep smiled and said, "All right, Sarah, you're done. We'll get back to you tomorrow on our decision." The next day she got the news— she had the job.

DIAGNOSIS

Sarah had read the situation correctly. The point of the stress interview wasn't to find out what she knew. The group wanted to know how she behaved under stress. Sarah's response was very appropriate. She didn't get defensive or allow the group to unnerve her so that she couldn't think. Instead she played the game, which, of course, won the day and the job.

Rx

Interviews make all of us sweat a little; no one really enjoys them. But they are the standard process for selection so it behooves you to be prepared. Many books are available on how to interview. If you are feeling unsure about your interview skills, learn as much as you can about how to interview. For starters, if interviews make you nervous, make certain you know how you behave when you are nervous (e.g., rubbing your hands together or clearing your throat frequently). During the interview, make certain you avoid those mannerisms. Try instead to concentrate on getting to know the interviewer and the company in order to think about how you might make a contribution to this organization. You will find that if you concentrate on understanding the company's needs instead of focusing on making a "good impression," you will kill two birds with one stone. You'll impress the interviewer and you'll forget about being nervous.

One last word. If you are feeling desperate about getting this job, you are in the wrong frame of mind to carry off a good interview. Before the interview, figure out how you can survive if you don't get the job for which you are interviewing. Then move in and give it your best shot. If it works, great. If it doesn't, you know you will still survive. The main thing is to remain poised and focused.

As for stress interviews, remember that the game is about handling pressure. So focus on playing and play it for all you're worth.

WHAT TO DO WHEN THE TEAM YOU'VE JOINED DOESN'T WANT A NEW PLAYER

When Marlene was offered the job of developing training materials for a small consulting firm, she was ecstatic. It was exactly the type of work she wanted to get into. The position even included producing video tapes—Marlene would write the scripts, help select the cast, and edit the tapes.

Marlene knew she had a lot to learn about the firm's methodology and philosophy if she was to do the job successfully, but she hoped the rest of the development team would help her get up to speed.

Such was not to be. What Marlene didn't know was that she had joined a very troubled company. The employees in the firm had gone without a raise for the past year. They deeply resented the boss spending money on a new salaried person when they were not being given the raises they had been promised. What Marlene also didn't know was that the company was limping along payroll to payroll. (She was hired because they needed to get the product to market quickly and improve their cash flow.) The boss was spread too thin to stay on top of the day-to-day decision making. Everyone needed his time and his input. As a result, morale was low and employees were becoming increasingly disenchanted with the company.

Enter Marlene on her first day of work. The boss came in long enough to introduce her to the rest of the staff. However, he was the only one who smiled, let alone talked to her. The office administrator looked at Marlene and said "welcome aboard" in a tone that meant "get lost." The others politely acknowledged her and turned away. Marlene was at a loss. Why weren't people welcoming the new recruit? What was going on here?

The boss drew her aside and said that there had been a little upset in the office and that for the time being it would be better if she worked in one of the offices down the hall rather than with the development team. He gave her some material to study, told her to take a few days to get acquainted with the programs, and said that he would check in a few days. He told her she would start working when she had digested the reading materials.

So there Marlene sat, alone, reading background papers in a back office. No one talked to her, the boss was on an extended business trip, and she felt totally isolated and useless. This went on for three weeks. Finally, one of the consultants who did contract work for the company befriended her. He explained why the staff was so angry and what her hiring meant to them. He described the stress the staff was under because of the financial difficulties and an absentee boss. Finally, Marlene understood what was going on and why she had been ostracized.

Marlene's first action was to ask for a meeting with the office administrator to lay out for her what she had learned from the consultant about the effect her hiring had on the staff. Marlene expressed regret that the new position appeared to be at the expense of the overworked, underpaid employees and asked the administrator what she could do that would, at least, be helpful—short of resigning from the job.

Luckily for Marlene, the office manager was sympathetic to Marlene's position. She told Marlene that the boss was erratic and difficult to work for. He was away a lot and yet wanted to make all the decisions, so the staff was frustrated on a number of levels. She told Marlene that she would be leaving as soon as she found another position. For now, she would help get Marlene office space with the development team so she wouldn't feel so isolated. Otherwise, Marlene was on her own. Relieved to have even a small bit of encouragement, Marlene was then able to use her interpersonal skills and gradually become one of the team.

DIAGNOSIS _____

The little drama could have gone a number of ways. Marlene could have joined with the boss in a "we versus they" scenario. She could have confronted the rest of the staff and demanded an explanation. Or she could take a wait-and-see attitude. In this situation, the wait and see allowed her time to figure out what was going on before she did anything rash. It wasn't that the employees were a nasty group out to get Marlene; it's just that her hiring represented the last straw for a group of people who were deeply frustrated in their jobs. Best of all, she did not take the cold shoulder treatment personally because she knew there could be nothing she had done to create these reactions since she had never worked there.

Rx

You never know what you will confront when you start a new job. In this case, Marlene was ostracized for reasons outside of her control. In other circumstances, new people may be ignored or scrutinized closely and tested as part of the hazing process. Being the "new kid on the block" (regardless of how old you are) means you live through the process of being assimilated into an existing group.

Two things are going on when you start a new job. You are being closely scrutinized by the group for your technical or knowledge base. But you also are being looked at in terms of your ability to fit in. Your "worthiness," if you will, is being evaluated from the moment you walk through the door. That scrutiny is coming from all sides—your boss, your peers, your subordinates, and/or the support people.

The depth of scrutiny/initiation/hazing will vary. In part, it will depend on how common it is for new people to join the group. It will also depend on the nature of your new role—are you a potential ally? a competitor? a replacement for a favorite team member? It will also depend on the relationship that the existing group has with their supervisor. Joining a team that is working well together is one thing. Joining a group that is in the midst of civil war is quite another.

The "hazing" process can take on different meanings. Depending on the hostilities or openness of the group, the process can range from raw pain to benign indifference to sophomoric pranks.

But make no mistake—each constituent will be testing you and watching how you behave. All will analyze your behaviors to formulate an early opinion of you and your ability to fit within the group and the organization.

The hazing process can start with others testing out your opinions on things—the company, the management, how you like your new job, how your work is progressing. The best response is a pleasant neutrality. Complaints are as inappropriate as effusive bubbling about the greatness of your situation. (If, in reality, everyone thinks your boss is a complete fool and you rave about what a fabulous person he is, your credibility score will be zero.) It takes about three months in a new situation to get a legitimate feel for things. Sharing premature judgments or acting recklessly will not serve you well.

Another early common test is that of keeping confidences. It is important to be seen as someone who can show discretion. This relates to the gossip chain as well—better to hear it than start it or spread it. To be seen as an effective team player, it's important to know what's going on, but not to be considered a gossip. Keeping your ears open and mouth shut will save you a lot of grief later. Early testing will also include some scrutiny of your background—in other words, why did *you* get this job? The best advice is modesty, especially if, in the eyes of the others in your group, you are an unknown and untried entity. That is, they've been in the department, and you haven't; therefore, you will gain credibility only by demonstrating what you can do. You may refer to your prior accomplishments and work experiences, but most of the time, no one is terribly interested, so be discreet.

Another important note. Don't say "We used to do it this way" or "At XYZ, we did." That turns others off. Instead, when you've had a chance to assess how things are getting done, offer your suggestions about other ways to do them. If you need support for your idea, you can explain that you've seen it before at XYZ. This way you're seen as a more original thinker who can draw on your past but not dwell on it. And whatever you do, avoid describing your past workplace as superior to this one. (After all, if it was so good, just why did you leave?)

LIVING UP TO YOUR OWN PRESS REPORTS

A phenomenon of these past two decades is the inflation of resumes. Modest accomplishments get blown up to "saving the universe" scenarios, limited exposure to a specific area of expertise gets restated as being one of the few in the country who really knows that field "in depth."

So it was for Sam, who took his narrow experience in manufacturing as a trainer and parlayed it into a project team management position with a new company. He claimed to have expertise in reengineering. The company hired Sam believing he could lead the company's reengineering program due to start in six months.

In truth, Sam had only observed some reengineering efforts. He had also conducted some training classes in process evaluation. Using that and knowing some of the jargon, he had put together a convincing story in his interview. In his new job, though, it became evident that Sam was not equipped to handle the project. When the boss caught on, he confronted Sam. He asked him, somewhat bitterly, "Exactly what do you know about reengineering?" Sam had two choices:

he could continue to misrepresent his credentials, or he could fess up. Sam followed his first instinct, which was to lay out a string of "accomplishments" which he hoped would act as a smoke screen. But his boss saw through it and reminded him that the reengineering program was too important to the company to be led by an amateur. He suggested Sam draw up a plan that stated explicitly how he would implement the reengineering program. He asked that Sam get back to him in 48 hours.

Sam was terrified. He knew he had overstated his experience, but he thought he could wing it, especially with a boss who seemed to know even less than he did about reengineering. After a completely sleepless night, Sam realized he was unable to put together a credible project plan. He offered to resign, but added that he hoped to be a part of the reengineering effort and would do whatever he could to make it a success. His boss told him that while he appreciated his candor, he wasn't sure Sam was cut out for this company. As for the reengineering team, that would depend on who the company hired to do Sam's job and what the person thought Sam had to contribute. He offered to support Sam if he wanted to try for a position in the training department, but felt he could not commit to any more than that.

DIAGNOSIS _____

Sam succumbed to a temptation familiar to most of us—the urge to make more of his abilities and experience than is true, especially in a highly competitive job market. He also succumbed to another temptation—believing in his ability to wing it and fool other people. Both attitudes show a lack of integrity and have the potential to ruin an otherwise promising career. In most cases where you take on a new job, there will be a learning curve. You don't need to make the transition more difficult than it already is by having to live up to a false image.

Rx _____

Don't over-inflate your resume or pump up your past work experience. Naturally, you want to describe your past work experience in the most positive light possible, but there is a fine line between enhancement and blatant exaggeration. Misrepresenting your credentials crosses that line. As for fooling the boss or anyone else for that matter, remember that old saying about how you can fool some of the people all the time and all of the people some of the time, but you can't fool all of the people all of the time. And it's on that note that we rest our case.

THE SCUT WORK:
Team Player or Lackey?

You often have to do some of the scut work to prove yourself early on. In many cases, this means doing the work that no else wants to do. Consider the situation in which Jim found himself.

Jim was a new junior financial analyst in his company. He moved into a department with two other juniors, each of whom had been in his job for about nine months, and four seniors, who were very experienced. When he first started in the group, he was doing fairly simple work—tallying up numbers for the seniors, calling the divisions for information they needed, and entering data into the computer analysis system. He was also doing backup work for the other juniors.

In the early months, Jim was so excited about the new job that he didn't mind doing the grunt work, although he wasn't too happy about the work he had to do for his peers. At first he wasn't too sure if they were all dumping on him, or if this was the role he needed to fill. He finally decided to give it more time and doubled his efforts to perform high-quality work with quick turnaround time back to the requestor.

His efforts paid off. The seniors were pleased with his attitude and his timely work and, as a result, began giving him more challenging work. While the department continued to work together well, the other new hires were no longer able to pass along their grunt work to Jim because his assignments were now high priority. In time, one of the seniors moved out, another junior moved in, and took over the "scut work" role Jim had originally played. The cycle of the department continued with the newcomer playing the role of "grunt."

DIAGNOSIS

As a new person, you have to pay your dues. The payoff is that not only will you learn a lot—but people will see you as a team player, not a prima donna. There may be hidden dividends in being seen as willing to pitch in. As more senior members ask you to do some of their grunt work (everyone's always looking for someone else to do it), you may very well end up getting involved in highly challenging projects that can provide visibility and continued learning.

Rx

You want to be a good team player, but don't be a lackey. There is a fine line between being a grunt and being someone who's willing to do the scut work. The latter is someone who adds to the group's productivity, the former is a dumping ground. Continually assess the value of what you are doing, and how it is perceived. You can often tell by analyzing closely the type of work you're getting. Are you developing the background numbers which are tedious but needed, or are you standing at the copy machine for endless hours to produce the report? Either is okay within the context of your responsibilities, but if it seems out of synch with your job level, you may need to take action. If you question your contribution, or want to see where that fine line is—and if you've crossed it—have a heart-to-heart talk with your supervisor and any senior members of your group who you think can honestly assess the situation.

Another caution—some people will take advantage of a willing-to-do-anything-to-get-the-job-done type. Beware of those who will use you and give you no credit for your efforts.

One last note—whenever possible, be sure to put in extra time to work on big projects near deadlines. People will appreciate it and remember who was there until 9:30 P.M. to get the work done on time. For example, three months into his new job, Jim was called to work on a project late in the project schedule. Rather than complain, he stayed with the project team until 11:00 P.M. to finish an important aspect in time for an early morning meeting. The project manager remembered Jim and included him in his somewhat elite group

Christmas party that year—and all those invited knew Jim "had arrived" and was now part of the inner circle.

GETTING PAST THE "OH, AIN'T-IT-AWFUL"

Imagine this scene. It is during your first days in the job, and one of your coworkers offers to give you the lowdown on the place. He then proceeds to tell you the following:

> The place is really run by a mysterious group of very powerful investors.
>
> All the guys who report to the CEO are his flunkies.
>
> The president's secretary is having an affair with the CFO.
>
> The company just sold one of its divisions, and the new owners fired all the employees and brought in their own people.
>
> The level of mistrust is so high employees whisper even in the rest rooms.
>
> Your own boss, the one who hired you, is on her way out, and the president is bringing in his son to run the department.
>
> Morale stinks and cocaine is available internally.
>
> When employees are not fighting the boss, they're busy thinking up schemes to either get each other or the organization.
>
> This place would be making all kinds of money if the top brass knew what they were doing.
>
> The big boss has a "thing" about new hires—he likes to test them by seeing how much abuse they can take from him.

DIAGNOSIS

Shall we go on? If you've been around awhile, you will undoubtedly recognize a common thread in these scenarios. It's called "Oh, Ain't-It-Awful." We are the first to agree that some work situations are as destructive as they seem. People are greedy, even vicious. They can back-stab, they do lie. They make enormous mistakes that cost other people their jobs. However, some employees make a career out of "Oh, Ain't-It-Awful." They are especially eager to grasp on to new employees and run them through the lunchtime brainwashing. They may be personally embittered and need to continually feed their own angst—each new incident confirms their suspicions. They get off on bad news.

Rx

Is it all as bad as some people would have you believe? Possibly. However, short of living on another planet, you are stuck with human nature as it exists and operates. Prescription for the new employee? Keep a low profile; watch and learn. Be sure you find out for yourself how things really are and try not to be swayed by the nay-sayer types.

HOW TO HIT THE DECK RUNNING

Mitch knew that the first few days in a new job can be critical. He knew that people tend to form their opinion of newcomers in the first few minutes of meeting them. He also knew a lot was expected of him. His boss had made it very clear that the company needed him to bring his expertise to a project deemed critical to the division's success. He had been assured that it would all come together and that the other project team members were looking forward to having him on board. He also knew that the job was a tough one and the pressure for results was heavy. So Mitch had some sense of the task that lay ahead. He was pretty confident he could make a difference.

What he couldn't know was that he was walking into a work situation that had defeated the project leader who preceded him.

The problem was that although the project team needed to work together to streamline processes, they operated as individual units and had almost no communication between them.

Mitch's boss compounded the problem with his style of micromanagement. There was no feeling of empowerment at the project team level (the manager's style of making decisions defeated the team's actions), and the commitment of the project team had faded.

Mitch was determined to make this project work. He recognized right away that there would be no honeymoon period—he had deadlines to meet and this was a do-or-die time for his career at the company. He had already decided that he wanted to be seen as a doer, a team builder, and as reliable by his manager. His goal was to nail down the project and to get results in a positive way—not at the expense of others through alienation or autocratic management skills.

Mitch started by assessing the project status and finding out where the problems were. Rather than concentrating on what had gone wrong, he used his time to determine what were the goals, milestones and roadblocks to the project's completion. He worked actively to meet all the players involved in and peripheral to the project. He focused the meetings on the issues and needs, not a re-hash of the problems, mistakes, and people that had caused the project to be in such a bad state.

Recognizing his boss's style of micromanaging, he met with him frequently to test out his plans for the project activities and to get buy-in on the team's work.

The biggest problem Mitch had was the team itself. They had been through a lot of negative experiences, and each member seemed to be scrambling to keep his or her job secure (after all, the team leader was already replaced—who might be next?). This contributed to the lack of cohesion and coordination of efforts of the team as a whole. Mitch recognized early that he had to change the dynamics of their interactions, focus the group on common goals, and build the team's morale to get the results he needed.

Mitch started his team-building efforts by taking the group off site for a two-day retreat. The first afternoon, the group participated in a "fun" exercise that was designed to make the members realize their interdependence and recognize that the results of a team are better than the results any individual can achieve. The group then went out for dinner together, which further broke down the walls between them. By the time they arrived for breakfast the next day, the atmosphere in the meeting room was considerably more amiable and relaxed than usual.

The agenda for day 2 was very focused, with the team working together to identify the actions and schedule needed to complete the project, the problems they might encounter, and contingency plans to deal with the problems. By the middle of the day, the group was humming.

Mitch engineered the next step very carefully. He knew how his boss would want to make his own imprint on the project, so he invited him to the meeting near the close of the day. Recognizing his boss's need for control, Mitch asked him to address the group and discuss his expectations and objectives. The group then presented its work plan as well as a list of resources it needed to implement the plan. Together, all agreed upon the plan of action.

WHAT IT TAKES TO KNOCK THEIR SOCKS OFF
WHEN YOU'RE A NEW HIRE

Do's	*Don'ts*
Meet as many people as you can—set up orientation meetings, stick your head into people's offices to introduce yourself.	Complain about your desk, office, boss, the cafeteria food, parking space, anything.
Learn about the company's total operations, not just your own unit's.	Talk too soon in meetings until you get the lay of the land.
Make it known—diplomatically—to your boss when you need help or information.	Look for continual feedback (it just doesn't happen).
Come in early and stay late (but do also recognize what expectations you are creating).	Leave your area for long periods of time without letting someone know where you are.
Keep your eyes on the politics and undertones of the organization.	Order every possible item for your new desk from office supply.
Show enthusiasm.	Spend a lot of time calling your old friends.
Network, network, network.	Talk continuously about your former companies.
Bring in some personal items so it looks like you plan on staying awhile.	Criticize anyone.
Attend after hours events.	

DIAGNOSIS

In today's tough work environment, you need to get in and make your mark quickly when you start a new job. In this case, there was a very real need to get the project on the right track immediately. Other circumstances may not be as dramatic, but you will start to create an image soon after you begin, and as we all know, first impressions do last.

The orientation time typically is brief, but you can take advantage of this break-in period when you don't yet have a reputation sealed. You can take advantage of this by learning quickly and then moving forward in a positive way.

RX

Soon after you start in a new area, you should be able to put together your agenda—what you need to do, how you want to be perceived, what you want to accomplish. Mitch made a conscious decision that he would make the project work through the team, and so that directed his actions. When you have a model in your mind of the kind of person you want to be, you can direct your actions accordingly. The resulting actions will make the image a reality.

PAYING YOUR DUES TO GAIN THE COMPETITIVE EDGE

When Linda was hired as a scientist by one of the country's largest companies, she thought she had died and gone to heaven. She had completed her degree from a leading university, she was working for a prestigious company, and the money was excellent. Her first assignment was routine; she had to carry out a series of tests to identify the molecular structure of various components. While the work was not complex, she was able to complete her assignments and report her results on schedule without loss of motivation.

So far so good. Later, the assignment involved some traveling, which made the job a little more interesting. But as the months wore on, Linda became increasingly disillusioned. The work was so routine she could do it in her sleep. Moreover, she saw some of her colleagues getting the promotions she coveted. In despair, she finally broached the subject with her boss. "What do I have to do around here to get ahead? I do everything I'm assigned. My performance is satisfactory. What do I need to do?"

His response surprised her. He told her she needed to find an area and develop her expertise in that area. He said somewhat bluntly, "You only follow orders. You don't initiate. You don't investigate. You haven't developed a reputation in the technical field." He went on to explain that the criteria for advancement included becoming an expert in some areas and that only after she had developed a reputation in a technical area would she be considered a candidate for a supervisory position. He went on to chastise her for being so passive, for not taking the initiative to identify what she could specifically contribute to the company. He told her that she needed to find a way to stand out in the crowd, that just doing the job correctly was not enough if she hoped to move ahead. He used his own career as an example, pointing out that he first became the industry expert in a specific technology before he was able to make his move into management.

DIAGNOSIS

While Linda's situation is common in that every field or functional area requires some degree of technical competence, there are specific areas such as engineering, computer programming, and the sciences where the development of a technical competency is of critical importance.

Skill and competence—the reputation for having a solid technical grounding and the credibility that goes along with that reputation—are absolute prerequisites to advancement in a highly technical environment. If you can develop a skill and become an expert with in-depth knowledge in an area, you'll be seen as a valuable contributor and an intelligent individual and you will stand out among your peers.

Linda needs to become the recognized expert. The strategy will vary by field, but in general, your best bet is to establish an area that is of specific interest to you and of particular value within your job function. One way to assess the potential value of the expertise is by looking at the organization as well as industry trends. That way your expertise can be parlayed into advancing internally and moving ahead externally if you ever need or wish to leave the organization.

Rx

Certainly, your own research and awareness of company and industry trends will help you determine where you might concentrate. Ideally, you should try to connect with a senior specialist in your field who can encourage and enhance your efforts as well as provide some structure and insights to your efforts. (This can give you the added advantage of a mentor.)

If you work in the field you've decided on, and develop your expertise in addition to carrying out your routine work responsibilities competently and with a good attitude, you will develop a definite advantage over the many others with whom you'll be competing. This is the competitive edge required to stand out and move ahead.

THE SECRET TO ACHIEVING STAR QUALITY

In some fields, it is not just their technical expertise that moves people ahead. It can be reliability, attitude, and initiative that give you the competitive edge. Consider Lou and Carla, for example.

Lou started as an expediter in a medium-sized retail store. His responsibilities were to ensure shipments were moved from the receiving area to the department sales areas. The work environment was casual—some of his coworkers wore jeans—but Lou wanted to stand out. He endured the laughter of his fellow expediters when he wore a tie and nice clothes to work every day. He was friendly to everyone in the company and always smiled when doing his work. He showed a real sense of pride, regardless of how menial the task and was the first one to go the extra step to get a job done.

In his early days on the job, there was a lot of skepticism toward him—almost a snobbery. "Who does he think he is? He acts like he's a manager here," was a comment from one of the managers. But the reactions soon changed from smug, looking down at him, to respect as he proved himself on a daily basis. People liked to have him around—he was an "up" guy and was completely reliable.

When a job at the next level opened up, Lou was the hands-down choice. The greatest irony was the sorrow people felt when they met his successor in the expediter job—another "typical" young guy in jeans. Lou had made his mark and would be missed.

Carla's first job was a management trainee. She wanted to bowl over her managers and to prove to them that they'd made the right choice. She also wanted to set a solid foundation upon which to build her career.

As soon as she got her first assignment as a sales representative, she realized that the management was testing her ability to "eat dirt." The territory was in a major urban locale, and she was a bit frightened about some of the areas where she had to make sales calls. She was determined, though, not to let it get her down; she used well-thought-through safety precautions and worked hard to get results.When she went into the headquarters office, she always talked to the product managers to give them her sales input and to learn more information to help her with her sales calls. She joked about her territory (the "war zone"), but she didn't complain.

Carla attacked every new assignment she was given with the same enthusiasm. She worked hard to meet the people whose work overlapped with hers, trying to bring some information or idea to them so she wasn't doing a one-sided take. She showed great (and genuine) enthusiasm for her new assignments, even when she wasn't quite so sure what they were doing for her career. Her attitude was universally seen as a great asset.

DIAGNOSIS

Companies value specific qualities in employees. Diligence, reliability, cordiality, initiative, and a positive attitude are most typically the qualities that can help you be successful. Interestingly, these qualities are most important early on in your career—they can help establish you as a valuable commodity in your organization. As you move up, there is less emphasis on these as success elements. Overall, though, good patterns started early on will stay with you and continuing demonstration of these assets can help you throughout your work life.

Rx

If you recognize that you have a shortcoming in one of these qualities, you can put together an action plan to strengthen it. It's best to work one issue at a time and continuously reinforce it to assure real improvement. For example, if "positive attitude" is not a strong point, you can improve it by

> Being consciously aware of your attitudes and reactions to events, then evaluating your response.
>
> Asking trusted friends to give you feedback about how your behavior comes across to others.
>
> Talking to yourself to remind you what you want to be.
>
> Watching others' actions to evaluate how they respond to issues, people, and so on.
>
> Reading appropriate magazine articles or books.
>
> Identifying the people who are valued in your company and analyzing their qualities to compare them to your own. Where there are gaps, develop action plans that can help you enhance your personal style. The value of personal attributes can never be underestimated.

GIVING AND RECEIVING FEEDBACK

Julio had been recently promoted into an analyst job providing technical support to a key area of the company's operations. He hadn't been working long, so he was still figuring out what people expected of him as well as the technical aspects of this job. He was very enthusiastic, though, and his supervisor, George, was pleased with his work results. Some of Julio's habits sometimes bothered him, however, and George decided to discuss them with him.

At the end of one of their update meetings, George told Julio he was doing quite well, but there were some areas for improvement. Julio was surprised when George started going through them—most were style issues: asking too many questions in group meetings, voicing negative reactions early in discussions, interrupting people when Julio wanted to make his point. Then, the real clinker: George told Julio that his appearance, while neat, didn't serve him well. Julio's sports jacket look was not in line with the standard business suit attire of the office.

Julio's initial reaction was indignation. How dare George tell him how to dress? And how could he learn what was happening if he didn't ask questions? He was so angry that he started to shut down. He told George he would consider the input and left.

Julio did some heavy-duty soul searching that night. What message was George giving him? How legitimate were his comments? By the end of the night, after thinking through the hurt and anger, Julio came to the conclusion that George's motivation was not to put him down, but instead to help him. As a new employee in the group, Julio was not aware of some of the subtleties of the department. George's input, though hard to swallow, was invaluable to Julio's development.

The next day, Julio went to see George. He explained how he was at first upset with what he heard, but that he valued George's comments. Together, they discussed how Julio's actions and image were perceived and where some changes would make him more effective in his role.

DIAGNOSIS _____

Often, people don't tell you the things you need to hear the most because it's not easy to do. When you work with someone—a boss, coworker, even a member of your staff—who will give you the "straight skinny" on how you are perceived or what you're doing wrong, you will be receiving a great gift. One caveat, though: always be sure to try to ascertain the motivation of the giver.

Rx _____

Receiving Feedback: Hard as it may be, try to make it easy for others to give you feedback. You may even seek it out, but be sure of your own motivation when you do that (don't ask in an attempt to get a pat on the back). The best way to receive feedback is to

1. Paraphrase what you've heard. "You think I don't look professional by the way I dress?" "I don't come across as knowledgeable when I ask questions?"
2. Ask for clarification when you need it.
3. Thank the person for their input.
4. Assess what you heard and decide for yourself if it is valid and if you need to adjust something you're doing, then make the needed changes.

Giving Feedback: Another important skill is the ability to give feedback to others. Because there will be times you will need to give input to your staff, coworkers, team members, even your family members, you need to be able to do it gracefully and helpfully. The "grace" part relates to keeping the person's esteem intact; the help comes from being as specific as possible.

Feedback can be positive and negative; ideally, you should be giving feedback on an ongoing basis, when things go well and when they're not doing too well. If you create an environment where the feedback is continuous, it makes it less of a "cause celebre" when you have bad news to deliver. The best way to give feedback is to

1. Describe what has happened—what behavior occurred, what action took place. Be as explicit as possible. Include how it affected you: "Joe, I was proud of the report you delivered today. It was concise, clear, and comprehensive." "Carol, it upset me when you complained about my team's actions at the meeting this morning."
2. Describe what effect the action had on you and others: "Joe, the report made our unit look reliable and credible." "Carol, you may have been unhappy with a specific action the team took, but the others in the room may now doubt my team's capabilities."

3. Discuss what you would like to happen and its consequences: "Joe, I hope that your next report capitalizes on the work you did today. I will be giving you the next high-visibility project as a result." "Carol, if you have complaints, please bring them to me privately. Then our departments will be better able to work together."

Practice giving and receiving feedback and encourage those around you to do the same. The result will be a more productive and developmentally oriented workplace.

WHAT THEY WON'T TELL YOU

Your Boss	*Your Peers*	*Your Subordinates*
When you have plateaued	When they can't stand you	How the rest of the subordinates feel about you
When you are working harder than you need to	When you don't "get it"	When you have made a fool of yourself
When you aren't going to get the promotion you want	When they are jealous of you	When you're obnoxious
When you don't fit	When they are competing against you	When you have hurt them
When you make him or her uncomfortable	When you are a royal itch	When you are acting like a jerk
When you're not smart enough	When they have gossiped about you	

SIDE-STEPPING CORPORATE SHOOTOUTS

Jane's new job was as a member of a five-person team. She reported to a supervisor, who in turn, reported to a manager.

The group was hard working and had been together for more than a year. Its supervisor, Mark, had recently been brought in from another area of finance. Mark had been hand selected by the manager in part because the manager believed in Mark's potential to make a significant contribution to the department. Jane joined the department three months after Mark arrived. Because it took Jane a while to figure out the dynamics of the group, initially she played it neutral and maintained a friendly relationship with everyone in the group. She was new and wanted to be well liked, to fit in.

However, it soon became evident that the group was not one big happy family. Most of the staff disliked Mark—they found him to be too strict and not as easygoing as his predecessor. One woman, Karen, spent most of the lunch hour complaining about Mark and pressuring the others to agree with her. Since Jane was still new and wanted to be a part of the group, she joined in the conversations, adding her own comments about the reasons why Mark was not the greatest supervisor. The group decided to do something about him. They decided it was time to stand up and be counted. Mark had to go.

Karen elected herself spokesperson for the group and set up a meeting to meet with Mark's manager. She spent 45 minutes outlining all the group's grievances and ended with an ultimatum—either he goes or we go. However, the manager backed Mark and told Karen the group was totally out of line. Even worse, after his meeting with Karen, the manager told Mark about the meeting and the concerns of the staff. Naturally, Mark was extremely displeased. When he met with the staff individually to discuss his concerns (and theirs), it became obvious to him that the one who was the most vociferous in her complaints was Karen. She was also the one who had the biggest axe to grind (her performance in the department was the poorest). As he talked to the other members in the group, they told him that they missed the old supervisor but were trying to adapt to his new style and that they never meant to let the situation get out of hand.

Jane, the newest recruit, was at a loss about how to respond to Mark when he asked what her role in all of this had been. She tried to explain what had happened, but, in the end, she had to admit that she had joined in with the complaining group.

Mark was deeply disappointed with Jane. She was new and he had personally selected her, privately hoping that she would be his ally in the group he knew was having difficulty accepting a new supervisor.

The crisis passed, but the group was never able to pull together until Mark moved Karen out of the group. With her departure went the negativism that had spread like a disease through the group. Once Karen was gone, the group members were able to again focus on their jobs and build a good relationship with Mark, although it took a lot of time and hard work.

DIAGNOSIS

Jane did well—or so it seemed—in handling the break-in period with her peers. She "fit in" and tacitly agreed to join into the agenda of the group. She missed a critical opportunity, however, by not remaining neutral, which then labeled her as a malcontent early on in her career. She failed to use good judgment in handling that delicate, tenuous balance between her peers and her boss, a mistake that could have torpedoed her budding career.

The politics of this situation might have been obvious to an outsider. For the novice, bunching up and going against the boss may have seemed okay. But it's a very dangerous game. Even if Mark was not the world's most effective manager, it's not a justification for a palace revolt. Karen was basically destructive, and she was leading her merry band of warriors on a suicide mission.

Rx

Jane was fortunate in that Mark understood and accepted her behavior; he chalked it up to being new rather than malicious. Jane was smart enough to begin supporting Mark—in his presence and in the presence of the other group members. She had learned an important lesson in dealing with the politics of office relationships. Often these politics can suck you in and cloud your judgment. Try to step out of your situation at times and take a good close look at the dynamics of what's going on and why in order to help you pick a course of action that takes you where you want to be.

PROMOTING YOUR CAREER HEALTH—
Getting Started

This stage of your career is the critical foundation for your success. To successfully navigate through this stage and to maximize your career health, you need to understand where to concentrate your efforts and to recognize the blockades you may encounter. Only then can you be sure you're starting off on the right track.

What you need to master

- How to take orders
- How to accept a low-level position in the hierarchy—dealing with the loss of status; gracefully accepting the role of peon while still asserting yourself as a professional
- How to perform under pressure and produce in the usually frenetic workplace of the '90s

- How to produce quality work, regardless of how routine it may be
- Who the key players are—and what makes them so (position in the company, relationships with key executives, specific interpersonal or technical skills)
- How the system works—-how things get done, who works with whom, what are the issues and activities that get attention
- How to work in a team
- How to continually learn from your actions—and others'
- How to identify what is valued in your organization

Barriers to success

- Inability to deal with routine, boring work
- Don't fit the culture
- No mentor or sponsor
- Can't build a personal network
- Getting tied into the "out" crowd—choosing friends that are negative, poor producers, not seen as the players for tomorrow
- Incompetent boss

Payoff for you and your career

- Meaningful work
- Getting paid as a professional
- Chance to work with outstanding people
- Build foundation for future growth
- Broad networks of contacts within the organization
- Developing skills that will continually help you throughout your career

PLAYING THE GAME

Keeping Your Career on Course

SCHMOOZING—
The Organizational Lubricant

Lisa was a quiet individual. She liked autonomy and independence and would usually work with her office door closed. She didn't lunch with the department, and only rarely would she make an appearance at the office social gatherings. When she did attend parties, she'd say a general hello and then quickly escape back to her office.

Lisa's department was a very social, team-oriented group. To accomplish their individual goals, there was a great deal of interaction and collaboration. Many of the ties built within the group were developed on task-related projects, but they were strengthened over a cup of coffee, a sandwich, or a birthday cake.

Last month, Alice, one of the support staff, lost all her belongings in a fire that wiped out her apartment complex. The department rallied to help her; they took up a collection for a security deposit on a new apartment. They collected clothes and furniture. They bought both of Alice's daughters new winter coats. They even filled in for her until she could get settled down and work full time again. Throughout all this, Lisa maintained her distance. She donated some money when asked, but she avoided any involvement in the "Alice project." The experience drew the group even tighter together, but their newly found cohesiveness only highlighted Lisa's isolation.

DIAGNOSIS

By her lack of involvement, Lisa missed a lot of the camaraderie developed in the department. She was seen as a loner, not willing to give part of herself to the group. As a result, when she needed information or help, she was unable to draw on personal relationships to get what she needed. She didn't cultivate favors—and others would not rush to help her since they felt she was in it for herself only.

Eventually, Lisa left the department. What did people say about her? She was smart and did good work, but she was a loner. She did not benefit from the input and actions of the group, nor did she give much back. She was perceived as self-centered when, in fact, she was basically shy.

RX

It's quite obvious that, in certain areas, strong people skills are a requirement. If you work in such an area, and you are not naturally a gregarious person, you may need to push yourself to interact with others if you want to succeed.

Force yourself to ask someone in your area to lunch once a week. By doing this on a systematic basis, you'll expand your network. If the idea of a one-to-one lunch makes you uncomfortable, ask two people. With three people at a table, there are usually few lapses in conversation.

If it makes you more comfortable, schedule meetings, tasks, and discussions over lunch—it will give you a focus for conversation.

Try to visit others' offices if you have questions or information for them—don't just call them on the phone, talk to their machine, or use electronic mail.

Attend the department's social events—anniversaries, birthdays, baseball games—even if just for a short while. Send cards in honor of personal contributions to show you care. Be seen at the public gatherings. Get involved with the local cause, whether it's an "Alice project" or volunteering for the English as Second Language class.

In most organizations, those that succeed have shown their ability to work socially within the company. They have their ear to the grapevine, can get along reasonably well with others, work effectively within groups and demonstrate the graces of good social skills. Social "moles" don't do well in corporate life. So head for the coffee machine early and often, because that's where much of the action is.

THE LITTLE THINGS THAT COUNT A LOT

Careers are often made on a person's ability to do something well or important such as developing a new product, figuring out how to save the company a half-million dollars or being the best salesperson on the West Coast. But careers can be thwarted by the small things— those nuances of behavior or attitude that jar others just enough to put them off. For example, Thomas was the company's most competent plant manager. He could move men and machinery through speed-ups, breakdowns, retooling, you name it. He was a master conductor. Yet for those who have had to work with him, he had one small habit that put people off—he talked with food in his mouth.

Now, talking with food in your mouth won't get you fired. But it doesn't make eating with you a high point of the day. In Thomas's case, it made the president think twice before inviting Thomas to important lunchtime meetings with key customers. Because the president could never bring himself to say anything to Thomas, he solved the problem by asking Thomas to stop by and catch a cup of coffee or he left him out of the lunch (and breakfast) meetings altogether.

Thomas was totally unaware of his own eating habits. And he was most certainly unaware of how others felt who had to sit across the table from him.

When we talk about the little things that count, it includes other types of things as well, not just table manners. To give you a sense of those other little things, read through the following descriptions to make sure none of them do or can ever fit you.

Body Language

Gloria stands too close to people. When people meet her in the hall to stop and talk, she moves in so close that her coworkers find themselves stepping back. If the conversation goes more than a few minutes, the pair of them can end up against a wall with Gloria still pushing the space limits. While the distance between conversationalists differs with each culture, in this country, about two feet is the range within which most people feel comfortable. More than that is too distant, but any closer causes the person with whom you are talking to feel pinned down or smothered. The posture can even take on an "in-your-face" connotation—and that's how people feel when they have a stand-up conversation with Gloria.

Jim sits with his legs spread eagle over the arm of his chair. Those who believe in psychoanalysis think there is a secret message to his position—something to do with suppression. Others simply find it annoying. Women find it crude.

Mary Ann does a lot of skirt scootching. When she sits down, she flips her skirt underneath her. Then she gets up again and does the same thing over again. Only this time, the skirt goes up a little higher. This jumping up and down goes on most of the meeting. The men love it. They vie to sit across the room from her. The women just shake their heads and wonder.

Susan sits at meetings grim and staring, her arms folded tightly across her chest. She is always frowning, speaks very curtly, and doesn't find anyone's jokes funny, not even the boss's. One day someone asked her if she was angry about something. Her face reddened, the veins in her neck bulged, and she answered "I'm never angry. Never, never, never." In truth, she is angry and her anger makes people hesitate about talking with her, especially if they think she may get angrier.

Appearance

Maggie could be on the best-dressed list, but only if the contest were held in a nightclub. She adores silky flowing dresses with plunging necklines and chiffon panels. She adorns herself with enough jewelry to rival Cleopatra with no less than four rings on each hand as well as multiple necklaces and drop-dead earrings. Her favorite look is rhinestone. Actually she looks great, but not corporate. As a result, she is not taken seriously.

Dan has that "good ol' boy" look—loosened tie, short-sleeved shirts all year round, no jacket, and a paunch that hangs over his trousers like a great watermelon. Lately he's been substituting suspenders for a belt—a look that is highly fashionable among the Ralph Lauren crowd, but not particularly flattering for the "Fat and Fifty" gang. Dan would look right at home in a saloon, but he works for a buttoned-down, dark-blue-suit organization, and while he is respected for his abilities, which are considerable, he will never be considered for an officer-level post given his appearance.

Jeff likes to wear his moccasins to work. He also loves his beard and his country-style haircut. He likes it even better when someone comments. It gives him the chance to explain he is not like the rest of the "sheep" who dress to please the boss. He also can't understand why he is not getting ahead.

This week, Jenny has fingernails that spell words. Last week she was psychedelic. Her deep pink nails were covered with bilious green dots. The week before the theme was black. She spends a lot of time with her nails. She has even been known to leave a meeting if she breaks a nail (she calls that E-m-e-r-g-e-n-c-y S-t-u-f-f). She also chews gum (A-l-l t-h-e T-i-m-e).

Communication Style

Lloyd says "you know" a lot. At the beginning of every sentence, after the first two words, in the middle, and at the end. Lloyd may be a very bright guy, but he sounds dumb.

Bruce doesn't know when he doesn't know. He freely offers his opinion on everything and has never met a subject he hadn't already mastered. He lectures a lot. He never listens. He's also left alone a lot.

Deborah comes across as haughty to many people. She has an air about her that signals danger. People feel that she is constantly evaluating them and that they always come up short. She is quick to describe her high standards to others with the clear inference that they aren't up to her level. She sees it as a way to keep other people on the defensive. Other people see it as a reason to avoid her.

Donald is always slightly out of it. One moment he's part of the group, the next minute he's turned in his chair and is doodling on his paper. He walks down the hall and doesn't see anyone. Even his comments are out in left field. It's a test of tolerance to have a conversation with him.

Work Style

Katherine likes details. Details like Katherine. She lives, eats, and breathes details. When she comes to a meeting, she brings along piles of documentation. Heaven help anyone who asks her a question or requests information. She drowns them in minutia. She surrounds them with data. She flattens them with exactness. And she wears them out with her nit-picking. Individuals have been known to have passed into corporate unconsciousness in her presence. People are beginning to find ways to "disinvite" her to their meetings. They do need information from her, they ask for it "in 25 words or less" or better yet, "put it on E-mail."

Robert runs the supply office for his company. What he is good at is keeping everything in order, monitoring the inventory, and seeing that orders are delivered on time. What he does is vital. How he does it drives people crazy. Robert is methodical. If he needs to refer to an order book to answer a question, he first finishes whatever he is doing (filing, rearranging, writing a memo, whatever). He never interrupts himself in anything he does. Thus, if you show up at his door with an emergency request for five flip charts for the director's annual meeting that is beginning in 10 minutes, he first looks at you for a while, reads through your order sheet at the rate of two words per 5 minutes, then finishes whatever he is doing. Only then does he make a move toward the flip charts. His final remarks are sure to include some comments about people who don't have the sense to plan ahead.

It's not that he is trying to make life difficult for people, this is his work style. However, the effect on those who have to deal with him ranges from teeth gnashing to tearing out their hair to schemes to secretly place a bomb under his desk.

DIAGNOSIS _____

We all do things that grate, annoy, or even disgust others, but we seldom realize we are doing them. Unfortunately, they are the type of things people don't feel comfortable giving us feedback on.

We can all laugh about the little horror stories involving people who walk into a meeting with toilet paper stuck to their shoe or with buttons not buttoned or zippers not zipped. While embarrassing, those types of things unto themselves do not ruin careers. The danger lies with those ongoing actions and attitudes that we are not aware of and that can have a negative effect on the way we are perceived..

As one wise man once said, "It's all in the details." Whether its your body language, your appearance, your communication, or your work style, it all counts. So be your own best friend by becoming your own toughest critic.

Rx _____

If you wonder if you could be damaging yourself unwittingly by doing things that turn off people, you need to find a trusted "other" who is willing to level with you. The conversation could go something like this: "Jim, I've been reading a book that describes how people can foul up their careers by doing things that irritate or annoy people, but how the person is often unaware of his or her effect on others." (Give a few examples.)

"I want to make a deal with you. I want you to tell me if you ever see me doing anything like that—or if you already see something that I don't realize but need to know. In return, I'll do the same for you."

IN A FIRE, GRAB YOUR ROLODEX:
The Importance of Networking

Kevin was a scientist who loved his job and knew he was on the rise. He was very good technically and interpersonally as well. In addition to having good relationships with his peers and supervisors, he also had been active in the American Chemical Society as well as the local chapter of his college alumni association.

One day his boss came to him with some very bad news. His division was to be sold, and the new owner already had his own research staff. Kevin, among many others, would no longer have a job. His boss told him that with his years at the company, he'd be given six weeks' severance pay.

Kevin was beside himself with anger and distress. How could his company sell out to someone who would fire so many employees? How could he find a job? What would become of him? And while the issue of career was important to him, for now, he had a mortgage to pay and needed a job.

Then he started using his network. He called everyone he knew, or had met, or who knew someone he knew. He left no stone unturned. When he heard through a professional contact that a job was open at XYZ Company, he immediately was in hot pursuit of that plus one other lead. He did some checking about XYZ and found that a fellow alumni worked there, and he realized this person could be a great contact. Through her, he found out XYZ had lost a big contract in another division and had some shaky times ahead. With this knowledge, Kevin decided to pursue the other job, which he eventually did land. In the end, he saved much anguish because he avoided putting himself in another shaky situation.

DIAGNOSIS

It's been said that you know you are over 30 when the first thing you reach for during a fire drill is your Rolodex. Although not really age-related, the most valuable resource you will have *throughout your career* is your network. Whether this is your Rolodex file or your personal notebook, your contacts are critical to your career success.

This network is cultivated as you move from department to department, group to group, association to association, job to job. As a resource, it will provide you with invaluable data as you grow and need professional expertise. It also has the potential to provide you with advice or information should you decide to change jobs, get a new job, or want to find out what's in the marketplace.

Networking is no longer a choice. It's a necessity. The rules of the workplace have changed. Nowadays, it is highly probable that you will have to act as if you are self-employed, which means you must build and maintain a large network.

RX

Networking begins with who you know. The list needs to include past and present coworkers and supervisors, friends, neighbors, members of clubs or professional associations, old schoolmates who may now be influential alumni, key players in your community such as the small business owners, the doctors, dentists, and lawyers, the real estate professionals, the local chamber of commerce, the health clubs, the YW/YMCA's, the service clubs (Rotary, Professional Business Women, etc.), members from your church or temple, the barber or hairdresser, members of your professional associations—the list could go on, but you get the idea. Everyone is a potential contact.

You build your network by developing relationships with as many of the people with whom you interact as possible. For example, when you attend meetings, go with the objective of meeting people and "working the room" rather than just chatting with your old compatriots. You may not use your network until and unless you have to. But it is there for you when you need it even as you are there when people in your network need you.

If you do need to use your network members to move your career along or find a new job, call them, explain why you are calling, and ask them for the names of people you might contact. Do not ask your network to find you a job. The idea of a network is to have people who can put you in touch with the right people. For example, your neighbor may not be a big shot in the ABC Company, but she may know someone who works there and who could introduce you to the decision maker in that organization.

Building and maintaining a network is serious business. Effective networkers keep a record (3 by 5 cards, their PC or Rolodex) of their network. If they are conducting a job search, they keep a careful record of who they talked to, when, and about what. They also make sure they loop back to the people they initially contacted in their network to let them know what happened.

Part of the art of building a network is becoming a good member of other people's networks. That means giving attention when others call you for information, contacts, or job leads. You never know when you will need someone's help. While you may not be asking for assistance from the same people you helped out, in the end, it will balance out. It's a little like casting your bread upon the waters.

So yes, in a fire, grab your Rolodex. But do prepare now, so you're sure that it's worth taking with you.

READING THE WHITE SPACE:
What the Organization Chart Doesn't Tell You

Theoretically, the greatest amount of power is located at the top of the organizational pyramid and to lesser degrees in the descending layers of management. But in all organizations, there are both formal and informal power systems; therefore, it is critical that you be able to identify and assess the informal power system. To ignore the informal system is to walk through a very active mine field.

Idealistic employees have a particularly difficult time with the informal system. They expect that life and corporations should run on certain principles. They get especially upset if the principles that the company officially espouses are different from what the company is doing in reality.

Laura was such an employee. She was assigned to work as finance manager with the group that was putting together a new advertising campaign. Her specific responsibilities included handling the budget and monitoring the expenditures. She soon discovered that one of the vendors with whom the group was doing business had a very tight relationship with a manager in the group (translated—vendor making very big bucks and taking good care of manager). What's more, the vendor appeared to be running the group. The vendor was making most of the decisions, and the project was already over budget. When Laura tried to discuss the situation with others in the group, she was brushed aside. The message was: "If you don't like what you're seeing, close your eyes." Laura became angry. She hated cozy "scratch-my-back-and-I'll scratch-yours" arrangements, and she was indignant that an outsider was virtually running the project.

She felt her only recourse was to let the president of the division know what was going on. After all, she was responsible for the budget of the project and the budget was out of control. So she asked for an appointment with the president and told her story.

Now guess who got clobbered? The vendor? The manager? Not on your life. It just happened that this same vendor had a long-standing relationship with the president of the division—they were golf buddies and social friends. The vendor took very good care of "his boys" as he called them and the president was on the vendor's "very special person" list.

Laura's punishment was not clear at first. The president thanked her and asked her if she would be more comfortable in another assignment. The "other assignment" turned out to be some rinky-dink accounting job in the company's version of Siberia.

Laura realized too late that she had made a serious mistake.

DIAGNOSIS _____

_____

Laura's anger and indignation was appropriate because she saw the company standards and procedures being compromised. But she failed to read the informal system that supported the vendor's position.

Laura was right about what she saw going on. But the way she handled it was naive. She had not checked out the system to see why such an arrangement was allowed to happen. Had she done so, she would have quickly learned that this particular vendor had 90 percent of the company's advertising contracts and that 90 percent of senior management had overlooked the cost overruns in advertising for many years. She would also have learned that this vendor was one of the president's "advisors" and that the president often invited him to the company's top level strategy meetings.

Was Laura morally right in blowing the whistle on this guy? Of course. But her decision to go to the president with her accusations bordered on a death wish. Laura didn't have the power to affect the way business was being done in her company. She had only the power to keep her own store in order. And as wrong as it may seem, there isn't a lot a first-level manager can do in any organization about how the president runs the business.

Rx _____

_____

Look before you leap into the corporate morass of power and politics. Find out who hangs out with whom. There are all sorts of unseen and informal power relationships that are not reflected on the organization chart.

If you feel that senior management is conducting business at the expense of the shareholders, then you may have a forum. But, of course, you should expect to pay a high price for being the bearer of the news.

Finally, don't for one minute give up on or compromise your own standards for inappropriate business ethics. The company needs more people like you, whether they know it or not. But don't throw yourself into a volcano thinking it will bring down the wrath of heavens on corporate business practices. Save your voice and your sanity for another time and occasion—when what you do about the problem can make a difference.

Better yet, turn your attention to getting ahead and becoming the company CEO. You already know where you can save a lot of money, right?

LEARNING HOW TO PLAY THE POWER GAMES

Power has become a dirty word in some companies. People grab it, abuse it, lose it, and fight for it. Power is one of those great intangibles that you can never quite see or touch, but whose presence is unmistakable. It's a little like gravity. You don't think about the force of gravity as you make your plans for the day, but from the minute you roll out of bed you are living with and being affected by gravity. So it is with power. It permeates all relationships, whether it's family, community, or organizations. Wherever you find people gathered together, you find power.

Our purpose in bringing up the subject of power is to increase your awareness of it and to help you to identify and use your own power base. To give you a sense of what this business is all about, consider this next episode.

Elliot was undoubtedly one of the brightest systems developers in his company. He could outthink, outstrategize, and outdesign anyone, including the head of his department. Two years ago he was assigned a key position in a project that, if it panned out, would mean very big bucks for his company. His job was to bring his vision and brilliance to the design team. To do this, he needed to gather data from the other members of the team and guide them in the development of the software. He had never been this close to a project with such high promise and visibility, and he was highly motivated. He wanted very much to make it all work. However, six months into the project, Elliott thought the group was on the wrong track. He set up a meeting with his boss and told him (from Elliott's very technical perspective) that they were going down some blind alleys. But his warnings fell on deaf ears.

Elliott was furious that no one would listen to him. After that, he became more isolated. He shared less information. In return, the team members shared less with him. Now two years into the project, the group is foundering. People have built their little kingdoms, and the project is already into costly overruns to say nothing of the deadlines it is missing.

Elliot thought his expertise should have ruled the day. But it didn't. He didn't know how to use persuasion as a power base. Even his boss was not persuaded that although Elliot is bright, he is right. He believes it's up to the team to work things out.

Janet's story takes a different turn. She doesn't understand why some people are powerful even when their title suggests otherwise. Recently, she called the secretary of one of the vice presidents to get background information for her project and to set up an appointment with the vice president. The secretary challenged her on giving out the information. She said it was proprietary and she would need the vice president's permission to release it. Janet saw red on this one and asked the secretary just who she thought she was. You can guess the rest of this story. Janet is getting the cold shoulder treatment from the secretary, which in turn is impacting on her ability to communicate with the vice president.

Janet did not understand the dynamics of the marketing department. This secretary has been given a great deal of power because the vice president trusts her so much and places high value on the secretary's judgment.

Fred's case demonstrates yet another consequence of misreading the power scene. He joined the senior management team of a medium-sized company as the director of finance. As such, he expected to be privy to the innermost workings of the company. To his dismay, he discovered that the company attorney, Richard, had the president's ear and in turn wielded a disproportionate amount of power. Early on in the new job, Fred decided to challenge Richard on some edict that Richard had announced concerning managing the company's pension fund. Fred saw that as strictly his own area of expertise and questioned Richard's plan. Within a half an hour of his discussion with Richard, the president called him into his office and told him to back off. If Richard wanted to get involved in the pension plan, he could. And that was that. Fred learned a powerful lesson in power—relationships may mean more than titles.

THE HIDDEN AND NOT-SO-HIDDEN SOURCES OF POWER

Formal Power	Power derived from a person's position in the hierarchy. As someone who has formal power, you may not be liked, but you will be obeyed.
Expert Power	Power derived from your ability and/or knowledge. You may not have a title that gives you formal power, but your expertise and know-how will earn you respect and, hence, the power to impact decisions.
Charismatic Power	Power derived from your ability to charm people or from the strength of your personality. Charismatic power is seductive. It is powerful, regardless of formal position.
Persuasive Power	Power derived from your ability to listen, determine what you can support in others' point of view and then to make a case for your ideas without making it a win-lose situation.
Barter Power	Power derived from what you have that other people need. Barter power is based on give and take, alliances, and calling in your chips.
Relationship Power	Power derived from who you know. Name dropping is one of the techniques used in this game. Relationship power often underlies much of what is called "politics."
Threatening Power	Power derived from your ability to threaten to withhold resources and to actually carry out threats when necessary. This type of power is usually played out like a poker game. The strategy is knowing who has the cards, what's been played, and how far you can go before calling someone's bluff. Threatening to use this power is often more effective than the actual use of it.
Raw Force Power	Derived from your ability to physically remove, eliminate, push aside, or neutralize the opposition. Wars are based on raw force power.

DIAGNOSIS

Power is that unseen force that is present whenever people work together. You must know who has power, what kind of power they have, and how it will affect your working relationships. Most important, you must never underestimate the role of power in the workplace.

Rx

For starters, read through the following descriptions of *The Hidden and Not So Hidden Sources of Power.* Choose which describe your situation as well as which types describe your colleagues. A careful analysis will help you direct your own actions toward using your own power sources more effectively. It will also alert you to the hidden sources of power in your workplace.

AVOIDING FLAVOR-OF-THE-MONTH FATIGUE:
Coping and Growing with the Changing Workplace

In some organizations, employees can count on at least one, if not more, major new training programs a year. One month, it's empowerment. Six months later, it's total quality management (TQM). Come the new year and it's reengineering. As you might guess, employees soon burn out if they already haven't dropped dead from boredom or exhaustion. As fatigue and cynicism grow, productivity decreases. As productivity decreases, the company looks for a new program to get people motivated. And so the weary cycle goes on. Small firms are less likely to have the resources or time to try out the latest management miracles, but as any employee of a large company can tell you, the fatigue from the "flavor-of-the-month" programs can be a real drain.

DIAGNOSIS

Many businesspeople are at their wits' end trying to cope with the immense change going on in the business world. What worked even five years ago is obsolete today. Markets have changed. Some have disappeared, while others have sprung up overnight to be exploited by those companies who can work smart and fast enough to capture them. Stability is out, as is job security. What we have now is a fearful work force working 60 to 70 hours a week just to keep their jobs. We have fearful bosses who are deeply worried about how to motivate their employees. Hence, the proliferation of a multitude of efforts designed to change how people work.

RX

Don't fight it. If members of management have fallen in love with GE's workout program, or Deming's quality movement, support them. They may not be ready or able to walk their talk, but the need for changing how work gets done is very real. If you are feeling tired of going to training programs or feel cynical about the latest round of posters touting empowerment or adding value, keep it to yourself. There's enough negativity in the workplace without adding to it.

It's not that you have to play "Gee whiz, this is great, boss!" but be a good soldier. Although the latest round of programs may hold little promise, given what's going on in your particular company, it still may offer something. If nothing else, you can spend the time analyzing why so many change efforts don't work and develop some insight about the difficulty in changing large systems.

If you can muster the energy, and can see that a particular program might help even incrementally, consider getting on the task force that is spearheading the effort. You'll gain a new perspective about what makes organizations tick, an appreciation for the role of leadership (whether it's positive or negative), and you might even have some fun.

Many individuals who have become involved in efforts to make changes in the workplace count that experience as being one of the most exciting (if not frustrating) times in their careers. It's also a great way to increase your network and gain visibility.

Knowing that you can't fight them, why not join them? You might have a good time, and you might, just might, actually make a difference.

ADDING VALUE—
Key to Success in the New Workplace

Adding value may sound like just one more of those buzzwords that enters into the jargon of the workplace, then fades into oblivion only to be replaced by another equally abstract, but catchy expression. The difference this time is that this particular phrase is being taken very seriously. It has become the standard for deciding the fate of many careerists.

It's also a phrase that is difficult to explain. What does it mean to "add value"? How would you know it if you did? How would you know it if you didn't?

Those were the questions Frank asked when he was told by his manager that he wasn't adding value.

Frank had started his career as an accountant for one of the large accounting firms. His job was to audit his company's clients. It was a good job: he learned the ropes; he knew what he was doing. However, 18 months into the job, his boss called him into his office and told him he was not adding value. Frank was surprised. He had always been given decent performance reviews. His clients had no complaints. He hadn't made any gross errors. He dressed appropriately; he lunched with the right people. So what was his boss complaining about?

The boss said, "Well, it's not always easy to put your finger on what adding value means, but it means at a minimum that you do more than what your job description says. The way we at headquarters view your work is this. We see you doing your job, not less, but no more. You do what is expected of you. But these days you have to do more if you want to stay at this firm. We can always find young people with your background. And we hire them just as we hired you. But for the long term, we're looking for those employees who add value."

Frank asked, "What didn't I do or what should I have done?"

His boss answered, "For starters, you took the job for granted. You did what you were told to do and did that well. But you didn't look past the space you were in to see what else might be needed and what more you could contribute. For example, last year you audited a division of TXZ. We had only a contract to audit the company's West Coast operations. TXZ has offices in many other states. You were in a position to have tried to sell TXZ on using our firm in its other divisions. That's one thing you could have done. You were an important contact once you started working in that part of the company. You had a golden opportunity to build that relationship and keep it alive. Instead you went in, did your job, and went on to your next assignment.

Frank protested, "But, I wasn't hired to market, I was hired to audit." His boss nodded. "I agree, you were hired for your background in accounting. But the market for our type of service has become so competitive that we need all our employees to wear a marketing hat when they're servicing a client. We need you to see the bigger picture, not just focus on your own assigned task."

DIAGNOSIS _____

Frank had a very narrow definition of what his job should include: his definition was based on a model that is rapidly becoming obsolete. In today's highly competitive marketplace, you must be more than just competent in your specialty. You must add value in other ways. In Frank's situation, enhancing his relationship with the customers would add value.

Rx

Take a close look at your present job and ask yourself if there is anything else you could be doing that would add value. Adding value could include something as obvious as going the extra mile for a customer or keeping in touch with customers as a way of building and maintaining relationships. It could include developing more efficient processes or ideas for saving money for the company. Spotting a problem before it turns into a catastrophe can be of enormous value. Coaching a new hire adds value. Helping out a colleague in a tight spot adds value. Teaching someone a new skill adds value. Anticipating the needs of your boss adds value and Brownie points (not to be lightly dismissed). Adding value is not about being political. It's also not brown nosing the boss or tooting your own horn. It's using your intelligence to figure out how you can do more than meet the basic requirements of your job even if it means going outside your area of expertise. Adding value is not a luxury reserved only for the get-ahead crowd; it's part of the basic strategy for surviving in today's world.

THE OFFICE AFFAIR

Maryanne had worked with Peter for three years and for the past year had reported directly to him. About six months ago, their relationship had become a romantic one.

They tried to be discreet about their involvement, but on occasion they would run into coworkers while going out. Eventually, everyone on the staff knew (but no one said anything) about Maryanne and Peter. For a while, the relationship seemed to have no effect on the department.

But, then, things seemed to change. Peter appeared to favor Maryanne's work and began spending a lot of time conferring with her behind closed doors about her projects. He put her in for a promotion within the group and pushed for a big salary increase based on her work. It seemed as if she could do no wrong. She was his right-hand person who effectively executed his every directive.

Their coworkers started to talk about Peter's favoritism of Maryanne, about the time they spent together, about how incompetent Maryanne really was and what actions really led to her promotion. Department productivity declined.

Peter's boss, Matt, eventually heard the rumors about Peter's relationship with Maryanne and had a chat with Peter. Based on what he heard, he started to question Peter's judgment. A cloud fell over the rationale behind Maryanne's promotion as Matt started to put two and two together and understood why Peter had fought so hard for the big raise that accompanied her promotion. Matt also queried Peter about his department's productivity and, after nosing around the unit a bit, realized that Peter had lost his staff's loyalty and was providing ineffective leadership to the group.

Matt assessed correctly that Peter was not performing his managerial responsibilities in an appropriate manner and transferred him from the list of fast trackers to a staff role. Peter's star quickly faded; his name was removed as a "Hi-Po." Now Maryanne was under a shadow; her skills were questioned—was she good or had Peter overstated her abilities? Ironically, she was as good as he'd thought, but her accomplishments were diminished by her liaison with Peter. She eventually left the company.

DIAGNOSIS

In some companies, boss-employee relationships are acceptable, and in some, they're not. Either way, they're bad business. For everyone's sake, one of the parties must be transferred. If that's not feasible, discretion and fair-handed treatment is critical. Peter would have been better off underplaying Maryanne's accomplishments because the allegations of favoritism are inevitable when others know of romantic relationships between a boss and employee.

Rx

If a relationship leads to marriage, most companies will require that the boss and employee not be in the same line of management and department. If you're in a relationship that you think may lead to such a denouement, you might consider getting a transfer early on—the end result will be the same but you may save two careers in the meantime.

If you're a coworker to a Maryanne, you're obviously in an awkward situation. The best advice is to not get heavily involved in petty office gossip about the relationship—you'll be seen as much more mature by keeping out of it. If you feel that you're at a disadvantage by the boss's relationship to your coworker, you might consider speaking with your human resources department to discuss *your* treatment from the boss. You may also consider talking to your boss' manager. This is a sticky situation (see "When Your Boss and Secretary Are an Item"), so carefully assess the politics and possibilities before you proceed.

The Office Affair: What to Do

If you see it:

- Don't leap to conclusions.
- Don't stare.
- Don't tattle.
- Don't ask questions.
- Give advice only if asked.
- Ignore it unless it threatens you.

If you're part of it:

- Be very, very careful.
- Examine the consequences of the relationship.
- Look for ways to limit the damage to your careers.
- Avoid any hint of favoritism.
- Separate your career from your love life as soon as possible.
- Assume more people know than you care to believe.

If you're the boss:

- Schedule a heart to heart and lay your cards on the table.
- Help the individuals deal with their career issues.
- Remain firm, but friendly.
- Don't get too judgmental about their behavior. Love, after all, is blind.

When Your Boss and Your Secretary Are an Item

This is a no-win situation. If you are to survive this one, it will take all your ingenuity and it still might explode in your face.

Let's look at a situation in which the employee almost didn't make it out "alive." The situation was just as the title suggests, "the boss and the secretary were an item." Dennis was the manager who was caught in the middle. He worked for a very large organization, so large that things like office affairs, while not encouraged, were overlooked rather than confronted. Dennis, however, became very upset when he realized what was going on. First, he suspected that his secretary was feeding his boss detailed reports about how Dennis managed the department. This meant Dennis could not trust her or the boss. He worried that the two lovers were discussing his work, which made him feel very uneasy. He checked with other members of his department and discovered that the affair had been going on for some time and he was one of the last to catch on.

As the affair grew more flagrant, Dennis's anxiety increased. He began to discuss with his colleagues what should be done. Dennis felt strongly that he needed to let senior management know what was going on—that it was unethical and that they should do something about it. He tried to talk some of his colleagues into joining him in the exposure plan, but they all refused. White Knight that he was, he went riding into one of the senior management's offices and blurted out his "discovery." He soon saw from the vice president's face and demeanor that he had made a big mistake. The vice president thanked him politely for his concern and ushered him out of his office. Sometime later, Dennis learned to his dismay that this vice president had been involved himself with another employee some five years ago and he was still very sensitive about it.

Dennis didn't know what to do next. He didn't dare go back to the vice president. He thought briefly about resigning, but that seemed foolish. After all, why should he resign—he wasn't the one having the affair. However, he was still concerned about the effect the relationship might have on his career. While he and his secretary had a decent working relationship, he had never felt she was part of his fan club. So he decided to sit tight and to keep his eyes open for another job somewhere in the company.

Six months later, there was a major reorganization in the company. Dennis's boss was one of those who got the pink slip. Dennis was moved to a new division and inherited a new secretary with whom he got along very well. Dennis learned later the big brass had known for a long time about the affair and the restructuring gave them an opportunity to get rid of his boss.

DIAGNOSIS

Dennis had a close call. He let himself get pulled into something that he would have done better to ignore. His responsibilities did not include policing who did what with whom off hours, and it certainly did not include playing whistle-blower on his boss. He should have ignored both the situation and the gossip, kept his suspicions to himself, and let the organization take care of the situation. Dennis obsessed over what the secretary might be saying in private to his boss. Instead, he should have focused on doing a good job (better yet, excellent job) and let the record speak for itself.

RX

This can be a no-win situation, but you need to conduct yourself with professionalism and aplomb. Avoid and stay clear of office affairs. Shut up. Don't discuss them, and above all, don't run around announcing them to senior management. They still shoot messengers as well as horses.

HOW TO RECOGNIZE "PERNICIOUS OFFICIOUSNESS" AND PUT AN END TO SUBTLE SABOTAGE

Pernicious officiousness is a fancy term for pains-in-the-posterior. You've met them. They range from well-intentioned busybodies to destructive meddlers. Our case is about the latter.

It all began when Jane went to work as a buyer for a large retail chain in the West. After seven years on the East Coast with its high-pressure culture, she was ready for a change of pace. She liked the people she met during the interview process, and she liked the area.

Her first day on the job was sheer joy. Members of the executive team took her to lunch. Her boss spent the afternoon talking to her about the company and the job. Her fellow buyers asked her to meet them for dinner at their favorite Mexican restaurant. So when Howard came around on the second day and asked how he could help, Jane thought she had died and gone to heaven. Howard was a group vice president; he had been with the company for over ten years and knew the ropes. She could use someone like him to help her get off to a smooth start. Thirty minutes into a lunch meeting with him, Jane sensed something was amiss, but she couldn't quite put her finger on it. Howard wanted to know if she had gotten her new driver's license. He asked about her housing situation. He wanted to see to it that she understood the local tax laws. He insisted she let him show her the area.

As time went on, there was no escaping Howard. Wherever she turned, Howard was there looking for ways to help her. It started making Jane crazy. It wasn't just that he was married and she was single. Although that bothered her, he didn't appear to be seeking that type of relationship. Rather, he seemed to want to be her chief advisor and counselor. While Jane had appreciated the help early on, it began to wear thin quickly. When she arrived to work in the morning, there was already a message in her E-mail to call Howard. He always wanted to make sure she got to work okay. Then it was, "Do you have someone to lunch with?" If not, Howard showed up as a more than willing escort. He pried her with questions about who she talked to. He shared the latest gossip. He gave her feedback on what she was wearing. ("It goes with our culture" or "It doesn't fit this organization.") He even had the audacity to ask her boss if she was getting the training and experiences she needed to succeed. When he found out that she was going to meet with a new insurance agent, he insisted on accompanying her. When Jane said she didn't need that help, he ignored her and appeared at the insurance agent's office just as she walked in.

By this time, Jane was doing her best to get rid of Howard. She dropped hints. She stopped answering his E-mail queries. She deliberately set up lunch dates to avoid him. But Howard was not so easily put off. When Jane was out sick for three days, Howard called her two to three times a day to see how she was. In desperation, Jane took her phone off the hook, a move that Howard took to mean she was in danger. He showed up at her apartment during lunch the third day to "make sure she was all right."

Jane was beside herself. Her job was too new for her to pull out, so quitting was not the answer. She needed to talk to someone, but she didn't know the company well enough to know who was safe. She had tried letting Howard know that she could operate on her own and, in fact, preferred it. She thanked him for all his kindnesses, but told him she was sure he had other concerns, especially with his *family.*

Howard was obtuse. Nothing she said seemed to make any difference. She knew from coworkers that Howard was a fairly powerful executive—powerful enough that someone at Jane's level should be careful of crossing him. But the day came when Jane could stand it no longer. Howard had come into her office on a Monday morning to ask her if she had a nice weekend and what did she do and what time and where. Jane lost it. She told Howard that he was driving her crazy. She thanked him angrily for all his help, but told him to lay off the favors and to get out of her life.

Howard's first reaction was to apologize, excuse himself, and leave her office. And for the next few days, he left her alone. And then began a subtle, but very effective, campaign called sabotage. The first hint of trouble was when her boss told her that Howard had brought up her name at the weekly staff meeting. Howard had described to the group how he had made a point of going out of his way to help Jane, but he now questioned whether she fit the culture. He told Jane's boss to keep an eye on her to make sure that their decision to hire her had been the right one. Jane quickly shared her long story of woe with her boss, who although sympathetic, told Jane that Howard was a very powerful person and that he as a boss was now on the defensive. A week later when Jane had to make a presentation before senior management, Howard acted as the grand inquisitor. He questioned her facts, he wondered aloud how she came to the conclusions she did, and he finished by suggesting she go over her data one more time to make sure she was on the right track before she submitted her recommendations.

DIAGNOSIS

Beware of corporate executives bearing gifts. Jane's antennae should have been up when Howard went beyond what most of us would consider offering normal assistance. Ingratiating behavior has its special markings. It usually appears unsolicited. The bearer of gifts disguises his or her offerings as "I only want to help you"—which usually disarms the reluctant recipient. The offers of help go beyond the norm: the helper crosses personal boundaries. The offer of help usually includes learning personal details about the recipient's life. In fact, there may be a voyeuristic quality to the helper's inquiries. Clever gift bearers walk such a fine line between being helpful and being nosy that only an experienced victim can spot the difference early on. They can also use their ingratiating behavior as a chance to control you.

Once this type work their way into your life, they are like leeches. Loosen their grip on one part of your life, and they grab you in another. A familiar pattern to many people is the neighbor who just can't seem to do enough for you. It is only later that the meddlesome quality of the relationship can be discerned.

Howard is walking a fine line between being a harasser in disguise and being a pain in the neck. He has been clever enough to avoid any hint of an interest in Jane sexually, although at some level that element may be present. But he could also be someone who likes to get into people's lives to gain control. It is typical of such people that they punish those who refuse their "favors."

Jane may have unwittingly contributed to this little scenario by acting helpless and more grateful than she really felt. Her attempt to "get along" with Howard may have sent signals to him that she was a willing participant. For Jane, this is a painful way to learn just how pernicious some officious people can be.

Rx

Jane will have to pull out all the stops if she is to counter Howard's not-so-subtle campaign to punish her for her "ingratitude." For starters, she needs to talk to someone in the company about what has happened. Perhaps she can go to the human resources representative who can then act as an intermediary in trying to contain the damage. Jane should also approach her boss for help unless he and Howard are in cahoots. She will need his support while Howard works his damage. She might ask either her boss or the human resources representative to meet with her and Howard. The agenda for that meeting is to address the working relationship of Jane and Howard. With a third-party witness, Jane can thank Howard for all his help, explain why she blew up as she did ("I'm a very independent person and I go crazy when I feel crowded"), and ask for his support as she develops her job. If Howard takes this as a signal to get back into her life closely, Jane will need to restate her need to be left to learn on her own in a friendly but firm manner. She also needs to document what is going on so that she has a record of the encounters.

NEVER UNDERESTIMATE THE SHARKS

Learning to swim with the sharks has almost become a rite of passage in corporate America. If you haven't been in or near a shark attack, you haven't really been through the ropes. Surviving an attack moves you from the position of callow young neophyte to a robust seasoned corporate warrior.

But as we know all too well, not everyone survives a shark attack. Our subject in this next case, Kelly, did not.

Her story began at the corporate headquarters of a large bank where she was in administration. Whether this was a "normal" bank or not is beside the point. It was the 1980s when banks were running high and handsome during the exploding real estate market. The executives who ran the company were making so much money for themselves and their stockholders that they could run the whole game. No one was interested in how they did it as long as the dividends made everyone richer. The bankers themselves had developed a sense of invulnerability—they had the Midas touch.

This was the setting for what happened to Kelly. The president, Archie, was from the "old boys" school of Ivy League and country clubs. He didn't even interview people who didn't have pedigree coming out of their dress socks to say nothing of which schools he considered in and which he considered out. He hobnobbed with the boat people (yacht crowd, that is); he threw lavish parties for the visiting brass (bank commissioner and folks like that). The fourth floor executive offices rivaled the French palaces—oriental rugs, artworks, mahogany paneling, china. This was indeed the good life.

Archie had a couple of idiosyncrasies. One was that he liked to bait people. He stated that the best way to measure a person was to challenge him on everything—to see how the person would "take the heat." So as part of his management-by-walking-around, he would saunter up and down the corridors looking for the poor fool who was unlucky enough to come through the halls at the wrong time. Archie would pin the hapless individual against the wall and begin his executive-friendly grilling. The idea was to try to bust the employee. Later Archie would regale the other executives with his stories. This, however, is a shark just nipping. To see what a full-blown attack looks like, read on.

Another of Archie's pastimes was hiring and firing. He was particularly fond of people he met while partying. If they met his criteria (the "right" people), he was inclined to offer them a job, even when none existed. Mysteriously, an opening always somehow appeared. That's where Kelly came in.

On one glorious Monday morning in May, Archie asked to see her. He brought her into his private office and began to talk to her very earnestly about the new manager of public relations who had recently been hired. Archie seemed to know a great deal about the young man's performance and all of it was bad. Kelly was surprised. The young man reported to her and she had kept close tabs on his work. So far, she had been very pleased with him. He had demonstrated a real flair for the business. But Archie seemed to think otherwise. Finally, Kelly, exasperated, challenged Archie. Archie leaned back and said, "Kelly, do I have to spell it out for you? The guy has got to go. I have someone else for the position. I'm giving you three months to document this man's performance and then you are to let him go." Kelly protested, but Archie made it clear she had no choice. If she didn't, her own job would be in jeopardy. She asked for time to think it over. He gave her until the next morning. His final words were, "If you can't do it, I can get someone who can."

So Kelly did it. She marked down the manager's performance and carefully documented his failings. The young man was distraught.

Now Kelly feels dirty. This is a game she has no stomach for. Now she wonders about all the other firings she witnessed.

One more thing. Kelly now knows that if Archie wants to fill her job with someone else, he will have little difficulty getting her boss to do the dirty work. That's how it works in this place.

DIAGNOSIS

Kelly has done something that will, no doubt, haunt her for a long time. But what were her choices given the situation? This is one of those devil-and-the-deep-blue-sea dilemmas. Any way she turns, Kelly is caught. The sharks are swimming, and she is in the water with them.

Rx

First, Kelly could have tried just saying no. Archie may have backed down if he couldn't get someone to do his dirty work. He has some of the hallmarks of a bully, so standing up to him just might have worked. But Kelly would have to be willing to risk her job when she called his bluff. If Archie followed through on his threat to "find someone who will," it would have given her a little time to deal with the consequences, which might include looking for another job.

She might have told Archie she was too uncomfortable doing something like that and appealed to his basic instincts, which may at this point be extinct. But it might have bought her some space. She might have challenged him directly by expressing her shock and horror at his directive. It wouldn't necessarily have saved her job, but it would have thrown a dose of reality into an otherwise Alice-in-Sharkland situation.

Learning to swim with the sharks, however, does not mean allowing them to force you into doing something you know is wrong. Archie is a human being run amok. He has lost his sense of decency. Sometimes you just have to make a bottom-line decision about the person you want to be and the price you are willing to pay in the corporate world. Only you can decide how far you'll swim with the sharks.

TEN SIGNS OF SHARKS IN THE WORKPLACE

1. Highly competitive—about everything
2. Ambitious—to the point of being ruthless
3. Has to win—will go for the jugular if necessary
4. Probes for the weakness of others
5. Always looking for an opportunity to put someone else down.
6. Cynical about any efforts to cooperate or collaborate
7. Self-centered, focuses on own agenda, not organization's
8. Exploits other people
9. Clearly looking out for number one no matter what
10. Totally indifferent or insensitive to other people's problems

How to Survive a Shark Attack

1. Develop good relationships with as many powerful people as you can. Make certain they understand your value to the workplace.

2. Demonstrate that you are 150 percent on board and will go the extra mile.
3. Avoid drawing blood. Corporate sharks attack out of a sense of insecurity heightened by a dose of sadism. Support their fragile egos.
4. Be open about your own sense of values, but avoid self-righteousness.
5. Limit your exposure. Avoid working with them whenever possible.
6. If attacked, stay cool. Remember, part of their fun is seeing you squirm.
7. Don't let them draw you into a dogfight. Instead, support them in public, even compliment them when you can. Your approach will confound the enemy and point out to everyone else the gap between your way of working with people versus theirs. And hang in there—what goes around, comes around.

HOW TO HANDLE BATTERING

The scene could have been out of a movie. Bill, the director of information systems, was standing at the head of a large oval conference table. Two rows of chairs circled the table. One row was drawn up to the table. Another row was pressed against the back wall. As the management team arrived for the meeting, Bill motioned where they were to sit. Some were directed to sit at the table, others were told to sit in the chairs in back. No one said a word; the faces of the men and women were tense. When one frazzled latecomer started to sit down at the table, Bill's voice boomed out, "Just where do you think you are going?" The man looked up, dumbly. "Get back to the wall with the rest of your bunch!" The man stumbled over to a seat against the wall. Bill paused. The tension was so palpable that some of the employees closed their eyes. Others stared intently at the floor.

Then it began. Bill was doing another one of his famous humiliate-and-abuse scenes. He pointed out that the people seated at the table were there for a reason. They are the "team players": they're loyal, they take orders, they don't make mistakes, they think. And they never forget who they work for. Bill then began to discuss them one by one. "Look at Ron. Ron has worked for this company for over ten years, and he has never, ever given me any problems. He listens, and he executes." "Look at Judy, she's another one. Totally competent. Knows when to come for help." And so it goes. The underlying themes are loyalty and a willingness to fight the forces outside the department. Bill is big on "us against them." Bill paused, began to eye the group seated against the wall and then he started again. "In marked contrast," he says, his words dripping with disdain, "is the bunch in back. The reason I told you to sit where I did was to show you who is doing his job and who isn't."

He pointed to the group in the back, then accused them of disloyalty, general stupidity, and keeping company with the enemy. He kept pointing his finger at them and asking, "Are you listening to me? I just want to make sure you understand." At different points, he asked the group at the table, "Am I right, John? Am I right, Mary?"

The tension in the room was painfully heavy. Some people broke out in a cold sweat. Bill paused as if to gear himself up for another tirade. Then unexpectedly, he stopped, looked around the room and said, "Meeting is over." Without a backward glance, he turned and exited. The rest of the group was momentarily paralyzed, then quietly left the room.

The scene was vintage Bill. His capacity for humiliation and abuse was legendary. However, he was also known as one of the smartest information systems professionals in the industry. The other executives were so intimidated by him that they abdicated all technical decisions. Bill had his kingdom all to himself. What's more, he delivered the goods. So he went unchecked.

Bill's downfall came when the company decided it needed a new system that integrated its national and international businesses. Marketing couldn't talk to manufacturing. Distribution couldn't talk to sales. The vendors couldn't talk with distribution. The information from the customers had to be hand-fed to the buyers. Bill, of course, was the obvious person to head such a project. Bill was to report later that he looked at every consulting firm in the business and that none could do it as cheaply or as quickly as his department could. Of course, he would have to hire a few more people. In short, give him the budget he needed to do the job and a free hand to do it his way, and, in two years, the company would have an integrated information system.

Three years and $7 million later, Bill was called in by the president of the company. He told Bill that he had been looking into the possibility of outsourcing information systems and that he had decided to cancel Bill's project since Bill's group had nothing to show for their work. He also told Bill he was fired.

As one might guess, Bill was shocked. He packed up and left the building almost immediately. Word spread quickly that Bill was gone. It was like the day after the storming of Bastille. The prisoners were free. Employees roamed the halls, grinning and laughing. At long last, the tyrant was gone.

DIAGNOSIS

So what has all this to do with learning how to play the game? If you're lucky, nothing. But the possibility of running into a sadistic boss is real, and you must know how to deal with it. And given the careericide potential inherent in this type of situation, you can do irreparable damage to your career.

RX

If you work with a batterer, you have but one choice; that is, to leave. There is no other option. It won't do you any good to redouble your efforts in the hope of gaining approval. The abuse and penalties will continue. It won't work if you play nice-nice. You'll only get abused more.

If you fight and confront this type of manager, you should expect to lose. That doesn't mean you shouldn't stand up to bullies. Although you may need to contend with a sadistic manager, you want to get out of there as fast as possible.

People who try to hunker down and survive often report feeling deeply fearful and powerless. Ultimately, they become paralyzed, unable to make even the smallest decision without the manager's consent. They begin to resemble prisoners, becoming increasingly suspicious of everyone and everything. Some employees never do recover their confidence even when the tyrant has gone. They become the walking wounded of the corporation.

If you can't get out right away, what do you do? First, take control of the situation. Make up your mind that you are going to survive this one by not doing anything irrational or suicidal. Buy some time to build your strategy. That may mean enduring the humiliation and abuse for a time. But your entire being should be focused on getting

How to Assess Managerial Sadism

Behavior					Frequency				
Never	Seldom	Sometimes	Often	Always					
0	1	2	3	4					

Behavior	Frequency				
1. Launches into screaming rages	0	1	2	3	4
2. Verbally assaults employees in public	0	1	2	3	4
3. Humiliates employees when giving feedback	0	1	2	3	4
4. Denies what he or she has said or ordered	0	1	2	3	4
5. Practices character assassination at all levels	0	1	2	3	4
6. Threatens and carries out vindictive behavior	0	1	2	3	4
7. Severely criticizes everything	0	1	2	3	4
8. Deliberately exposes weaknesses of others	0	1	2	3	4
9. Withholds positive reinforcement	0	1	2	3	4
10. Tolerates no dissent	0	1	2	3	4
11. Demands obedience	0	1	2	3	4
12. Capriciously rewards and punishes	0	1	2	3	4
13. Sets rules and enforces them arbitrarily	0	1	2	3	4
14. Curries favor, rewards friends	0	1	2	3	4
15. Is moody—may be seductively charming, then capriciously brutal	0	1	2	3	4

Scores 0-15	No problem
Scores 16-30	Red flag scores
Scores 31-45	Definitely in the running
Scores 46-60	Full-blown case

away, including getting a job in another company if necessary. Keep your plans to yourself unless you are very certain of relationships. Tyrants usually have pipelines to ferret out disloyal employees.

Make finding another job your total focus. Don't think that you can sit this one out and that it will all go away. Until and unless the tyrant is removed from his or her job, you are in danger, your career is in danger, your health is in danger—your emotional well-being is in danger. Keep a low profile. Use E-mail if available to communicate with the boss. Avoid discussing things with the boss. And beware if the boss tries to get cozy with you. Most abusers have two sides: one is the side that we know all too well, the sadistic side, but often abusers can have an almost seductive side to them. They are often able to convince the unwary that they are really nice guys after all. They may even do you favors to hook you.

If attacked, don't internalize the criticism. Remember, you are dealing with an irrational person. The person's judgment is, at best, unreliable. If you have to live with the situation for a while, get yourself to a counselor in order to remain emotionally intact and relatively undamaged. After it's all over, count yourself in the company of those who have been to the battlefield and survived. Give yourself a medal for holding your own while being subjected to enemy fire in extremely hostile conditions.

BLOOD IS THICKER THAN WATER:
The Pitfalls of Working in a Family-Owned Company

John works for a business that was started over 50 years ago by a highly inventive engineer who developed and patented a unique process. The second generation turned it into a big business. Now it's in the hands of the third generation, and the process isn't working any more. The grandson who was appointed president is fighting with his younger brother who thinks he's God's gift to production. The oldest sister (the one none of them can stand) thinks she knows how to market. The other sister is on maternity leave, but is trying to run the show from the nursery. Pa and Ma are in Florida, supposedly enjoying retirement. But neither can keep their hands off the telephone. They not only call the family members to check on their decisions, but they countermand those decisions they don't agree with. John is going nuts.

John is a midlevel manager in the personnel department. Because he's been around a while, the family members see him as their confidant. Each gives their side of the story except Ma and Pa who just yell at him just as they yell at the family. Staff meetings are a nightmare. No one trusts anyone else. They accuse each other of dogging it or trying to take control or say that the other person is an ignoramus or that "Ma and Pa never intended you to be a part of this, you just horned your way in" or "Who said you were such a hot shot? Where would you be today if Ma and Pa hadn't handed you your job on a silver platter?" and on and on and on.

Up to now, the business has survived because of the strong customer base established over the past two decades. But foreign competition has finally come to Grover City, and the company is losing market share.

The question is: Can John do his job (which he likes in spite of everything) and survive the family feud? Ever since the third generation took over three years ago, there has been a 25 percent turnover in managers. A number of them resigned, but others were let go because they couldn't focus on their jobs and handle the politics of the infighting.

John didn't fare very well either. He developed a close relationship with the brother who ran production. John thought it was probably good for his career that he was "in" with at least one member of the family. Wrong! John was very quickly drawn into the battle and forced to take sides. Production still loves him, but the president (whose vote is the one that counts) doesn't see John as "having managerial talent." Which is a nice way of saying he's finished. He'll never go anywhere in this company.

DIAGNOSIS

John is in a no-win situation. His strategy to ingratiate himself with one of the family members has backfired. The chances of the family straightening itself out are not good. If it stays on its present course, it could infight itself out of business. John is not only dealing with the normal everyday slugfests that characterize many companies, but he is in the middle of a family feud that has minimal chances of being resolved given everyone's strong feelings.

Since family-owned businesses account for 95 percent of all U.S. businesses and 45 percent of all jobs (one third of *Fortune* 500 companies are family-owned), chances are good that you may work for a family-owned business someday (or already do). What are the risks and how do you manage this tinder box?

Rx

If you work for a family-owned business, you must first read the relationships accurately. You must avoid siding with family members and give your support only to those positions and decisions with which you really agree. Your basic integrity is what will carry you in this type of situation. All family members must see you as someone who is committed to the well-being and success of the company, even if it means disagreeing with one of them at times. Taking sides will never work, even though you might get some short-term gains. An important caveat—never talk negatively about one family member to another, no matter how much they say about each other. (It's okay to criticize your own family, but no one outside the clan has that right.)

At this point, John needs to mend his relationship with the president. And he must convince the brother who runs production that in the interest of the company, he, John, needs to have a good working relationship with both brothers as well as with other family members. There is only one road to take in family-owned businesses and that's the high road.

John, as well as the other employees, must also accept the fact that he will never attain certain positions in the company if a family member wants the same spot. Regardless of the person's capabilities, blood is thicker than water. So John must make his peace on this one or look for a job in a publicly-owned company. (The one consolation may be that in large family-owned businesses, family members tend to occupy only the very highest levels, so there are opportunities for advancement in the middle- and senior-level positions.)

The greater danger for John is that the family will end up destroying the business or having to sell it in order to prevent fratricide. Either way, it poses security issues for its employees. If you work for a family-owned business, you need to assess its basic stability, and you need to assess whether you will be happy working in what may be a top-down leadership style. If you can take orders, you may be okay. If you want to be in on the decision making, you may be frustrated unless you have gained the trust of the family's ruling members. And if you want to become the boss, forget it.

WORKING FOR A FAMILY-OWNED BUSINESS

Advantages	Disadvantages
Family's pride and joy	Messy—lots of conflict around roles and relationships
Less bureaucracy, more personal treatment	Family members may be given preference because of who they are, not what they can do
Little or no pressures from stock market	
Focus on the long-term, no quarterly reports	Can become a family welfare agency
Tendency to plow profits back into firm	Family members often lack training and experience
Employees feeling as if they are part of the family	Board of directors often weak, ineffective
Greater flexibility with taking action	May stay wedded to outdated vision and strategy

CRAZY PEOPLE, CRAZY SYSTEMS

Wendy works for a sick organization. The CEO is biding his time, waiting for his golden parachute to kick in. The vice president of research and development runs his department like a despot. Manufacturing is out in left field playing games with just-in-time inventory and production. Whether the customers get what they have ordered on time is irrelevant; the average delay is over four months.

Marketing lives in another world—the one that vanished about 20 years ago. They still think they know what's best for the customers. Finance and administration is a monolithic monster intent on bringing everyone to their knees by enforcing their 2-foot-thick book of rules and procedures. The vice president of sales has her own thing going. She plays cozy cute with the president and has the board of directors wall-eyed.

In the midst of all this craziness, meet Wendy, the distribution manager. Five years ago she was an eager young MBA ready to storm the ramparts in manufacturing. Today she is a seasoned warrior with more than just a few scars to show she has been there.

Six months ago she was asked by the president to head up a new task force. The company had known for a long time that it would have to integrate its far-flung functions and services with new software programs. Because Wendy had good working relationships with many of the people in information systems and because she had updated her own department's technology, she was seen as a natural to run the project.

Her job was to form a team of users and programmers. The users were to tell the programmers what they needed, and the programmers were to develop the programs. Sounds doable—yes? Wendy thought so. She was very excited about this opportunity. It was the first highly visible task she had been given since she joined the company. She knew that the successful completion of the task would make a bottom-line impact on the business. She was assigned ten programmers who were to act as liaisons from the information systems group and ten representatives from the various business functions. The idea was to meet, hammer out a strategy, and get to work. There was only one hitch. The director of information systems thought he should have been given the job. After all, it was his department that would be "doing all the work." He announced to Wendy that he would be sitting in on the meetings to "monitor" his people. Wendy should have sensed something right then, but in the spirit of cooperation she said fine. So there he sat at meetings, glaring at her, not saying a word.

Three months into the project, things began to seriously deteriorate. The programmers said the users were unreasonable. They didn't understand technology, they didn't know what they wanted—and they didn't like what the programmers suggested. The users said that the programmers were arrogant and abrasive and only pretended to listen to their requests. As relationships broke down, the meetings heated up. Near the end of one particularly rough session, the director of information systems stood up and announced he was taking over the project. With that, he proceeded to order his employees to go ahead and write the programs as they thought were needed. He told the users that they could learn to adjust their procedures to the program.

He also told the users that the programmers would call them if and when they needed them, but all this user-friendly stuff "was going to stop." The company needed the programs and he and his team would produce them. The users would have to make the adjustments because that's how it was.

Wendy was shocked. She had never imagined in her wildest dreams that something like this could happen. She tried to protest, but the director announced the meeting was over and he left the room. Wendy tried to speak with him, but the director waved her off saying he had too much work to do to waste his time with her.

Now, in a normal company, Wendy could have gone back to the president and protested. After all, it was the president who had asked her to run the project. In a normal company, the president would have never tolerated this type of usurpation of power. But this, as you will recall, was not a normal company. This was a crazy company. So Wendy went to the crazy company's crazy president and told him what happened. He told her that sometimes that's how things work out and that it was probably for the best. (Yawn.) Then Wendy went to see the Operations Director. He just shook his head and said "What a shame." In desperation, Wendy decided to take the information systems director head on. She marched into his office and began to state her case. Halfway through, he interrupted her and told her she was basically incompetent, that no one in his department had any respect for her or for that matter anyone else on the task force, and that he, the director, was keeping the project. He was very matter of fact. That's just how it was.

Now Wendy thinks she may be losing her mind. She can hardly believe that the company would let such a thing go by. She doesn't know whether to laugh or to cry. It's gone from tragedy to comedy except the joke is on her. She is five years into her career and she's hit the wall.

DIAGNOSIS

The company is obviously poorly managed. Wendy has little or no support from senior management. She may have lost too much credibility in this last debacle to recover. The question for Wendy is: Does she want to work for this company enough to do what it will take to get through this crisis and get her career back on track?

If she stays, she may become infected by the sickness that pervades this company's culture. Its employees are deeply fearful: they worry about their jobs, about the future of the company, and about the capricious nature of the senior executives. Productivity and morale are at an all-time low. Absenteeism is up, as are disability claims. Sooner or later, Wendy may become sucked into this vortex of despair. She may decide that looking for a job outside the company is the best strategy.

Rx

Wendy underestimated the power of the director to sabotage her project. She acted naively when she set up her team without taking his strong feelings into account. She could have gone back to the president and expressed her discomfort with the arrangement and asked that the information systems director be accommodated in some way. That might have helped to deflect some of his anger. She also could have gone directly to the director, put the issue on the table, and asked for his input and cooperation. In some way, she needed to negotiate a relationship with the director that would support him and the project. This was one situation where the groundwork was needed before the task force started its work. Wendy also could have done team building with the task force members. The parties had such different agendas from the beginning, that even without the interference of the director, the task force was in trouble.

As for the present, should she decide to stay, she needs to have a discussion with the president concerning her role and responsibilities. She needs to come out of that meeting with enough clarity and support to continue in her position.

The bottom line is that the company itself is the problem. It behooves anyone looking for a job to find out as much as possible about the culture before saying yes.

Ultimately, the answer to this one is to not ever get into it. But sometimes it happens. It can be very difficult to assess a company's relative health before beginning a job with it. Many organizations have great public relations and look good on paper even though the inside is like a rat's nest.

Rule of Thumb: If the system is so crazy that you are beginning to feel nuts yourself, it's time to go. Don't rationalize it. By the time you get to where you really can't stand it anymore, you may have thrown away the best years of your life with a lot of grief—and maybe psychotherapy bills—to show for it.

HANDLING THE INEVITABLE CONFLICTS

Patrick works in an area that has a hot product that has to get to the market quickly. But the team responsible for the production side of the project is faltering. His boss has been pitting his staff against each other. The team members are engaged in what appears to be institutionalized back-stabbing. Each person understands that he or she must be on guard at all times against possible attack and in turn often continually and aggressively works to make others look bad. There are concerns about how realistic the project schedule is, and thus there is posturing among the team members; all of them are looking to protect their roles to be sure they don't get blamed if the project does not meet the schedule.

On top of all this, one of the department supervisors has charged that the environment is hostile and reeks of sexual harassment. She claims that several of the employees made inappropriate remarks about her physique when she passed their work area or lunch table.

Patrick was eating lunch with some of the other guys on one of the days the incidents allegedly occurred. While he did hear some kind of a remark, he is not *exactly* sure what it was since he was talking to someone at the table behind him when it happened. He does think there was a sexist remark made, though. Now he is in the middle of this mess; he is a friend of the supervisor who has made the complaints and has good working relationships with the other employees. The last thing he wants is to be in the middle of this one.

Patrick already feels overwhelmed by the conflicts he encounters in his job. Although this isn't the first time that someone has tried to pull him in on his or her issue, this one could blow up into a major firestorm. Patrick feels as if he is in a no-win situation. Each side wants him to testify for it. The pressure has become so intense that Patrick feels he is the one being prosecuted.

DIAGNOSIS

Patrick does not like conflict; it makes him uneasy. He avoids arguments and actually leaves meetings if the discussion gets too heated. He is having an especially difficult time with this latest situation because, up to now, he has been one of the few team members who has managed to keep some semblance of a working relationship with the feuding factions. Now he is getting pulled into battle where the outcome can only be increased bitterness and dissension.

Although not all workplaces or teams are as full of conflict as Patrick's, conflict is a way of life in many group efforts. Since conflict is inevitable, the place to start learning how to handle it is to assess where you are in terms of your own style. If you are satisfied with your style and are getting the results you want, strive to continue to hone your skills. If you feel you need to learn to deal with conflict more effectively, get yourself to the nearest library and read the how-to books on handling conflict. As for the corporate conflict that pervades most workplaces, make your peace with it—it is inevitable. What you can do about it is to become as effective as possible in dealing with conflicts that include you personally.

Rx

Patrick needs to learn how to deal with this conflict. Because he tends to avoid all conflict, this situation is extremely stressful for him. He is very uncomfortable if he thinks anyone is angry with him or might get mad at him. He spends a great deal of energy and time trying to avoid the conflicts in his department; as a result, he is seen as a pushover, someone who is easily intimidated.

Patrick needs to tell all the players that he heard what he heard (or didn't), whether that makes them angry or disappoints them or whatever. No matter what he says, he is bound to make one of the parties angry, and he will have to live with that. Patrick needs to experience the consequences of taking a position on something and testing his assumptions about what might happen to him as a result. His present assumption is that he will acquire enemies, and he might. But he might not; he might gain respect and be seen as someone who has the courage to tell the truth regardless of the consequences.

Coping with Conflicts: What's Your Style?

Handling conflict is difficult for most of us. Unless we had very skilled role models when we were growing up, we never learned how to handle disagreement well. However, there are well-developed techniques for learning how to deal with conflict. By identifying your own style for coping with conflict, you will have taken the first step in the process.

King of the Hill

- Highly competitive
- Get what you want at the expense of others
- In-your-face approach
- Survival-of-the-meanest mentality

The Doormat

- Make no demands on anyone
- Plays victim

- Avoids rather than speaks up
- Sometimes becomes passive aggressive

Love-Sweet-Love

- Cooperate to a fault
- Can't say yes fast enough
- Plays "I'm-all-right-I'll-stand-outside" (when it's raining and supper time)

Scratch Each Other's Back

- I give a little and you give a little
- "Even Steven"
- Let's cut the baby in half
- Measure it very carefully to make sure it's fair

Let's Help Each Other

- Here's what I need. What do you need?
- Let's stay with this until we both get what we need
- Tell me your concerns and I'll tell you mine
- Let's collaborate; that way we both win

YOU'RE A VISIONARY, BUT CAN YOU IMPLEMENT?

Susan has been told by her manager that she is being moved out of her job and that she needs to find herself another job internally or externally, if necessary. The reason? He says that she is great at seeing the big picture, and can even get others around her excited with her vision of what could be, but that when it comes to planning and executing the plan that could make it all happen, she loses interest and energy. As a result, her projects are not on track, and her work is causing a negative effect on the company's bottom line.

Last year, the company wanted to offer a new line of promotional products that customers could use as "give-aways" to their own customers, such as pens with the individual's name on it, calendars that advertised the company name or monogrammed datebooks. Susan's job was to come up with new ideas, develop the designs, and cost out production. She was also part of the manufacturing task force that helped troubleshoot the manufacturing glitches, and she was to oversee the projects through to completion.

Susan did excellent work on the idea generation and design aspects of the project, but lost interest and follow-through when it came to the production side of the job. Her lack of executional skills were seen as directly related to the missed deadline and delayed project schedule that caused the company to miss an important show that would be attended by potential customers.

Her boss explained her accountability for the project and told her that while they valued her as an idea person, they needed someone who could stay with the idea and see it through all its processes. He told her that she avoided the cost analysis task and skipped those meetings that bored her.

He also reminded her that he had given her the same feedback a year ago, but she hadn't changed. Susan protested his description of her performance by reminding him that she had been hired for her creativity, not for her skills in production. But he stood firm and insisted that, although she had been brought on board for her ability to be a visionary, he had told her that she had to learn the other parts of the process and actually carry them out. He said that it was her failure to learn as well as to implement that was her difficulty and that he could not afford her if she insisted on such a narrow role.

DIAGNOSIS

Susan is right about her strengths. She is the idea person. But everyone in her organization needs to wear more than one hat. Susan wanted to do the work that appealed to her and to avoid the work that didn't. Thus she limited her value to her company. The story could have been reversed. Many people are good at execution and getting something accomplished, but they have a difficult time when it comes to developing a vision or creating new ideas.

For Susan to survive, she must learn to do those things she doesn't enjoy or do well so that she makes a greater contribution in her organization. Her payoff will be that she will get a chance to also do what she likes best, creating ideas for new products.

RX

For the present, Susan needs to talk her boss into giving her another chance to show her stuff and to lay out specific learning objectives so that he can see her commitment to developing herself. She could ask for a six-month trial period to show him what she can do. Although it's late in the game, he just might go for it.

Susan needs to understand just how important such learning could be for her career. If she could discipline herself to become involved with all phases of production, she could become a highly valued employee with the potential for a high-level position. As it is now, she is perceived as a good idea person who works well with everyone, but as someone who lacks follow-through.

Whether you are a visionary or tactician, you must learn to do those parts of the job that have less appeal for you. Organizations today need people who can do many things well and a few things very well.

If her boss gives her another chance, Susan can also work to delegate the implementation aspects to others, either her staff or other team members. Not all people can do everything, but the successful ones will compensate for their shortcomings by surrounding themselves with people whose skills are complementary and/or by working to offset their weaknesses.

Are You a Tactician or Strategist?

There's nothing wrong with either, but you must realize that the most successful people at the top are visionaries, not just implementers. People who see the goal and then develop programs to meet them will go farther than will those who simply get the job done. Just remember, both types are required to sustain an organization.

Read through the descriptions that follow and decide which description fits you more closely. If you are more of a visionary, you will need to make sure you lay the groundwork for making change happen. It won't be enough just to see how the future might be shaped. You will need to get down in the trenches and do some of the spade work. If you are more of an implementer, you bring another type of value to your company. You are good at getting things done. What you must be careful about is discounting the visionary. While some of that type of thinking may seem far out to you, companies need their visionaries as certainly as they need people like you who are grounded in reality—the nuts and bolts of how to get things done.

Do You Have What It Takes to Get Ahead in Your Organization?

Assess the importance of these factors to your company's environment; circle the appropriate score. Assess the extent to which you currently demonstrate each factor; circle the appropriate score.

	Importance to Company	Your Level of Competency
	High Low	High Low
Interpersonal skills	5 4 3 2 1	5 4 3 2 1
Communications skills (oral/written)	5 4 3 2 1	5 4 3 2 1
Political skills	5 4 3 2 1	5 4 3 2 1
Networking ability	5 4 3 2 1	5 4 3 2 1
Technical knowledge	5 4 3 2 1	5 4 3 2 1
General business knowledge	5 4 3 2 1	5 4 3 2 1
Physical appearance	5 4 3 2 1	5 4 3 2 1
"Dress for success"	5 4 3 2 1	5 4 3 2 1
Sense of urgency	5 4 3 2 1	5 4 3 2 1
Ability to make decisions quickly	5 4 3 2 1	5 4 3 2 1
Tolerance for ambiguity	5 4 3 2 1	5 4 3 2 1
Importance of the team	5 4 3 2 1	5 4 3 2 1
Importance of the individual	5 4 3 2 1	5 4 3 2 1
Significance of status/hierarchy	5 4 3 2 1	5 4 3 2 1
Degree of formality in the environment	5 4 3 2 1	5 4 3 2 1
Need for high energy	5 4 3 2 1	5 4 3 2 1
Ability to think strategically	5 4 3 2 1	5 4 3 2 1
Ability to get things done quickly	5 4 3 2 1	5 4 3 2 1
Customer orientation	5 4 3 2 1	5 4 3 2 1
Planning and organizational skills	5 4 3 2 1	5 4 3 2 1
Creativity, innovation	5 4 3 2 1	5 4 3 2 1
Ethics/integrity	5 4 3 2 1	5 4 3 2 1
Competition among peers	5 4 3 2 1	5 4 3 2 1
Collaboration among peers	5 4 3 2 1	5 4 3 2 1
Risk taking	5 4 3 2 1	5 4 3 2 1
Patience	5 4 3 2 1	5 4 3 2 1
Team player	5 4 3 2 1	5 4 3 2 1
Loyalty	5 4 3 2 1	5 4 3 2 1
Social conscience	5 4 3 2 1	5 4 3 2 1

Analyzing the Results

1. Identify gaps of 2 to 4 points between your rating and the company's rating;
2. Of these, identify the five that are most important to you;
3. Develop action plans to close the gaps; or
4. If you cannot reconcile them, consider another company.

Strategist/Visionary

Develops the plays
Sees into the future
Plans ahead
Thinks conceptually
Sees the forest from the trees
Creatively puts together diverse concepts and ascertains effects on the
    business.

Tactician/Implementer

Carries out the plays
Focuses on the here and now
Relies on ability to handle it when it happens
Thinks more concretely
Likes clearing the forest
Develops creative ways to implement changes in direction

PROMOTING YOUR CAREER HEALTH—
Playing the Game

Your career success is dependent on you being attuned to the idiosyncrasies of your individual workplace, on your antennae working
nonstop to understand the inner workings and relationships, and on
your capacity to deal with the changing tableau of the business world
today. Your ability to "play the game" will have a direct and ongoing
effect on your career potential.

What you need to master

- Where the power is in your organization
- How to work with difficult people
- When and how to take risks
- How to recognize, analyze, and deal with sensistive situations
- How to handle conflict

Barriers to success

- Inability to read situations and relationships
- Making political faux pas

- Avoiding dealing with conflict and its effects on your relationships with others
- Taking risks that are too big for your level of expertise or responsibility
- Naive about the power relationships in your organization

Payoff for you and your career

- Getting closer to the power centers
- Being seen as a player who understands the organization
- Not being blindsided by others

Chapter 3

HEALING CAREERS IN CRISIS

What to Do If Your Career Goes Off Course

CAREER TRAUMA:
The Modern Malady

Career trauma is the result of an incident or a series of incidents that impacts your ability to function at your normal level. For some, trauma occurs when the job suddenly disappears or they are unexpectedly fired. For others, the trauma is the result of months or even years of psychological wounding such as working for an abusive boss, sweating out extended periods of job insecurity, or even something as common (but equally lethal) as working too hard for too many hours over too long a time.

The result is a loss of spirit, the diminution of motivation and energy, and a general feeling of powerlessness that whatever you do, it's never enough; the whole situation seems overwhelming.

Not all trauma, however, is the result of what the company does to people. Some career trauma is self-inflicted. For example, Francine has been on the fast track in her organization, which positions her as potential officer material. However, as her level of responsibility has increased, so has her cockiness and recklessness. Her temper tantrums are part of the company legend. In fact, people were beginning to wonder if part of getting ahead in this company was dependent on one's ability to stage ear-shattering tirades.

Her last assignment was seen as "the big one"—the job that would make or break her. The new president gave her 18 months to turn around the sales department. The problems facing the department were formidable. What really doomed Francine's efforts, however, was not the massive resistance she met when she tried to turn sales on its head. Her real problems arose when she repeatedly locked horns with the new president. For the first time, she was confronted with someone who refused to put up with her "style" of management. When she protested her last evaluation and threatened to go over the new president's head to the chairman, he told her to go ahead.

When she met with the chairman she demanded a different assignment "or else." The chairman listened quietly, then suggested she take off a few weeks to pull herself together, and he would do what he could to find her another spot in the company. The weeks have now dragged on, and she's presently doing a "no-brainer" in a staff role. She feels alone, unsupported, and rejected. For her, career trauma is a very real and painful situation. She's lost her punch. She wonders if she can ever again find the energy and willpower to be the dynamo she used to be.

Kurt's case is different. His trauma is the result of a long-term erosion of his self-esteem. He worked for over four years for a very demanding, abusive boss. Kurt is so demoralized that all he can do is say "yes, sir" and "no, sir." He has developed a noticeable tic above his right eye. Kurt is past the point of working on building a career. He simply wants to survive, one day at a time. His soul is gone. Should he ever face a layoff, he would probably be incapable of dealing with the stress, let alone mount a job campaign.

Dave works as a consultant for a large accounting firm. His trauma is directly related to the hours he puts in at work. Like Kurt, he's worn down, but in Dave's case, it's physical fatigue compounded by the intensity of the job. Ten years ago, Dave could handle the pressure and the schedule. Now he's deeply tired, and with that goes a lack of motivation, to say nothing of creativity. Dave feels he has succeeded if he can get through just one more week. The problem is that there is no end in sight. Career trauma for Dave is not a condition, it's a way of life.

DIAGNOSIS

You may not be experiencing trauma at the levels described in these three case studies, but you may be dealing with enough career trauma that you need to take the situation seriously. It is important to assess the level of your distress so that you can address the problems before they become a crisis. Read through the following statements and place a check before each statement that describes you most of the time. (An occasional bout of career trauma is like an occasional bout of the "blues"—you only need to pay attention to it when it becomes chronic.)

Give yourself one point for each of these symptoms that applies to you:

_____ 1. Gnawing doubts about your chances of making it

_____ 2. Painful, recurring memories of past mistakes, goofs, and personal disasters

_____ 3. Vague, but persistent, uncertainty about how you stack up, compared to others

_____ 4. Fear and trembling at the thought of what lies ahead

_____ 5. Anger and bitterness at the unfairness of it all

_____ 6. Free-floating anxiety about your career and its improbable success

_____ 7. Feelings of longing to fold up your tent and get out of the rat race

_____ 8. Paralyzing inertia due to corporate battle conditions

_____ 9. Bewilderment and confusion over the constantly shifting playing field

_____10. Burnout and exhaustion from trying to stay even, to say nothing about getting ahead

Total Score_____

Scores 1-3   You are carrying on as well as can be expected given what's going on.

Scores 4-6   You are looking shaky. You have probably sustained injury, but nothing that you cannot fix if you get the right treatment.

Scores 7-10 You are in deep trouble and you don't need a checklist to tell you about it. You may even qualify for battle honors for performance above and beyond the call of duty. You may want to analyze where and when you were wounded, that is, mergers, acquisitions, downsizing, purges, abusive bosses, relentless expectations, and so on.

Rx

Surviving Career Trauma Surviving any trauma always includes working through your emotions. This means that if you have a high score, you may need to find someone to talk to about what you are feeling. Once you have dealt with the feelings you have about what has happened to you, you are ready to approach the problem in a more objective manner. The following exercises will help you to work through your career trauma in a rational and effective way.

Step 1. Assess the troublesome situations in your workplace.
Step 2. Identify those situations over which you have control.
Step 3. Identify those situations over which you have no control.
Step 4. Take action only in those situations where you have control.

Situations You Can Control	*Situations You Can't Control*
1.	1.
2.	2.
3.	3.
4.	4.
5.	5.
Take Action	*Take No Action*
You can choose how you want to respond to different people.	You can't change people who don't want to change.
You can choose how to feel about people, problems, and issues.	You can't move immovable objects through brick walls.
You can develop your own goals and action plans.	You can't influence or impact every event.

Don't

Feel helpless.
Feel powerless.
Feel you can never change.
Feel sorry for yourself.
Play victim.

Do

Understand what you can and cannot change. Use good judgment to know the difference.

Know when to back off and let go.

Reduce your own need to control the uncontrollable.

Focus on what you can change and do something about.

Remain optimistic. Optimists live longer and are more successful than pessimists.

COPING WITH CAREER DERAILMENT

Many people think that derailment is something that happens only to trains and top-level managers. But no one and no level is secure against derailment. The potential for careers to go off track is always present. Sometimes employees can sense that all is not well, but the derailment can also happen abruptly without any hint about what's ahead. Such was the case with Elizabeth. When she got a new boss two months ago, there didn't seem to be any problems. Everyone continued to do what they had always done while the new man settled in. Because Elizabeth had been the trusted assistant for the vice president who had retired, she had no apprehensions about her value to the company.

Elizabeth wasn't concerned when she was called into her new boss's office on a Monday morning. To her total surprise her boss told her that her job was being eliminated. The boss explained, "We are becoming more customer oriented, and we have redefined the job you do to include a high percentage of time building customer relationships. We see your skills as having value, but not here at this time." The boss offered to support her while she looked for other positions within the company.

Elizabeth was dumbfounded. She shook her head and then looked at the boss. "Where did I go wrong?" she asked. The boss became very quiet. Finally, he answered. "There just wasn't support for you from upper management. And I am not in a position to build that support for you. Whatever went on before is beyond my control. I'm sorry, but that's how it is." Elizabeth's first reaction was anger. She told her husband that evening that it was all about politics and she had lost her position because she didn't play the game.

However, as Elizabeth reflected on it, she remembered that in the past three years she had crossed swords with a number of the senior-level people on issues of company policy. Elizabeth felt strongly that since she was the expert, what she said should go. When people disagreed with her, she held firm and never yielded. She saw herself as upholding the integrity of the company. People who disagreed with Elizabeth had a different explanation for her behavior. They saw her as stubborn and as someone who became very angry when crossed. No one who worked with her was surprised that her nit-picking, black-and-white approach to complex problems had caught up with her. In fact, few people felt sorry she had been removed. She was difficult to work with and for.

Diagnosis

Locking horns with senior management is always problematic, but to do it on a consistent basis almost guarantees career problems. Elizabeth had always explained away her run-ins with senior management, and her old boss had always been able to buffer her or mediate the issue. However, once Elizabeth lost her protector, she was, as they say, history.

Elizabeth derailed because she was too rigid. When she was asked to interpret company policy on some issue, she immediately took a position and would refuse to even consider other possible ways of addressing the problem. She made company history one year when she sent out a memo to the vice president of finance informing him that he had used one more vacation day than he was entitled to. When the vice president tried to explain the situation, Elizabeth was intransigent. She told the vice president that policy was policy and that the vice president owed the company money for that day. Elizabeth would not budge. As a result, her boss had to intervene and work out a solution. Elizabeth had always looked on that incident as a moment of triumph. Others would say it was the beginning of her career demise.

Rx

Elizabeth needs a world and a job where there is no ambiguity. She sees the world in black and white. She had no tolerance for the gray areas. Her intolerance for ambiguity puts her at a disadvantage in any job where the problems cannot be answered by a simple "yes" or "no."

Elizabeth also needs to understand how she contributed to her own derailment. Her rigidity coupled with her naivete about company politics ultimately caught up with her. Instead of building relationships with senior management, she gave them a hard time. She never saw her job as that of serving the customers. To her, fellow employees were people who needed to understand how "her" programs worked. It was her job to make sure there were no deviations from policy. Whether that met the needs of employees was not part of her job.

Rigidity is a difficult problem. Elizabeth will need to look for a job that does not involve ambiguous data, one where the issues can be literally interpreted and where the enforcement of standards is valued.

Given the black mark she has on her record with this company, she needs to repair the damage quickly if she is to find something else within the organization. For starters, she needs to sit down with the new boss and describe to him her rationale for how she performed. She also needs to acknowledge that she underestimated the effect her approach to problems had on senior management as well as on other employees and to ask for the new boss's advice as to how to get back on track.

She also needs to identify her strengths, which include her ability to master a complex body of knowledge and to stay highly focused on what she is doing, regardless of distractions. She will do better working with data than with people.

Finally, she needs to learn when it is time to play Custer's last stand and when it is time to sound a retreat. As any old soldier can tell you, it is much better to choose your battles based on the odds of winning versus going at it when you know from the start you are outnumbered, outgunned, and outranked.

Causes of and Cures for Career Derailment

Derailment is more common than most of us want to admit. In fact, it is so common that some social scientists have conducted in-depth studies as to its causes and cures. We have listed several of the most commonly identified causes for derailment, based on some of the research. We have also suggested cures for them. Read through the causes and cures in order to make sure you don't engineer your own derailment.

Causes	*Cures*
Being such a hard driver that you leave your colleagues breathless and bruised	Pay attention to your relationships. Build them, maintain them, and mend them.
Making sure that when someone has made a factual mistake they hear from you about it regardless of the situation or the importance of the error.	Learn to keep observations to yourself unless the "correction" is critical to the situation. If you must correct someone, do it diplomatically. Most important, do not cause others to lose face because you have caught them making an error. People dislike people who make them look foolish; sooner or later they find a way to return the favor.
Arguing for the sake of it, knowing that you are usually right or can outargue or outlast the other person.	Hammering on people because you are getting a kick out of it never wins friends or influences people. Remember, not everyone enjoys the role of getting beat up by your verbal jousting. Most people prefer persuasion if they are to change their minds. And, if you're just doing it for fun and games, they will find someone else to play with.
Losing confidence in yourself at crucial moments. Secretly believing that sooner or later the rest of the world will find out you are a phony.	This is commonly known as the "impostor syndrome." It occurs to more people than you would believe. In fact, the majority of people in the workplace worry that they really aren't as good as others think they are. Remind yourself that you have earned your position and that it is your talent and hard work that brought you to this level. The real danger for those who suffer from the impostor syndrome is that they will try to compensate for these doubts by becoming perfectionists or procrastinators. If you feel those types of reactions creeping up on you, talk to people that you can trust. Ask what they see in you in terms of competencies. Chances are they will tell you that your self-doubts are unfounded and that you need to relax and enjoy who and where you are.

Causes	**Cures**
Being a real ball of fire, but lacking depth or follow-through.	Keep up the energy, but learn to discipline yourself to do the necessary preparation and follow-through. Otherwise, you will be just one more of those corporate comets who burned out before making it to earth.
Depending on your mentor, boss, or champion to carry you along with him or her.	Having a mentor can be very advantageous in your career, but long term, it may suggest that you can't make it on your own. If you are beginning to worry about being seen as too dependent, extricate yourself from the relationship as gently as possible. You may need to explain to this person who has brought you along that you have got to demonstrate you can make it on your own. If your mentor has your best interests at heart, there should be no problems.
Having difficulty following the rules, doing things by the book, or taking orders. Finding yourself questioning management decisions to the point you become a professional pain in the neck.	While the workplace needs people who can think outside the box and aren't walking robots, it also needs people who can work within the system regardless of its flaws. If you are one of those persons who constantly is at odds with the company, you may be struggling with unresolved authority issues. Be careful your rebellious nature doesn't propel you to the great outside where you are free to make all the decisions, but don't have anyone to work with or pay you a salary.
Having a brilliant mind, but believing that your intelligence is so special that people ought to defer to you because of your natural and obvious superiority.	IQ alone is never enough unless you can earn your living by scoring high in intelligence tests. You need to be able to get along with people if you are to sell your brilliant ideas. Otherwise you remain an undeveloped genius. As for your natural mental superiority, enjoy it for what it is, a gift.

(continued)

Causes	*Cures*
Having difficulty switching gears and moving into new or undefined areas.	If you find yourself growing irritable or anxious when faced with a new situation, count to ten and remember that all people have these feelings to one degree or another when faced with the unknown. You might try imaging yourself dealing with the new challenge by walking yourself through the steps you will take to master or deal with it. It's like a mental rehearsal for what you may be doing. You might also ask yourself what you would have to do to fail in this enterprise or even what failure would look like. You will do better to get your worst fears on the table where you can deal with them rationally than to allow them to surround you like a dark cloud that distracts and impedes your journey into the unknown.

MISSING THE "WAKE-UP" CALL:
How to Recognize the Early Warning Symptoms

Robert works for a large retail firm, and he has had the same position for over seven years. He's in charge of manufacturing forecasting. When he first got the position, he was elated. It meant new responsibility and more pay. He was now considered eligible for the company training and education programs. Moreover, he really liked the new job. That is, he liked it for a while. Then he began to feel bored, that there was nothing new to learn. He knew he wanted and needed to move on, but nothing happened. So he continued to do a good job and waited and waited. Several years later he is still waiting. He's running on empty and feels he is not getting anywhere. But no one has said anything to him, positive or negative. He doesn't know where he stands, he just knows that he has been doing the same thing for seven long years.

And now, he feels stuck. Many of his colleagues have moved past him into more exciting jobs. Robert doesn't know why that hasn't happened for him. Lately he's found himself worrying about his abilities. He wonders if his dream of a career in management was unrealistic. He's starting to lose confidence in himself and he's becoming a little angry with his company. He's afraid to quit and he's afraid to ask his boss for the truth about where he stands.

DIAGNOSIS

Robert is finally answering his "wake-up" call, but it may be about three or four years too late. *That* he didn't get another opportunity some time ago was the signal. He needed to have seen it and then to have done something about it. At a minimum, he should have asked his boss for some feedback on how he was perceived and what his career outlook was. If his boss gave him the runaround, then he should have seen that as a signal. Bosses have no problem telling high-potential people they have a great future. But bosses do have a problem leveling with "adequate" performers who have only a modest career outlook.

Even if Robert couldn't have that discussion, all sorts of bells and whistles should have gone off when he realized his colleagues were moving up and he was not.

Now he needs to take a hard look at his aspirations and make some decisions about what is important to him.

Rx

Robert should go to his boss's office and discuss his situation. He needs to let his boss know about his career goals and his disappointments, and he must ask his boss for feedback on how he is perceived. Robert may be encouraged by his boss's comments, and together they may develop a plan that helps Robert achieve some of his career objectives. But Robert's boss could tell him it looks as though he has gone as far as he can in that company. Robert can then decide what he wants to do. Stay, with some degree of security, and settle in, or strike out and look for a company where there is more opportunity for him. Once Robert knows the score, he needs to decide what matters to him and then make his plans accordingly.

In today's environment of downsizing, people will stay longer in their jobs than they have in the past. However, you need to continually build your technical knowledge and skill set to help keep yourself promotable. Then you must continually review your career progress and look for signals that tell you how you are doing. The absence of feedback *is a signal*. It means something. Being left in the same job for more than five years may be a signal. Getting passed over for promotions is a signal. For the get-aheader, no news is usually bad news. Don't wait for the company or your boss to let you know where you stand. Take the initiative and ask, even if you're afraid of what you'll hear. The penalty for waiting until the job fairy taps you on the shoulder is lost opportunity and time, and remember, although opportunity knocks, it doesn't nag, so get moving.

SURVIVING CORPORATE UPHEAVAL

Ten years ago, Maggie believed she worked for one of the best organizations in America. The firm was a leader in its field, and it was making all kinds of money. The company was like one big family and the employees were happy. Now it's a very different story. The company was acquired not once, but twice. Her company, the little fish, now lives in the belly of a shark who is being slowly digested by a whale.

Gone is the fun, the feeling of camaraderie. Instead, the place is overrun by "numbers" people who appear to operate in only one gear, quarterly returns. In the year since the last buyout, morale and productivity have plummeted. Maggie is reeling from the change and the loss of the world that she knew and enjoyed. Now Maggie feels herself taking a very long time to do anything. She used to be very creative—now she feels her creativity has dried up. She has a hard time getting to work on time, and once she is there, she puts off doing her work as long as possible. She is surrounded by coworkers who feel as she does, that the "whole thing stinks." Mourning has replaced working, and Maggie is feeling so discouraged she is ready to throw it all in and quit.

DIAGNOSIS

Maggie has lots of company. Thousands of employees in hundreds of organizations are feeling and acting like Maggie. Newspapers and magazines are full of stories describing the massive demoralization of many American workers and the ensuing drop in productivity and creativity. But no one can rescue Maggie or her friends.

Outside forces and events can have enormous impact on our lives and our careers. The lack of control that we have around such things as leveraged buyouts, lousy leadership, or the economy is a reality.

The only thing we can control is how we respond to these forces. In Maggie's case, she is stuck in the past, mourning the good old days. She's paralyzed emotionally and psychologically.

If you find yourself falling into the "oh, ain't-it-awful" abyss, realize that there are other ways to deal with these uncontrollable events. One is to decide to remain in control of yourself, your attitude, your productivity, and your career. That's not to deny feelings of sadness that come with the end of a good thing. Those feelings need to be acknowledged and expressed. But then it's time to work with what *is*. What can you salvage? What can still make the work you do worthwhile to you personally? Forget the profits that are getting made or not getting made or that it's your sweat that makes stockholders rich. Those are some of the out-of-your-control happenings that you can't change. Don't waste your precious time on things you cannot change, and get on with the business of living.

Rx _____

If Maggie is to survive this corporate anomie she will have to do it on her own. Resigning from her job is not necessarily the answer given the enormous investment she has in her career with this company.

The first step for Maggie is to accept that the company has changed, that it will never be as it was before. Until Maggie can do that, she will not be free to move into the present.

The second step for Maggie is to decide whether she wants to continue to work for this company. After all, no one is forcing her to stay. If she decides to stay, she must find within herself the resource for making a commitment to her career in this organization, regardless of what is going on around her. It will be a real pulling-herself-up-by-her-bootstraps deal, but no one is going to throw her a rope. So if she doesn't climb out of this hole, she will be stuck there.

Decide to bring back the joy to your work that you had before—in spite of the sharks and the whales. Focus on the half of the cup that's full and build from that.

The Secret to Managing Change

Most people think that change involves moving from the old to the new. However, the middle stage, limbo, is a critical part of the change process.

The most important thing we have learned about managing change in organizations is that the losses must be acknowledged and the limbo stage must be experienced before individuals can move into the future.

COPING WITH CHANGE

Stage I: Old,	Stage II: Limbo,	Stage III: New,
Losses	*Uncertainty*	*Vision*
Way things were	Disoriented	Options
Meaning	Grieving	Possibilities
Control	Wandering	Goals
Certainty	Inactive	Plans
Identity	Restless	Action
Future	Waiting	Regain control

The secret to managing change is to allow yourself to go through the stages and to experience each stage. For example, if you have lost out on a career opportunity, you will need to mourn the loss and what it may have meant for your future. Then you have to allow some time for regrouping. This will be the limbo period in which you will feel like there is no clear path or way to go. After a period of time, you will begin to see other possibilities for your future, and as these options become clearer, you will again enter the cycle of planning and pursuing goals.

Steps to Successful Change Management

This model applies to all types of changes, whether it is loss of a job, promotion, a relationship, or of a way of life.

1. Losses must be acknowledged and felt.
2. The limbo period must be experienced.
3. New vision will be formed from the ashes of what is lost.
4. Allow yourself to go through the stages. Experience your grieving. Get comfortable in limbo. And be ready for the new vision as it unfolds. Then get back on that horse and ride!

WHEN THE DREAM JOB BECOMES A NIGHTMARE

Ryan was hired to be a sales rep in a small company. In his interviews, the regional manager told him about the territory's great sales potential (translation: big commissions), especially since it had been a neglected area (the job had been open for three months). The potential for a rep to go into the territory and drum up new business was limitless.

Ryan was very excited about this job, not only because of the money potential, but because the career path (so he was told during the interviews) was the way to get into marketing—Ryan's ultimate goal.

The first few months were very tough. Customers told Ryan that his products represented the old technology and yet were priced higher than the competition's state-of-the-art technology.

The territory itself was primarily in a depressed economic area where no amount of effort or sales promotions or contests seemed to make a difference—the sales just did not come through. To make it worse, Ryan learned from other reps that this was a "dog" territory. Even the executives knew the territory was a loser; they routinely assigned naive sales reps to the depressed place because no one "in the know" would willingly take on this area. Belatedly, Ryan realized what a pack of lies they had told him during the interview.

Ryan was mad—mad at himself for being such a dolt and madder at the company for sticking him with a "no-win" assignment. His motivation went down and his sales results followed. He lost his enthusiasm and his energy. He stopped running sales promotions for his territory and did just enough to get by. At the regional sales meetings, he kept to himself, suspecting that the other reps were laughing behind his back about his bottom-of-the- barrel territory. Instead he spent his time reading the classified ads and calling headhunters, trying to find a new job. When he went on interviews, however, his negativism toward his present situation would inevitably surface, and Ryan would not even get a second interview. His behaviors became a kind of death spiral; each act contributing to its downward movement.

DIAGNOSIS _____

It's not what happens to you that matters; it's how you respond. Ryan defeated himself by placing the blame on his company and regional manager, then sought to "stick it to them" with his poor sales performance. He assumed no responsibility for what happened and completely lost focus of what he could take from an otherwise bleak situation.

His original objectives were twofold: make a lot of money and move into marketing. When he realized the first objective was not realistic, he lost his drive toward the marketing objective. He changed his objective to getting out as soon as possible and put all his energy into escaping from his current job.

Sometimes it does make sense to direct your energy to moving on. A word of caution, though: Your resume should always be protected. Most times, it is best to try to stick it out for a full year before changing jobs. You can use that year to analyze your current situation, learn what went wrong, and most important, *protect your resume.* Changing jobs frequently can make you look like (in recruiters' parlance) "a jumper"—someone who moves from company to company. No one wants a jumper—it looks as if they can't stay around long enough to get results or must have other problems. Recruiters know the past can be a good predictor of the future.

Rx

In this case, Ryan could have turned an awful situation into a learning one. He could have tried different selling skills to see what worked better than others. He could have networked with the other reps to try to learn from them. He could have started graduate school at night to help him get the marketing courses he would need to succeed in that function.

Ryan could also have spoken frankly—but not accusingly—to his boss to see if the boss would help him improve the territory—or maybe realign it—or at least give Ryan some hope about the payoff (the marketing job). Rather than going into a funk—in results and in his self-assessment—Ryan should have focused on learning from experience. That would have given him a good story to tell on future interviews, and a good foundation to build upon as he encountered other disappointing experiences in his career.

HANGING ON AND LOSING OUT:
When It's Prudent to Take a Risk

Like most people, Terence thought that the "only way was up." He had a series of promotions in the manufacturing area. Starting as a group leader, he had been promoted to a foreperson, then to manufacturing supervisor, and then manager. His performance reviews were excellent; he was seen as having very good management skills and was technically up to date on manufacturing processes. He felt the next "natural" move for him was to be promoted to director of manufacturing.

Terence was very surprised when he was asked by the director of quality assurance to consider a Q.A. manager position in his area. The director assured him that, even though the job was a lateral move with no salary increase, it would be beneficial to his career to broaden his area of expertise.

When discussing the opportunity with his current boss, the director of manufacturing, Terence indicated that since he had no experience in Q.A., he was concerned about leaving the manufacturing area, where he had such a good track record, and taking the job in Q.A., which had some risk. He also emphasized that his next move should be "up," not sideways. The director told Terence that he would expand his knowledge about manufacturing and the overall company operations if he took the job in Q.A. and that, although there are always risks when changing functional areas, it could be a good "proving" ground for Terence's development. He said to him, "While I can't make you take it, I think it would be a smart move. Naturally, I'll continue to support you if you decide not to. But you may be making a mistake."

Terence thought for a long time about what his boss had said, but finally decided that it just wasn't worth taking on new responsibilities and risks without a pay or grade increase. He stayed on in his role as manufacturing manager and continued to get his usual excellent reviews.

Eighteen months later, Terence's boss was transferred to a different location. Terence interviewed for the director job with the expectation it was his, he was shocked to find out that an individual from the logistics department (a peer of Terence's) was selected as the new manufacturing director.

DIAGNOSIS

What did Terence miss in his background that caused him to "fall out" as a candidate? Lack of breadth, mostly.

The manufacturing director job was a pivotal one in Terence's company. The individuals who had held that job often were later assigned to key jobs in the branches or promoted to the vice president of operations job, which would oversee the quality assurance, manufacturing, and logistics departments. Senior management felt that Terence's lack of experience outside of manufacturing would seriously limit his ability to move out of the director slot. His skills would be so specialized that he would not be able to easily move into other areas without high risk to the company. They didn't want a "blocker"—someone who gets into a position and can never get out—in such an important feeder job like the director slot.

Terence had missed a big opportunity to

- Prove himself in a new area
- Broaden his knowledge base in areas that complemented each other (manufacturing and Q.A. are intertwined)
- Prove he was savvy about what was needed at the top (broad skills and knowledge)
- Take a risk that had a strong probability of success since there were similarities in the jobs (especially since the company was willing to take the risk with Terence at that level)
- Demonstrate that he was motivated by team spirit and meeting the company's needs rather than by only promotions and more money

Rx

For Terence, the way to correct his career course would be to work effectively with his new boss and request consideration for other positions in the area to give him exposure to other departments besides manufacturing. He has lost valuable time, but since he has a good track record, if he stays on good terms with his boss and doesn't let his pride get in his way, he can succeed. In fact, he may be a valuable asset to his new boss, who had Q.A. and manufacturing experience, but not in his most recent assignments. Terence's state-of-the-art technical know-how can help his new boss, and his boss's knowledge of the many facets of operations can help Terence plan his ascent in a more effective manner.

Many companies and individuals are looking at lateral moves in new ways. The downsizing and removal of management levels has resulted in rethinking career paths. What used to be the traditional advancement pattern has been replaced by a strategy that uses lateral assignments to broaden employees' experience and knowledge base.

If you are considering a lateral or some other developmental move, ask yourself

- What skills will be learned?
- What skills are needed at the apex (the top of the career ladder you want to climb)?
- Will the new job provide skills needed at the top? Do they complement or add to what you have versus what you need?
- What has been the career path for others who've been successful in your area? Such information may provide a template for your developmental path.

Effective analysis of jobs at the top of the ladder and critical review of your own skills and abilities can help you plan your career. It may mean initiating developmental moves, but you have to get the experience and prove your abilities while you are still low on the ladder before companies will risk putting you at the top.

FATAL DISEASE:
The Cradle-to-Grave Mentality

Greg is in shock. It has finally dawned on him that he may not always have a job with his company. He can hardly believe this has happened to him. He had his world and his future laid out from the time he joined the company some 20 years ago. All that time, he did what was called for and more. He was totally loyal to his organization. He went the last mile, did whatever it took, and even sacrificed his family and personal life. Now when he should have been in line for a big payoff (a cushy senior position with a fat pension in the future), his world has been kicked out from under him. His job is in jeopardy, and he has lost the buddies who used to take care of him. He is running scared and feeling angry. How could the company break its promise of happiness and riches when he had kept his part of the bargain?

At this point, Greg has also lost his way and his confidence. He's pulled back from people, the old one-liners are gone. At his staff meetings, he sits glumly with a detached do-what-you-want leadership style.

Diagnosis _____

Greg has lots of company, if that's any comfort (we know it's not). What he is expressing is a widespread phenomenon—and it's not only the Gregs who are suffering. Many of these large cradle-to-grave organizations are having great difficulty in changing from stodgy, complacent bureaucracies to fast-moving, highly competitive environments.

When the company shifted to a more competitive stance, Greg lost power and prestige. His world of rank and privilege shrunk to carrying around a few company credit cards with a strict limit on where and how he could use them.

Greg's immediate problem is how he feels about himself, his career, and his company. He has given a large share of his life to his organization, and it's little wonder he feels betrayed about promises not kept.

But whatever the promises appeared to be, they were unwritten. Underneath his apathy, Greg is reeling from the shock of discovering that jobs can't be taken for granted. Like many people who started their careers in the 1960s and 1970s, Greg believed that if he paid his dues, he had it made. As a result, he didn't worry about whether or not he would have marketable skills or even what was going on outside his organization. He focused on his company and responded to its needs. Since it was an organization where people traditionally worked from "cradle to grave," Greg was not prepared for a different or more competitive work environment.

In today's environment, you should take nothing for granted. Consider yourself as self-employed and base your career on your skills and talents and your ability to market them. Assume that there will always be change and that you have to be ready for it. That means you work with one eye on the company and the other on the outside world. Keep your resume up to date and look for ways within your organization to develop new and marketable skills.

The new unwritten contract reads a lot differently from the one Greg operated under. Now the company promises rewards and developmental opportunities. In return, you are expected to turn in a first-rate performance and continually upgrade your skills. That's the deal. No long-term commitment from either party can be expected or promised in today's environment.

Rx

Greg's real challenge is to understand that there are no guarantees and that he still has a responsibility to his company to produce at his highest level. This will be hard for Greg. The psychological wounding has taken a heavy toll. If he can work beyond that, though, Greg can adapt to the new realities of the workplace and stop wallowing in self-pity. If he continues in his slump, he may nail the lid completely shut on his career, and the company may be inclined to replace him with someone whose attitude and work results meet their needs more than Greg does.

The Unwritten Contract: Implications for Your Career

The new worker needs to consider himself or herself *self-employed.* Paternalism is out. Entitlement is out. Those good old days are gone. Independence is emerging as the workers' choice.

So what does this mean for you? It means that you no longer look to the company for lifetime employment. It means that you look at yourself as someone who has a set of skills, competencies, and knowledge and that you market yourself. It means that you look at companies as your clients. And that you work for a client as long as it is mutually beneficial. But that you are ready to leave and go to another client if you need to or want to. It means that you look at each job as a way to gain valuable experience. Your obligation to your employer is to make as great a contribution as you can toward the organization's goals.

Is the new contract a better one? Well, that depends on what you need and who you are. If your security needs are high, you may wish for the old relationship—the "Ma Bell" world. If you are more entrepreneurial, you may relish the idea of being "self-employed." If you are somewhere in between, you may not like it, but you can learn to do it. Think of it as getting lemons and that you have no choice but to make lemonade.

SEMPER PARATIS (Be Prepared)

Sheri really disliked her company and her job. Not only was the business not growing, but there had been many layoffs. However, she felt that hers was a very specialized and important job, and so she was not worried about her job security.

For months, Sheri's friend had been after her to update her resume. Whether because of inertia or lack of interest, Sheri kept putting it off. Finally, late one Friday afternoon she sat down with her friend; together they developed a good resume.

Two weeks later, Sheri was flabbergasted when she was called in by her boss and told she was being terminated—her job was eliminated. Although not really over the shock, Sheri starting networking almost immediately. By coincidence, she answered her boss's phone three days after she had heard the bad news—the caller was a headhunter who also knew Sheri. Sheri told the headhunter that she was actively looking for a job as a result of the layoff. By sheer luck, the headhunter was working on a job order in Sheri's field of specialty. He told Sheri to fax her resume immediately. Since the resume was ready, Sheri was able to supply it and got an interview later that week. The following Monday, she had a job offer and walked out of her former company with a new position already lined up to start the following week.

DIAGNOSIS

Like many people, Sheri felt little need to update her resume. She felt secure in her job and, besides, writing a resume is not easy or fun. However, she had the good sense to listen to her friend and do what was needed to update her resume.

RX

No prescription needed here, except for the simple lesson that in today's economy, you should *always* have your resume up to date. Putting together a resume while trying to deal with the emotional and financial consequences of losing a job only adds stress at the worst time.

The intelligent employee will always have a current resume at hand so that if the "perfect" job comes along, the current job disappears, or a wonderful job opportunity opens up in the company, he or she will be prepared for it.

PLATEAUED AND PEEVED:
How to Resurrect a Stagnant Career

Someone (supposedly wise and knowing) observed that at some point in life we are all plateaued. Even President Reagan was plateaued eventually. In this case, it occurred when he was well into his seventies and had just completed two terms as president of the United States. We should all suffer from such plateauing. However, the real world of plateauing is not nearly as comfy as riding off into the sunset to a mansion in California.

Many, many workers, more than anyone can realize, have been plateaued. The get-ahead career track is strewn with the casualties from corporate plateauing. And the pain and sense of dislocation that accompanies plateauing causes inestimable anguish. So plateauing is not a ho-hum occurrence. It marks that moment in time when people become fully aware that their dreams of getting ahead are over.

For many, the shock is devastating. For others, it becomes a wound that never gets serious enough to warrant a doctor, but that never heals.

That's what it's been like for David. For the first 15 years of his career with a large manufacturing company, David was on the rise. He moved through the various levels of management with seeming ease. The company was growing, and there were many opportunities at the middle management level.

Then came the 1980s with all its downsizing. David's company was no exception. The company officers looked at the now-bloated middle management level, saw a place to cut, and did. Many jobs were eliminated, including David's. However, David was lucky: he was given the choice of taking a demotion or leaving. He took the demotion.

Now, five years later, David is very discouraged. He sees the younger hires getting the promotions and feels he has been sidelined. Unfortunately, his performance has paralleled the downturn in his career. He's indifferent to most of his work. He avoids the boss and his coworkers. He is churlish with the people who report to him. At 42, he feels it's all over.

His boss is beside herself. She doesn't know how to bring back the old spark and fire. She has threatened, cajoled, and pleaded with him. But David stays stuck. At this point, he is "unpromotable" on his performance appraisal—which is in David's eyes just one more "nail in his coffin."

DIAGNOSIS

In truth, David was never considered unpromotable until his performance fell off. The demoted people were not targeted; David was dumped with many other midlevel managers when the decision was made to reduce the levels of management. It was a totally impersonal decision. But David interpreted it as a comment about who he was, and he began to "live" the part he thought he had been assigned.

David needs to talk to his boss and lay out what has happened. Then he needs to enlist his boss's support in turning his career around. And then he needs to do whatever it takes to change how he is perceived by his company.

RX

When you take a hit like David did, you can't stay down. You have got to get back up and start at it all over again. To stay on the mat is careericidal. No one can pick you up but you. If you don't get up, you'll get to lay there—plateaued and passed over.

How do you resurrect a career that has taken such a big wallop?

You begin by making a commitment to yourself to do something about what has happened. You get rid of the anger and bitterness that would otherwise act as a drain on your energies and motivation. Then you go back to your job and do your darndest to be an outstanding performer. There will be two payoffs for certain: (1) you'll feel better about yourself and (2) your company will see you as a highly valuable employee. As for getting promoted, hang in there and look for opportunities. As Yogi Berra said, "It ain't over 'til it's over."

Up Against the Wall? You Don't Have to Stay There

Erica was a public relations manager in a large conglomerate. She had worked at the firm for more than ten years, following seven years in the insurance industry.

Erica started at the company as a public relations associate. In her early years there, she assumed more responsibilities and the titles to match. She later branched into the area of community affairs, then into legislative affairs. She has held her current job for about three years.

Erica has started to think that she's hit a plateau. There had been several senior-level jobs open in different parts of the company for which she'd be a good candidate, but she didn't get them. Some were filled before she even knew the jobs were open. She had interviewed for another but lost out to a younger, more aggressive individual—the "up-and-coming" talent. The irony is that she used to be one of those up-and-comers. Now she's wondering if she is going anywhere at all.

A job in the community affairs group in another division came open and one of Erica's friends asked her if she was going to throw her name into the hat for the job. "Forget it," Erica thought, "the job's a lateral move and I've paid my dues. I'm waiting for the next plum assignment." Before she completely closed out the option, though, she had several heart-to-heart talks with people who knew her and from whom she felt she could get confidential insights. With each, she asked,

- Do you think I should consider the job?
- How would taking a lateral move be seen?
- What would it do to add or detract from my opportunities?

She also openly discussed her frustration at what she interpreted to be her plateaued situation.

With the input of these conversations, she put together a list of the pros and cons of taking the move. Included in the upside was the broadening of her experience, the opportunity to show her skills in a new arena and develop more skills, and the challenge of new responsibilities. The downside was that she would pull herself out of contention for at least a year in the event a higher-level job opened up. She would also have to re-prove herself to a new boss and adjust to a new environment. Above all, though, she had to come to terms herself with the fact that maybe she really wasn't going to be the next director or vice president and that her opportunities for career advancement now might be more limited.

What pushed her to take the job eventually was the question posed by one of her confidantes: Do you see anything else on the horizon for yourself in the next 12 months? If not, what have you got to lose by taking on a new assignment? Erica knew the chances of a senior-level job opening up short term *were* pretty slim and that the open job was reputed to be a "good" one—good responsibilities, good boss. She took it.

Erica had a hard time in the beginning dealing honestly with the congratulations—"Congratulations on your promotion! Is it a promotion?" Since it was not a promotion, that part bothered her. Eventually, though, she just said, "It's a developmental move" and left it at that.

She also did a lot of soul searching to try to reconcile herself to the fact that she may have reached her career limit in her company. At times, the feeling of personal failure has been overwhelming and hard to admit to herself, let alone talk to anyone about. She also had to deal with the change in what motivated her—she had put in many hard hours with her "eyes on the prize." If the prize was no longer there, what would bring her to work every day?

So, as Erica made the job change, she also made other changes. She resolved to work less than the standard 10–12 hours daily she'd routinely been putting in. She wanted more balance in her work and personal life, and if the potential for rewards at work were not as strong as in the past, how much she gave would diminish as well. Erica also found a good friend with whom she could openly discuss her feelings and who helped her come to terms with herself.

The ending of this story? Well, Erica liked her new job a lot. She liked the people she worked with, the work she did, the satisfactions of the job itself. In some ways, she came to terms with the "status" issue. She began to recognize that status wasn't everything, and she looked to other things in her life to give her satisfaction and feelings of self-worth. She also started to think differently—more realistically—about her future working years and her goals and aspirations. Through a lot of soul searching and commiserating with others in similar circumstances, she reached a higher level of understanding and contentment about her life.

Diagnosis

What happened to Erica happens to everyone at some point and at differing levels in their careers. For some, it happens at the technician level, and for others, it is the senior vice presidential level. For many, it happens in their late thirties or midforties, times when it is common to rethink what's realistically ahead, from a personal and professional perspective. For others, it may happen in their later forties or fifties, when they are also starting to keep an eye on "when can I retire" from a financial perspective, when career growth will have an absolute effect on future earnings and therefore pension.

For each person, this moment of truth—the recognition that dreams of great success may not occur— is a crucial one. For some, it may be recognition that they've gone as far as they can in that company and that they need to move on if continued upward mobility is important. For others, there may be a balance of what they have invested in the company and what they are willing to accept—and at what price. If the investment already made in the company is important and adjustments—in thinking and attitude—can occur, the individual can become a motivated and productive contributor in the organization again.

Rx

It is important—when the time is right for you—to face this issue. You don't want to be a victim. It should be your choice to go or stay (assuming there are no organization changes, such as a restructuring or downsizing, or performance issues). You sometimes need to take stock of what is important to you at a given time and to see if the company can support it. If not, get out, and don't let yourself become a victim—"I was passed over and now I am a loser." A negative attitude will cause you to suffer in the organization—far beyond the disappointment of an unrequited career hope. You can be lost or bounced in the ensuing fallout. For those who maintain control over their own actions and activities, the opportunities for happiness and self-fulfillment are much greater.

You must also realize that personal fulfillment is still possible when you have hit the wall—whether that wall is a temporary block or appears to be a permanent, immovable concrete slab. The fact that you are not able to move up (regardless of the reason) at this time—or even apparently in the long term—doesn't mean that you should limit or decrease your contribution or ignore your need for intellectual stimulation. In fact, the realization that you are "in place" for a duration of questionable length can help you to plot out strategies for maximizing yourself. That includes maximizing your worth within the organization as well as within the "bigger picture"—your community, your family, within yourself. As much value and weight we place on our work, it is still only one component of the total life we lead. You can achieve a greater balance and ultimately a higher level of personal fulfillment by viewing your career in a larger perspective.

HOW TO COPE WITH A PLATEAU

On the Job

- Spearhead task forces and pilot activities.
- Identify/volunteer for/request special projects that are of interest to you.
- Consider a job rotation (temporary or permanent) with another individual to broaden your experiences.
- Solicit feedback about how you are perceived, then critically take that information into consideration. Good sources of this information include
  - your boss
  - trusted associates/clients/peers
  - human resource representatives
- Consider lateral or even lower-level jobs to keep your knowledge growing.
- Take training courses at work or through work. Look for appropriate classes; then go, learn from them, and have a good time.
- Look for opportunities to do something new or different in the company, or ways to do your job differently. These may or may not lead to a promotion or other opportunities, but it will keep your knowledge and interest high.
- Become and/or stay involved with technology, for example, the personal computer. You may learn a better way to do your job, as well as a critical skill for tomorrow's workplace.
- Continually advance your technical knowledge of your profession. It is critical to your future success (and continued employment!) to stay on the cutting edge of technical and professional knowledge. Continuous learning and development is key to staying current.
- Consider getting help with a professional career counselor.
- Be gracious (at least outwardly!) when changes/promotions occur for others.
- *Don't* think you are "dead-ended" and start acting that way. You will seal your own fate.
- Stay connected in your field—professional associations, headhunters, networking, and so on.
- Decide if it really may be time to move on or if you are willing to stay with your company, even if it is not at the higher level you desire.
- Always keep your resume up to date.
- Continue to work to keep yourself challenged and learning new things about your job, your company, your profession. Your level of performance is almost always related to the degree to which you are challenged and find your work interesting.

HOW TO COPE WITH A PLATEAU

In Your Personal Life

- Strive for balance between your home and work lives. Be sure you are working enough on each and that you are getting the return on your own investment.
- Assess how you can make your life more enjoyable and what would give you satisfaction in addition to your job.
- Take specialized courses to continually advance your personal knowledge, for example, art, music, history, language.
- Consider a related or nonrelated business on the side (as long as it doesn't interfere with your primary job).
- Take long weekends and minivacations in addition to your regular vacation to give yourself a break from work.

Balancing Your Life—The Value of Volunteering

Volunteering in activities outside of the workplace can significantly add to the satisfaction in your life. Volunteering can meet a community need, provide you with a way to meet new people, and help you "make a mark" on society. The activities you select need to be compatible with your interests and your life-style to ensure a long- term commitment.

You can find organizations in need of volunteers through your local United Way, church, temple, or even your company's community service department. To maximize your personal rewards from volunteering, try to determine what you are missing/not getting from your professional life. Then identify how you may apply those needs to a worthwhile cause. For example,

- Leadership: Look for board positions, officer slots, and so on, on planning boards, professional associations, or nonprofit organizations. The concept of becoming a "community trustee" is very appealing and satisfying to many people.
- Artistic/Creative: Arts, music, theater groups, newsletters, photography
- Altruism: Soup kitchens, social service agency volunteering
- Children and/or Sports: Little League, Girl/Boy Scouting
- Social: Organizing trips at work, joining ski clubs, going on group excursions

You might also consider publicizing your volunteer activities in local or company publications. It can help others to see you in a different light and may open new doors. The publicity you generate can also help the organization—all non-profits need and love publicity.

DEALING WITH THE "ULTIMATE INSULT":
What to Do If You Are Demoted

There used to be a time when a demotion was akin to being fired. The only difference was that demotion lengthened the agony. In today's workplace, demotions are being used to save people's jobs. Because many companies are reducing the number of midlevel managers, they are having to put former managers in nonmanagerial slots, or they are reducing the number of managerial levels, forcing many employees to do the same job with a lower salary grade or title.

Should that happen to you, how you handle it will become critical not only to how you perform in the future, but how you live your life.

Brad went through such a demotion. For the last five years, his company has downsized, then downsized again. Brad has survived all five of these downsizings, and for that he is grateful. However, last week his boss called him in, asked him to close the door, and told him that he had something he needed to talk to him about. Brad was puzzled. The last downsizing had picked the company clean. Everyone who was left was doing the work for three people, Brad included. What more could the company ask for? His boss went over this history of the last five years, emphasizing to Brad that each time his name came up, he was viewed as too valuable to let go. But, his boss told him, now the company wanted to get salaries and titles under control. They felt there were too many managers at Brad's level, and they wanted to cut out that whole level. While Brad would not take an immediate cut in salary, his status would be downgraded, and he would no longer be considered a manager.

Brad listened very quietly. He had worked many long, hard years for this company. He had given up weekends and vacation time and had come to work when he should have called in sick. And now this. He shook his head. It just felt very sad. Brad told the boss he appreciated hearing about it from him and thanked him for his continued support. The boss appeared to feel as badly about the whole matter as Brad did. But the boss could do nothing about it. The two men parted and Brad was left to think about what had just happened.

A part of him wanted to be very angry. This was a pretty shabby way to treat a loyal employee. At an even deeper level, Brad felt humiliated. He had worked hard to attain a good title. Now that and the executive perks that went with it would soon be gone. Even his business card would read differently. He would have to go home and tell his family that he had been demoted.

Brad had a difficult time concentrating on his work for the rest of the day. The demotion really hurt. Brad hadn't realized—until he lost them—how much his level and title meant to him. He was a little surprised that it affected him so deeply.

When he told his wife about it that evening, she seemed to take the news rather lightly. "Well," she said, "at least you still have a job." Brad wanted to scream, "But there is more to it than just having a job. This is my dream and I just lost it." But Brad said nothing. Instead he took a very long walk by himself. By the end of the walk he had made some peace with what had happened, and although he still felt a sense of humiliation, he decided that life was too short to consider his demotion a tragedy. When he returned to work that next day, he felt sad but calm and he was able to get on with his work and his life.

DIAGNOSIS

Being demoted is painful, but it will only be as painful as you let it be. You are in charge of the feelings you have about what has happened to you. If you decide to feel like it is the end of the world, then for you it will be just that. However, if you think that it is a sad event that you can and will survive, you are creating that result. It is important to remember the roles our titles and status play in how we see ourselves. The less we need the titles and status symbols, the less we depend on them to tell us who we are.

The more you can develop a sense of who you are and your value to yourself and others, independent of your career experiences, the easier it will be for you to take the ups and downs that often accompany all long-term careers.

RX

This scenario could have had an entirely different ending. If Brad had not developed a sense about what was really important for himself, he might have reacted very differently to being demoted. Instead, he managed his adjustment the way he handled other personal issues in his life—with long walks and lots of thinking.

At this point, Brad needs to take stock of what is important to his own long-term career goals and to determine if they will be met at his company. Once he is comfortable with his priorities (security, financial stability, career opportunities), he can decide if it makes sense to stay or to go elsewhere to meet his goals. Either way, if he handles the devastation of this demotion with grace, he will maintain his image as a top-drawer professional.

THE DREADED WORDS:
"You're on Probation"

No one wants to hear those words, but they are spoken more routinely than many people imagine. Being put on probation is a process whereby the company serves you notice that your performance has slipped and that you may be fired if it doesn't improve. Sometimes companies use probation to wake up employees who appear oblivious to the danger they are in. It's a move meant to get their attention.

In Jena's case, it was the latter. For the past two and a half years, Jena has become increasingly disenchanted with her job. What looked exciting five years ago has now become a dreary routine. Her job is to serve the major clients by helping their employees with their insurance problems. When she first started, she loved her work. She learned how to use a PC; she worked with some of the *Fortune* 100s. She knew many of her customers by first name. She received outstanding performance reviews from her boss. But now the job had gone stale and with that has come loss of enthusiasm.

Jena knew at some level her work was not up to par. She had stopped returning phone calls as promptly. She had been less patient with the nitty-gritty details that had always irritated her but that she had handled effectively. Even her belief in the company's goals was eroding. Whereas before she saw the company's role as a caring provider of services, now she saw it as a money machine that didn't always walk its talk.

Last year, Jena had made up her mind that she was no longer willing to work until 7:00 or 8:00 P.M., which was par for this company. At first, she packed up at 6:00 P.M., then 5:30 P.M., and then finally started leaving as soon as the clock struck 5:00 P.M. It wasn't that she was the only one to leave at 5:00 P.M., but there was an unwritten rule that you don't leave until the boss does, and her boss was a workaholic. Jena saw herself as becoming more independent. Her boss saw her as becoming less responsible. So when the boss gave Jena her yearly performance review, she told Jena that her work was not acceptable, that she was being put on probation, and that she had six months to clean up her act or she would be terminated.

Jena's first reaction was to protest. But her supervisor had done her homework, and she pointed out to Jena the specific examples that supported her contention that Jena's performance had slipped.

Jena asked for time to think about the problem—a wise move. It gave her time to absorb the news, and it allowed her the chance to reflect on what was going on in her life that had resulted in this slippage. Jena realized she had two choices. Come back and work very, very hard to reinstate herself, or consider other types of employment. When Jena analyzed the reasons behind her poor performance, she realized that she was basically bored with her job as well as less wide-eyed and naive. The real question for her became: "What do I want to do that would keep me enthused and productive?" She didn't find an answer to that question immediately, but she was able to go back to her boss and describe for her what she was feeling about her career. Jena said, "I know it's not an excuse, but I do want you to understand why I think it happened." She told her boss that she was now reexamining her career choices and would be making some kind of decision once she had sorted them out. In the meantime, she promised to deliver at 150 percent. The boss was impressed enough with Jena's honesty and professional attitude that she offered to get the human resource people involved in helping Jena work through her career issues.

End of story? Jena realized that she needed a job with much more challenge and variety. Routine not only bored her, it actually demotivated her, even with the customer contact she enjoyed. With the help of the human resources advisor, she identified a number of alternate career paths and began finding out more about each one. Her performance improved, she was taken off probation, and she was told that she had a job and her boss's support while she figured out her next step.

DIAGNOSIS

Being put on probation is serious business, but you can recover from it if you want to. The secret to how Jena handled this one so successfully lies in her lack of defensiveness and her willingness to admit to poor performance. She kept her cool, did not blame others for her situation, and developed a plan for surviving her crisis.

The worst response is to deny the manager's appraisal and to be self-righteous in your denial. The trick is stay calm, take your hits, and then figure out a strategy for extricating yourself from your situation. Even if you think the evaluation is unfair or untrue, you must still deal with the reality of your boss.

RX

The most important part of your probation discussion is the action planning. You need to understand fully what are the problems, what actions you need to take to rectify them, how your performance will be measured while on probation, what is the time line for improvement, and what are consequences at the end of this time. Even if you feel your boss is against you, you need to plan jointly for the improvement of your performance. Then, unless you do not want or need this job, you need to do everything in your power to carry out the actions.

You need to also maintain a positive attitude, tough as that may be. Don't lash out at your boss or the company, unless you really do want to end your job here and now. Swallow your pride and concentrate on doing what it takes to clean up your record.

Do not use it as an excuse for your poor performance, but if you have personal problems or, like Jena, have lost your enthusiasm for your job, do explain these to your boss. Use them as backdrops to your action planning—knowing you need to get beyond them—not as crutches for why your performance is not at an acceptable level.

One last point: If you feel that, no matter what you may do, the decision has been made to terminate you, you might consider asking for a severance package at the point you are told your work is not up to par. This may work best in a larger company; you should certainly do what research you can before you propose this. You obviously need to be ready to hit the street immediately if the company accepts this option.

Either way, do prepare your resume and use your time judiciously to start looking for a new job if you feel you will not make it successfully out of probation, or do not want to. Don't call in sick or take "dentist's appointments" while on probation—your attendance problems will aggravate an already bad situation—but do consider using vacation time to start looking for new opportunities.

YOU MUST BE KIDDING—
I'm Being Redeployed?

Downsizing, restructuring, rightsizing, redeployment—it's all the same for those who end up losing their jobs. To survive these types of reorganizations, you must learn how to play the game.

Let's take Frank as an illustration of what not to do. Frank had worked for his company for over 20 years. Those were good years for him and the company. Money was easy to make, there wasn't much competition, and no one was ever laid off.

Now things have changed. In the past, Frank's company always had the inside track making parts for the automobile companies. Sure, there were a few small companies who got a contract now and then, but his company had long-term relationships with the Big Three. As long as the company produced quality products, it had the contracts. Good business, good life, no sweat. However, when the automobile industry began to lose business, Frank's company found itself in tough times. The Japanese were not nearly as cooperative in their buying as were the old automobile firms. The company avoided layoffs until about six years ago. Then it began to cherry pick, a unit here, a unit there, a few managers, but no major layoffs. Frank felt secure. After all, he had seniority; he had good contacts inside the company, he knew the business. He didn't see how he could be let go without hurting the business. So he remained his relaxed do-the-job-and-go-home self.

Last month, however, the company announced there was to be a redeployment. Translated, that meant that the company intended to reorganize itself. The first step would be to figure out what it would take to succeed over the next five years. The second step would be to identify what type of skills would be needed to achieve those goals. Then the company would develop a new organizational chart based on those needs. In short, everyone theoretically would lose their job and then apply for one of the newly defined positions.

Frank's division was tapped as the first one to go through the process. Everyone in his division was notified that their positions had been eliminated, that there were new positions they could apply for and may the best person win. Frank couldn't believe what he had heard. Find a new position? Interview for a new job in the same company after he had put in 20 long years? He was in shock. He was also mad.

Frank had three weeks to think about it while the top-level management positions were filled. Then it was his turn to apply for those jobs for which he thought he was qualified. Frank was so angry he could barely focus on writing a resume. To him, it was all so ludicrous. He knew his job, he knew he was valuable. So why all this mickey mouse stuff about reapplying for a job?

Frank could not even bring himself to talk to his old boss about it, partly because his old boss was now in a different position himself, but also because Frank felt that somehow his old boss should have taken care of him. "After all," Frank reasoned, "I see lots of guys who are no better than me and they are getting jobs." Frank's anger turned to bitterness and he began to blast the company anytime he had an audience. As a result, Frank's inability to handle himself and his situation became well known. To his dismay and surprise, Frank found himself losing out to other people in his interviews. "You're close, Frank," they would tell him, but so-and-so "simply is more qualified."

At this point, Frank has gone for six positions and he has lost out on every one. In two weeks, the people who didn't get jobs in the redeployment process will go into outplacement, which means Frank will no longer be employed by the company, and at age 51, he will be on the street looking for work.

DIAGNOSIS

Frank's situation is not unique, unfortunately. He put in his hours, he did a good job. But with the increasing competition for jobs, he is not where he needs to be to make the final cut. For starters, he made a big error by not keeping his cool through the redeployment process. Whatever he thought of the company's methods for running leaner, he should have kept his mouth shut. However, playing it cool may still not have saved him if he was not up to date on the new skills needed by his company. Frank had become complacent over the years. While he saw change around him, he never saw the need to examine his own marketability. Now he must compete with a younger and highly skilled work force who are willing to work for a much lower salary than he can.

Rx

Part of surviving a reorganization is to keep your head. From the minute you suspect you may be vulnerable, you need to start networking to make sure that the key people know you are around and available. Better yet, pick up the skills you need to stay abreast of where your company is headed.

As for your anger and bitterness—get rid of that baggage as soon as you can. You will need all your energy and attention focused on surviving what comes next, which, given the business climate, could be yet another redeployment or downsizing.

YOU'RE OUT OF A JOB, NOW WHAT?

Wanda has been an accountant for over ten years. She had worked for a stable firm and thought she had a job for life. But like many, she was nailed in a downsizing, and now she is unemployed. Wanda has made a number of tactical errors that have proved costly. First, she declined outplacement by her company, since she decided she would rather temp and earn money. Looking for work would come in good time. Thus, she missed out on learning critical job search skills and developing a network. Second, she is having difficulty describing what she can do other than in terms of her past responsibilities. She hasn't made the connection that she must start thinking in terms of what she can do for a new employer, not just what she did for the former employer. Third, she has decided that there is a definite prejudice against female accountants, and therefore, she doesn't expect to get a job anyway.

Wanda's attitude shows when she is on an interview. Although the people who are interviewing her do not quite know what it is about her that makes them uncomfortable, they are put off just enough by her attitude that they cannot see working with her. Further, Wanda has no sense of appearance when it comes to interviewing. In her old job it was okay to come into work wearing a skirt and sweater. She still uses that same wardrobe to go on her interviews. As a result, she comes across as too casual.

Ben is also in trouble. His problem is that he is so unfocused about what he wants that he cannot sell himself at interviews. When asked for his past experience, he digresses and goes on and on about one situation or another, but never quite answers the question. When asked what kind of job he wants, he waffles because in his heart he wants anything they have to offer, whether it fits him or not. His lack of focus confuses people. Ben, like Wanda, believes that there is some kind of conspiracy against him. He hasn't learned how to interview, and his inability to articulate his career goals is working against him.

Jessica has problems of a different nature. She got her job through her father, who worked for the company, which meant that she never had to find a job on her own before. She has always been an executive assistant and that's what she is looking for again. However, she is too shy to call people to network for job leads. She has yet to go on one job interview. She sent out ten resumes to local companies, but didn't follow up with any of them. Now she sits at home, collecting unemployment and becoming more and more depressed about her situation.

DIAGNOSIS

Each of our cases demonstrates a different set of problems. One thing they have in common, though, is that their failure to find a job is as much a function of their job search skills and attitude as it is the tough job market. Finding a job is complex; it's not just writing a good resume. People often shoot themselves in the foot on the job search process because of their attitude. For some, they drag around their old anger toward their former employer. For others, they don't have self-confidence, or they think the world is

TOP TEN WAYS TO REDUCE JOB STRESS

1. Figure out what the most important tasks are and then set up a schedule for doing them. Get rid of the less important tasks by putting them on that proverbial "back burner."

2. When you start to feel agitated or stressed about small things, ask yourself who will really care about it a hundred years from today.

3. Stop trying to do a number of things at the same time. Focus on one thing and do it well and with a sense of pride and peace. Treat an unexpected break as just that—a break! Then sit back and enjoy.

4. Develop a sense of detachment about the game playing you see going on around you. Most of this is done for success via advancement without any real understanding of what success in life is all about.

5. Stop evaluating yourself and others in terms of how much you have or how much the other person is "worth." You will be surprised how much of a burden this will take off you.

6. Find time to be alone. At work, find some moments for yourself even if it means closing your door for a while. Walk alone after lunch or try to image the universe of stars looking down on you.

7. Start your day 15 or 30 minutes earlier than you really need to. Use that time to do something that is good for you. Walk in the early morning air, share toast and coffee with someone you love, read your favorite sections of the newspaper or favorite author. Some people find it very relaxing to play music first thing in the morning.

8. Avoid perfection at all costs. Perfectionists create enormous stress problems for themselves and others. Be glad that you are a member of the human race and that your membership includes making a few mistakes. No one has ever succeeded in the quest for perfection, so why should you expect yourself to do the impossible?

9. Learn to say no. Many people get themselves into impossible binds because they are more concerned about how people feel about them than they are about their own welfare.

10. Establish some life goals that are apart from the clutter and crazy pace that is part of your everyday world. Listen to your own drummer and pull away from the race for money, prestige, and status. You will discover a whole world of riches far more satisfying and one that is much less stressful.

against them, or they really would rather not work, but have to. Whatever that underlying attitude is, if it is negative, it will show during interviews.

Rx

If the unthinkable has happened, you need to do a number of things very quickly. Define what you can do, and write your resume. If your company offers you outplacement, take them up on it. That will help you construct a job search. Let all your friends and colleagues know about your situation and ask them for names of people they know who might be helpful. Get yourself down to your local library or bookstore and learn as much as there is to know on how to find a job. This topic is so broad that it is beyond the scope of this book to cover the subject. Our interest in this type of situation is the "what-not-to-do" parts.

Do not sabotage your own efforts. Once you have written your resume, done your homework on how to find a job, and contacted your network, take time to reflect and ask yourself if there is anything you might be doing unconsciously that could affect your ability to find a job. If you have an observant friend or spouse, ask him or her for input. You may not want to hear about yourself when it could be negative, but it could be the most valuable learning experience in your life.

One more note about dealing with conducting an effective job search: finding a new job is usually very stressful, especially when the market is tight. Most people struggle with all kinds of problems ranging from worrying where the next rent or mortgage payment will come from, to wondering if they will ever get a decent job again, to struggling to keep their self-confidence up in spite of being rejected for a job. Any way you cut it, looking for a job is stressful. People who have been through a job search often report that finding a way to reduce their stress was a critical part of getting through the process. We have listed some suggestions that you might find helpful, whether you are facing job loss or are under a lot of stress from your present job. Whatever the source of your stress, you need to address the problem.

PROMOTING YOUR CAREER HEALTH—
Healing Careers in Crisis

The most trying and yet telling time of your career is when you encounter one of the inevitable crises that will befall you during your worklife. You can let these situations take over your life and destroy your career potential, or you can take control over yourself, your actions, and your responses to these difficult and often traumatic times.

When you successfully deal with these crises, you will not only work your way through and out of the situation, you will also have developed self-reliance and maturity skills that will serve you through-out your life.

What you need to master

- How to respond when the crisis hits
- How to keep your disappointments to yourself—who you can talk to, who you shouldn't
- How to assess for damage totals and manage for damage control
- How to keep your sanity and balance in the midst of crisis
- When to cut your losses and get out

Barriers to Success

- Wearing your heart on your sleeve
- Persecution complex—thinking this could happen only to YOU, not recognizing it happens to everyone at some point in their life
- Letting the situation take control of you, rather than you controlling your response to it
- Carrying the tragedy with you, not working through it and moving ahead

Payoff for you and your career

- Being able to conquer the crisis and moving forward with greater fortitude
- Reassessing what you really want for yourself and what you are will-ing to pay
- Ensuring you are in a place that will help you meet your objectives
- Career maturity

Chapter 4 MANAGING YOUR BOSS

A Delicate Balance

HOW TO SURVIVE A BAD BOSS

Bad bosses abound. They are everywhere. You are not going to be able to escape them, so your best bet is to settle down and prepare for the worst. Surviving a bad boss is like a rite of passage. Everyone has to have had at least one bad boss to qualify as a true corporate warrior. However, the damage that bad bosses inflict on careers is not like a simple act of hazing. Bad bosses can do enormous damage to people and their careers. Bad bosses can make even entire organizations "sick." Employees become aware at some level that there is a degree of "craziness" in their organizations, that people are behaving irrationally, and that decisions are being made that actually hurt rather than help the organization.

To get a sense of the damage that a bad boss can have on a career, take a look at Ed. At 33, Ed was an up-and-coming get-aheader. He had all the prerequisites: a track record in sales, a reputation for really knowing his stuff, and a burning desire to make it to the top. In his first six years with the company, he progressed from being a "techie" in information systems to sales and then to a supervisory position in finance and administration. It was at the last station that Ed stumbled. Ed had accepted a position in this department to build his background in the business in general and in finance in particular. So far, so good. His boss was seen as well connected to the inner circle, and the department was meeting its objectives. What was not immediately apparent was that his boss was incompetent. He could not make decisions, he avoided conflict, he didn't keep his word, he abused his subordinates, and he did not have an in-depth understanding of finance. So why was he the boss?

In this particular company where relationships count more than skills and knowledge, Ed's boss did a superb job of managing the relationships of the people above him. He knew who he needed to know and he took good care of them. He also made sure his posterior was well covered. In fact, Ed's boss was a bit of a chameleon—he could change his colors to match any circumstance. However, with his subordinates he was only one kind of person—bad. He hammered on the staff about the smallest details, made sarcastic remarks about individuals, bawled subordinates out at staff meetings, and ruled his department with an iron hand. When Ed, like the others, became the target of his boss's wrath, he felt deeply frustrated with what was going on. The last straw came when Ed caught wind of a reorganization of his department. Jobs were to be restructured or eliminated. People were to be demoted, transferred, or let go. What's worse, the rationale behind the reorganization, which was to make the department more efficient, was seen as just a rationalization. Ed suspected that his boss's real agenda was to make a grandstand play with his ability to make tough decisions and that there would only be one winner—the boss.

Ed felt the reorganization would torpedo his career and saw the reorganization plan as one more piece of evidence demonstrating how bad the boss really was. So Ed decided he had to do something about it. He began by holding discussions with the other people in the department. He leaked the information about the unannounced reorganization plans and then began to develop strategies to fight the decision.

Ed became convinced that the only way to save his job, as well as the jobs of his coworkers, was to go around his boss and let senior management know what was really going on. His plan was to get all the people in the department to sign a letter about the boss and he volunteered to deliver it to the "right" people.

Ed never had a chance to implement his plan. His boss learned about it (remember, the boss was a master at operating the grapevine), and he confronted Ed. That's the end of the story. Ed wasn't fired. He was left to dangle in the wind. The reorganization plan went forward, and Ed's boss essentially told him he was on his own to find someone or some department who would take him—which, of course, was very difficult because Ed needed the support of his boss to move somewhere else.

DIAGNOSIS

Surviving a bad boss is part of getting ahead. Many seasoned managers see this "bad boss" as a powerful learning experience. They look at what the boss did wrong and figure out what to do right. Moreover, by surviving a bad boss, they have demonstrated to others in the organization that they can handle difficult situations.

TIPS FOR SURVIVING A BAD BOSS

1. Develop your network for a possible escape route.
2. Keep a low profile—no mutiny.
3. Be so competent you amaze yourself and confound your boss.
4. Console yourself with the knowledge that this too will pass.
5. Think about all you are learning about what not to do.
6. Try and make them look good so they get moved up and out.

What could Ed have done other than organize his own mutiny? He could have asked his boss (regardless of how he felt about him) to work with him to identify other opportunities within the organization and enlist the boss's support in moving on. And, of course, he needed to have developed his own network of relationships so that he could locate other opportunities within the organization. He also could have better spent his time organizing his coworkers to survive the reorganization rather than planning how to "get the boss." He made a very serious mistake when he tried to organize his coworkers to revolt. And, finally, going around one's boss is usually suicidal. However, there are times to blow the whistle. If the boss is doing something illegal or if the future of the company is threatened, then you must speak up. But departmental reorganizations are a way of life with many companies and not a justification for mutiny. Ed lost his cool and allowed his personal feelings of anger and fear to cloud his judgment.

Rx

Ed may have to eat humble pie if he is to remain with his company. He could try apologizing to his boss and ask for a second chance to demonstrate his loyalty and good judgment. At this point, his boss is too powerful to ignore, let alone alienate. He might also ask his boss how he could repair the damage he has done to his career and to the department.

The Ten Worst Boss Behaviors and Prescriptions for Your Survival

1. Publicly humiliates employees in front of peers and subordinates.
   Rx: Speak with the boss and ask that he or she respect you by discussing negative issues privately.
2. Forces their employees to endure his or her frequent temper-tantrums.
   Rx: Patience. Don't react emotionally or get sucked in. Your calm may help diffuse the anger.
3. Sets up employees against each other through gossip, innuendo, and favoritism.
   Rx: Don't play this game—the results can be horrifying. Stay neutral and be sure to protect yourself by making public statements that may refute bad stuff that's being spread about you.
4. Works a seven-day, 18-hours-a-day week, and puts down anyone who isn't "on board."
   Rx: Put in the hours that match your life-style needs. Be available by phone if needed in emergencies so it is obvious you're a team player. Recognize that your advancement may be limited if a 60-hour workweek is not for you.
5. Thinks everyone is out to get him or her. Listens in on phone conversations, reads employees' mail.
   Rx: Be discreet and take home your personal items. Be supportive so you don't contribute more to the paranoia.
6. Acts as if he or she is well informed, but makes decisions that ensure that the project will fail and then blames it on the employees.
   Rx: You can't tell others it was their idea that made the project fail, but don't accept the responsibility.

7. Holds the threat of firing over employees' heads. Uses it on regular basis.
   Rx: After you realize it's an empty threat, ignore it.
8. Backs off from anything controversial. Doesn't fight for programs or people.
   Rx: Find ways to convince the boss that there will be payoff back to him or her.
9. Cheats. Lies about expense reports, lies about what was said. Double crosses colleagues and subordinates.
   Rx: Stay away! Don't condone or duplicate that behavior. If you are asked to do something yourself that is illegal or immoral, recognize that if it's found out, even if the boss ordered it, you will be held responsible for the actions you took.
10. Plays the dictator. Is abrasive, nasty, vicious, dictatorial, punishing, arrogant, perfectionist, controlling, chronically angry.
    Rx: Keep your balance and try not to let them get under your skin or take it personally. See the behavior for what it is—irrational and not within your power to change.

WHEN YOUR BEST FRIEND BECOMES YOUR BOSS

Here's the scenario. You and this other person started working for the company at the same time. You became best friends. You are both smart and competent, and you both want to get ahead. Your boss gets transferred and guess who gets her job? Your best buddy. That "friend."

Now imagine the next scenario. Your buddy is a little unsure of herself. She wants to look good and certainly doesn't want to be accused of showing favoritism. And this is her big chance. Now what does she do with you? Well, she might sit down with you and discuss the situation—put the conflicts on the table and discuss how you might work together. But she might not do that—or she might not know enough to do that. She might do what Jeanne did when she was promoted over Chris.

When Jeanne was promoted, she abruptly stopped having anything to do with Chris. Instead she became very formal. To show how tough she really was, Jeanne laid down a new set of rules for the department, which included everyone being at their desks by 8:30 A.M. Before the promotion, Jeanne and Chris always met at 8:30 A.M. at the cafeteria for coffee. Jeanne also demanded that no one should have any contact with anyone else in the organization without going through her. She also announced that she would be carefully monitoring everyone's work with special attention to using company time for personal business.

Chris was dumbfounded. How could her friend treat her and the other people in the department like this? When she recovered from her shock, Chris realized she was very angry, and she decided to let Jeanne have it. She walked into Jeanne's office and reeled off a long list of accusations and complaints. Her final words were, "I don't know how you managed this one; I just hope you can live with yourself considering what it means for my career." Jeanne in turn went to her boss and complained about the "problem" employee whose "jealousy" was "ruining" the department. The big boss called Chris in and told her to shape up. Now Chris was really boiling. Enter revenge.

Chris began a campaign to systematically destroy Jeanne. She began by leaking stories about Jeanne's personal life. She undermined Jeanne at staff meetings and enlisted the support of other people in the department in sabotaging Jeanne. What did Jeanne do? Why naturally and, of course, she began to "write up" Chris, which meant that she began to systematically document Chris's performance. She gave her three months' probation and a long list of goals, which included correcting her "attitude." Chris quit.

DIAGNOSIS

Chris had plenty to be angry about. She not only lost a promotion, but she was reeling under Jeanne's new directives. The way she handled it, though, was disastrous. It cost her a good job with a good company—a company in which, up until this situation, she was considered one of their high-potential employees.

In the ideal world, the manager who promoted Jeanne might have pulled Chris aside and discussed her potential or career outlook. But life doesn't usually follow the ideal. So Chris was mad at the department head for not choosing her and angry at Jeanne for getting it. Certainly Jeanne's attitude and actions aggravated an already difficult situation.

But the responsibility for this mess rests with Chris. She could have handled the set of circumstances differently. Instead, she let her emotions take over, and she made a bad situation worse.

Rx

If this ever happens to you, swallow your hurt and your pride even if it chokes you. Keep your mouth shut as in *lips not moving!*

When you've simmered down and recovered your senses, find out why you didn't get the promotion. It may have nothing to do with you personally and then again it might. You need to know what went into that decision for your own peace of mind as well as for the sake of your career. If possible, ask to discuss the change in relationships with your former friend, now boss. If possible. If not, do your darndest to stay in role (subordinate) and help your new boss meet his or her goals.

What do you do if someone pulls on you what Jeanne pulled on Chris—the new rules and procedures bit? Again, try to get your new boss to discuss the rationale for the changes. Then, describe how it is affecting you and your ability to work productively. If that is not possible, then smile, grit your teeth, and live with it until you can get yourself to another place or position. If you wait it out, you may even find the tyranny phase will pass as the new manager becomes more confident in his or her role. A lot of people will be watching to see how you handle this, so give them a performance that would make your parents proud. Above all, *Don't seek revenge.* You'll end up suffering more damage than you can inflict.

As for your anger, work through it, then let it go. And get on with your life.

WHEN YOU BECOME THE BOSS OF YOUR BUDDIES

Teddy was aptly named. He was the plant engineer and a real "teddy bear." He was one of the most popular employees in the company. He dished up the hamburgers at the company picnic, ran the United Way campaign, and coached the baseball team. He was known as a hard worker who did whatever it took to get the job done. He was good at what he did.

Sound like the characteristics of a good plant manager? His boss thought so. After four years with the company, Teddy was promoted.

And that's when the trouble started. Teddy now had a new role and relationship with his buddies. He had to supervise them and do unpleasant things like evaluate them and give them performance reviews. He also had to do the disciplining when someone was out of line. Or, rather, those were the things he was supposed to do.

But he couldn't do them. He felt uncomfortable as the one in charge. When he sat in on all the high-level meetings with the other managers, or parked at his reserved parking place, he felt like he was betraying his old friends. He hated giving evaluations. He hated having to discipline people. He hated making demands on people.

As a result, production began to slip, and he began to miss his goals. He started spending as much time as he could working alongside of his old colleagues and as little as possible in his office working on his management responsibilities. He neglected his weekly reports, which resulted in his boss finally reading the riot act to him and telling him to shape up or else. It didn't take long before Teddy began to hate his job. He grew morose and moody and began finding excuses to leave early.

Teddy lasted 18 months at which time he was given the choice of going back to his old position as plant engineer or finding a new job. Teddy tried his old position, but it wasn't the same. The relationships had changed, and he couldn't create what he had before. Moreover, he had lost that sense of joy that he had always found before in his work.

DIAGNOSIS

The problem? Teddy had a very strong need to be with people, to have people like him and to gain their approval. His need for affiliation was stronger than his need for power and achievement. In fact, Teddy was uncomfortable with power or competition. He much preferred to be one of the boys, even though it meant a lower salary and fewer perks.

For the present, Teddy would be more successful in a staff position (like plant engineer). But his need to be one of the boys is depriving him of the opportunity to grow and contribute as a manager.

For Teddy to change, he will have to become aware of his emotional needs and how they are impacting on him at work. For him to take on a management role, Teddy will have to grapple with his need for inclusion and approval. He may need to forgo that at work, but could find it otherwise in other arenas—church, politics, social services.

Rx

If you have a high need for peer approval and affiliation, you need to consider carefully what role you want in your company. Being a manager is a tough, complex job, and if being in charge is not your best suit, you're better off in a staff position as an individual contributor. Managers have to be able to handle heavy responsibilities (such as evaluating poor performers—who may even be former colleagues), and it really is lonely at the top. If relationships at work are a major source of your job satisfaction, be wary of the management track. Like Teddy, you may find being in charge to be a painful experience, and, as Teddy found out, you can't go home again.

Transitioning to boss is hard work, but key if you are to be successful as a manager. There are ways to help ease that transition. If possible, talk to your boss about the difficulties of the transition; also talk to others who have made the leap. A supervisory-management course—at your company, a local adult school or college, or an outside seminar—can teach you the new set of skills you need to be effective.

Be open with your staff about difficulties that may arise—don't assume you are now expected to have all the answers. It doesn't detract from your stature to ask for more input; in fact, it helps build a team when you encourage everyone to participate. You and your subordinates are all experiencing a transition—wrestling with how to relate with you as the boss. Putting issues on the table and talking about them openly can help smooth that transition.

Even if you are comfortable dealing with increased power and authority and you do become a manager over your old buddies (or some other group), recognize that the initial transition will be a tough one, but the payoff can make it worth the sacrifices.

POLICY DU JOUR:
When Your Boss Keeps Changing Directions

On Tuesday, Karen's boss told her to prepare a memo to the senior management committee regarding a new expense control policy. On Friday, after she had finished the memo, her boss told her it made no sense to send the memo to the senior staff. Instead, it should go out to all cost center heads.

The next week, Karen's boss said the memo would have to be approved by two levels up. After Karen prepared the cover letter to accompany the request for approval, her manager told her to just go ahead and send it out to all the cost centers.

Huh?

DIAGNOSIS _____

Each day the message changes without fair warning. Karen can never tell why. What she may not know is that sometimes these changes result from discussions her boss has with his manager and so changes his directions based on those comments. Other times, her boss thinks through the initial directive and devises a new strategy. Other times, he just changes his mind.

Not all bosses are automatically endowed with well-thought-through plans or with a clear sense of how everything should be done. Karen's boss is obviously having difficulty making decisions that he feels confident about. As a result, he keeps changing his mind and his directions.

Rx _____

How do you cope with a boss who frequently seems to have the mind of a chameleon? For big projects, put your understanding in writing and be sure everyone buys in before you proceed. For day-to-day directions, try to repeat them back so that everyone is working on the same agenda. If your boss is one to change his mind frequently, it may pay to wait a day after he tells you how to approach something, then feed it back—"I've started drafting the letter for the cost center managers and we should be able to send it out by Tuesday"—to give him a chance to change course, if he's going to. The more you remind him of what you've both agreed upon, the better the chances that he won't swing into a new channel.

A few other points: Sometimes the policy du jour can work to your advantage. If you don't agree with an approach or don't like doing a specific assignment, you may be able to manipulate the purveyor of the policy du jour to adopt a strategy that is more agreeable to you.

Your manager may also want you to take the initiative, either to take the monkey off his or her back, or to give you the opportunity to act, learn, and be accountable for your actions. Otherwise—watch out—he or she may want to have someone to pin problems/blame on. So read the situation carefully and proceed with caution.

THE PERILS OF BYPASSING THE BOSS

John was unhappy with his manager, Sally. She had given him a performance review that he felt was unfair and inaccurate. He wasn't sure how best to handle his complaints, but finally decided to go to Sally's boss, George, who was the director of the department.

He made an appointment to see George and told George's secretary it was "personal." George saw this on his calendar and was unsure about whether he should mention the appointment to Sally. For now, he thought, he'd wait and see what John wanted. When the two men met, John described his dissatisfaction with his performance review. The first thing George asked him was what had his manager Sally said about their disagreement about John's rating. John sheepishly admitted that he hadn't told Sally how unhappy he was. George talked to him a while more about his working relationship with Sally and then advised John that the first step toward resolution would be for John to go back to Sally and discuss the review. If they did not reach closure, he could return and George would intervene.

Sally was not too happy when she found out from John that he'd gone over her head before trying to work out a resolution with her. Sally recognized, rightly, that George would take a closer look at her now that he knew Sally's people went around her. She had no difficulty discussing John's performance review in more detail, but in reality, she felt that her back was against the wall to stand 100 percent firm on her review of John so that George wouldn't think she was indecisive or a pushover. Further, if John did go back to George to discuss the poor review, Sally was prepared to stick to her guns, even if it mean discrediting John.

DIAGNOSIS

John broke two unwritten rules. First, he did not discuss his problem with his immediate supervisor. Second, he tried to bypass her and take the problem to the next level. The whole thing backfired when the boss refused to deal with John. In addition, John has put Sally in a corner. She has to support her review if she is to be seen as credible.

Unless the circumstances are extreme (e.g., illegal activities), don't jump the managerial chain and go past your boss. Consider this from the boss's perspective. If you are a supervisor and your employee has an issue and bypasses you to go to your boss, you will not trust that employee. No manager wants to look bad, and no manager wants surprises such as the boss questioning a decision without previous warning from the subordinate that there was a problem

Rx

To get out of the immediate situation, John should admit to Sally he had been unsure as to how to proceed, and that he had not pursued the resolution correctly. He should also let George know he learned a good lesson. Then the three of them may be able to open up a meaningful and productive dialogue about his review.

Jumping the Line—Downward

Sometimes, it is senior management that bypasses the chain links downward; that is, your boss's manager comes directly to you to work on a project. The best way to deal with this is to keep your supervisor completely informed about the project. The reasons that your supervisor was bypassed are immaterial unless you're advised by the top manager that they are investigating wrongdoing on the part of your supervisor, in which case you must respond confidentially. If you get into this type of situation, it will be difficult to handle. For example, if the supervisor is cleared but you were seen as an "accomplice" to management, you will not be trusted again by the supervisor. Fortunately, these cases are rare.

Since one of the most important relationships you have is the one you have with your immediate supervisor, you must actively work to establish and build trust with that person. Thus, advising your boss when you've been given a project "from above" and then keeping your boss apprised of discussions, updates, and outcomes can only increase that trust. You can do this casually so that you don't embarrass your boss who may have been bypassed (he or she can take that up with the manager; it's not your battle). Keep the updates informal; include your supervisor on copies of anything that you're sending upstairs (you can clear this ahead of time with the top brass or tactfully "cc" your boss on correspondence). Whatever your strategy, it is critical that you gracefully balance this very delicate situation.

WHEN YOU WORK FOR A TYRANT

The careers of many people founder on the shoals of a tyrant. Such was the case of Nelson who was assigned to work for Max, who was known as the meanest manager in the organization, which took some doing, because this organization ran on nasty. The meanest manager was not stupid, however. He had built his career on two principles. Be totally loyal to your boss and do whatever he or she asked. Period. No questions. Just do it.

Max was also extremely effective in working the executive circuit. He flattered, he followed, and he fared very well. However, he was a different person when it came to interacting with his subordinates. Whereas to his supervisors he was charming, agreeable, cooperative, and supportive, to his subordinates he was a real beast. He publicly humiliated his subordinates, screamed at them, demanded total obedience (meaning no discussion about anything!), and was famous for his scorching performance reviews. Employees who survived working for Max came out of the experience shell-shocked and scarred. Naturally no one wanted a job with him, so he convinced the big boss that he had a number of positions that were ideal for developmental assignments. This meant employees could be rotated in for a specific length of time.

Nelson was one of the "lucky" employees to be assigned to Max's department. Unfortunately, he did not survive. Actually, Nelson managed the initial experience of working for Max. What brought him down was his reaction to what he saw Max doing to one of his colleagues. Nelson had developed a good and even close relationship with the other people in the office (bad bosses create great teams—the group pulls together against their common enemy). So when the "schmuck," as he was called, began to give one of his friends a hard time, Nelson became very upset. The last straw occurred when Max gave his friend in the department an undeserved poor performance review. Nelson saw red on this one. He knew the employee had always been a top performer and that this was some kind of a setup. So Nelson went to Max's boss and blew the whistle. He accused Max of being deliberately malicious and a destructive manager who created a hostile working environment, which was a violation of company policy. As you might have guessed, Max went crazy. He not only denied all accusations, but he demanded that Nelson publicly apologize. As for Nelson's job—forget it. He wasn't just dead in the water—he was in permanent submersion. Eventually, Nelson managed to get transferred to another part of the company (he had developed supporters in his earlier assignment). However, Max's rage and power hang over him like a large black spot. He's around every corner just waiting to take a shot at him.

DIAGNOSIS

This is another survive-by-surviving situation. Nelson threw himself into a battle he could not possibly win. He had nothing on his side but his indignation, anger, and a smattering of self-righteousness. He was right about Max and his evil empire. But taking him on like he did was an exercise in corporate kamikaze. What could or should he have done?

First, Nelson was too emotionally wound up to be rational. Part of the problem with working for the tyrannical type is that their craziness drives everyone else crazy and normal people end up doing wild and crazy things like taking the "Max's" of this world head on. Nelson lost it, as they say, and allowed Max's behavior to make him crazy. Second, Nelson could have had a heart to heart with Max and described to him how his management style was affecting the group. It probably would not have done any good, but he would have gone on record as the voice of reason. At the least, Max would have heard how he was affecting people.

Nelson might also have sounded out senior management (or the director of personnel) on Max's tactics using a hypothetical situation to see where the company stood on violation or abuse of company values and policies. The "hypothetical" case might have inspired someone to do a little investigation on this one. They in turn could have used the formal company system to address the problem. Nelson was heavy on principle (fueled by his enormous and understandable distaste for Max), but light on power.

He was over his head emotionally and positionally, and Max's craziness made him reckless. It's not within Nelson's power to go into the ring with Max. Max can outbox and outfox Nelson anytime. What he has to do is first survive Max. The colleague who was being railroaded needed Nelson's support, but she was the one who needed to initiate any formal complaints against Max.

Nelson picked the right cause, but the wrong battle. The tyrants of our world usually self-destruct over time. Nelson would have done better to use his network and help his colleague escape Max, and then he should have followed her out as quickly as possible. The most destructive thing about this type, aside from their basic sadism, is the rage they create around them and the irrational behavior this rage engenders.

Rx

If you work for a tyrant type, escape as fast as you can. Focus on getting away—not on getting even. As long as you are a tyrant's subordinate, you are not free—you're a corporate captive.

While you are captive, though, strive to keep your personal balance and prevent the insidious chipping away at your self-confidence, which can easily result from working for this type. Often employees in this situation find professional counseling necessary to cope with their feelings of helplessness.

Does the organization need to know about the tyrants in the company? *Yes.* But how that gets done is an issue of strategy, and you won't be effective or successful until you cool down and gain some leverage.

Remember, this is a book about getting your career on track, not about martyrdom. If you want to make your group's salvation your cause, do so. But consider the consequences, including finding a new job.

WHAT TO DO WHEN YOU WORK FOR AN UNBEARABLE BOSS

1. Don't try or even dream of trying to change his or her behavior. It won't work.
2. Figure out how to minimize the pain. For example, reduce face-to-face contact.
3. Identify one thing the boss does that is helpful and let him or her know about it. Keep reinforcing the positive behavior—no matter how insignificant.
4. Develop a support system for living through this ordeal, but limit how much you talk to coworkers unless you have already developed a very close relationship of trust. You will need to talk about it, but you need to choose carefully in whom you can confide.
5. If, through your efforts, your boss could become so successful that he or she got promoted to a new job *and another place*—well, now you've got a reason to be motivated that works for everyone.
6. If "unbearable" is a loser and here to stay, then you have got to make the move if it fits with your long-range career plan. But don't let the unbearable boss be the reason you do something stupid to your career.
7. Give your boss's name to a headhunter who can find him or her a job out of your company.
8. If you can't escape and must simply survive, look upon it as a learning experience on how not to treat people. And remember, the situations that are the most stressful are often the ones that develop you the most.

THINKING OF SABOTAGING THE BOSS?
Beware, the One You Sabotage May Be Yourself

Jack has a new boss—Tom, an important man, well connected in the organization. Tom was brought in from another division, where he was well considered and "on the rise."

Jack is not happy. He thinks that the vice presidency that was given to Tom should have been his—he had worked hard for his group and had been told he was a valuable player. Now, all of a sudden, here is Tom, from a smaller division, in the job that should have been his. What makes it worse is that Jack has to help Tom understand the division's business, the key players, the policies and practices. It would have been much easier if they had just given Jack the job.

Still nursing his wounds, Jack decided at the last minute to take a few vacation days the week Tom started ("Serves him right! Now he won't have me there to help him!"). When Jack returned, he openly bragged about staying home to mow the lawn so that Tom would have to figure out on his own how to run the place. As the weeks moved on, Jack openly rebelled against Tom's directives. He reasoned that since Tom was still new to the group, he couldn't know that much. Jack thought that the projects Tom supported were not as important as the other things the group was already working on. He felt that the new direction Tom wanted to take with some of their projects didn't make sense, knowing the history of the projects. As a result, Jack made it very obvious in staff meetings when he objected to some things Tom wanted to do. Whenever Tom overruled him, Jack "pouted" and remained silent for the duration of the meetings.

Then Jack started "bad mouthing" Tom, in a subtle manner, with clients and coworkers. Because Jack disagreed about the direction Tom was taking with one particular new project, he decided to distance himself from it. When he sent out communications about the project, he made it very obvious that it was Tom's direction and that he didn't agree with it.

Jack was truly surprised when Tom called him in one day and told him that he was being terminated. The reason—"a lack of confidence" in Jack's managerial skill, not being a team player, undermining Tom's efforts. Tom told him he was sorry to see such a valuable employee leave, but Jack's attitude and actions had such a negative effect on the group that Tom could not keep him on.

DIAGNOSIS

The point of this story is obvious, but the frequency with which this same scenario occurs makes us realize that it is a common cause of self-sabotage. Not only was Jack's pride hurt, but he didn't agree with Tom's approach. While both could be reasons for Jack to act as he did, his behavior came back and hit him in the face. People started to dismiss Jack as a valuable player because he so blatantly brought his personal battle with Tom into the public arena. It made others uncomfortable, and it made Tom angry (it got back to him directly and indirectly that Jack was not "on board" with Tom's approach). When Tom found out that Jack, a key player, was gardening at home while he, Tom, was struggling to learn his new job, Tom was incensed. Regardless of how Jack felt, Tom expected him to act professionally.

Jack thought he could win this battle, proving to the organization that they had given the vice presidency to the wrong man. What he missed was that the *decision was made*. Management would back Tom at any cost, especially in the beginning, regardless of whether Jack or anyone else would have been the better choice.

Jack sought to discredit and sabotage Tom's credibility. The politics of this are blatant, but Jack missed them. Since Tom was now the anointed player—for whatever reason—he was in the driver's seat. Jack could not win this battle.

Rx

A key role of every employee is to support their boss (like it or leave it). Jack needed to deal with his anger and get on board with Tom. Jack had the opportunity to become a key ally to Tom. Tom was well considered and going places—Jack could have used his relationship with Tom to advance his own career.

Jack missed the opportunity to team up with Tom—who could have used his help—and so missed the chance to expand his options. In the clash between the boss and the employee, the boss almost always wins. If Jack doesn't learn from his experience he'll spend the rest of his work life shooting himself in the foot every time he comes in second.

BREAKING IN A NEW BOSS:
An Opportunity to Shine

Liz is an administration manager in a fast-moving small company. She has a new boss—Jorge, who has just joined the firm from a large, structured organization. Jorge has lots to learn—the politics, the processes, the people. Liz is no dope and sees this as a great opportunity for her to be of help—possibly to make herself indispensable—and, knowing the value of quid pro quo (I'll scratch your back . . .), she realizes Jorge's success can only help hers.

Right from the start, Liz has gone out of her way to be helpful to Jorge. She keeps him up to date on all her projects, introduces him around the organization, and identifies areas of opportunity. She realized early that Jorge was an "idea guy" and had an agenda for the things he wanted to accomplish. Liz also recognized that her ability to implement his suggestions, capitalizing on her knowledge of the organization and how to get things done there, would help him succeed in his transition. As a result, she became a real partner in the relationship by pointing out possible pitfalls, helping Jorge think through ideas, and letting him know how to get then done. She then implemented his ideas, acknowledging that it was Jorge's brain power behind it. Management is thrilled by Jorge's ability to get so much done so quickly. Jorge is thrilled because Liz made it happen. Liz is thrilled because Jorge knows she helped him succeed.

Diagnosis

A new boss can be a curse or a blessing. The curse can be unknown—style, interests, priorities, the untested—what does he or she want from his staff, what is important for performance, the frustration at having to break in someone new. The blessing can be the new ally—someone who needs (and, you hope, appreciates) help assimilating into a new company, the clean slate to start anew.

Rx

There are many things you can do to strengthen your ties with a new boss:

- No matter what you think or you've heard, give the new person the benefit of the doubt.
- Get together a list of your projects and goals and educate the newcomer on your area.
- If you supervise people, review your staff's skills, needs, aspirations with your boss. If possible, schedule a lunch or meeting with the new boss and your staff to allow everyone to get to know each other.
- Help your boss acclimate himself or herself to your organization. Brief him or her before meetings about issues and personalities. Don't, however, be negative ("Shirley from manufacturing is a loser" is a no-no). Better to say nothing than to paint a negative picture until you give the new boss time to form his or her own opinions.
- Don't badmouth your new boss to coworkers or clients. If he or she turns out to be a jerk, everyone who needs to know it will eventually.

But you may unwittingly make some statements early on that could come back to haunt you, especially if a competitive coworker is in earshot.

- Just remember, if you don't cooperate with your boss, there is always someone who will. This could be your downfall and your coworker's windfall.

WHEN YOUR BOSS NEVER HAS TIME FOR YOU

Carly's boss, Lori, is a mover and a shaker in her company. Lori manages a large department, is the team leader for a key project, and serves on an outside board of directors. Lori also has an attention span of about 5 minutes.

Carly is a supervisor in the department and is very competent, having been in her job for several years. For the most part, she likes the autonomy that results from Lori's style and schedule. Sometimes, though, she finds it very frustrating that she can't get in to see Lori or can't have a full 20 minutes without multiple interruptions. Carly schedules update meetings with Lori on a periodic basis. Typically, she arrives several minutes early, with her list of issues to be discussed. Most times, she waits outside Lori's office—sometimes 10 minutes, sometimes 30. When she finally gets into the office, Lori spends time talking about the project she is managing, or an issue that is bothering her (regardless of whether or not it affects Carly), or where she ate dinner last night. Then the phone rings; Lori will jump up and say "This might be the call I am expecting," then spend 5 minutes chatting with the caller, even it is not the one she was awaiting. By the time she sits down with Carly again, she will say, "We only have 10 minutes, what have you got?" Carly often leaves these meetings frustrated and without answers to some of her critical issues.

DIAGNOSIS

Lori's style can be detrimental to your sanity but, if managed well, not an impediment to your career.

Many managers, like Lori, think you will float to them the issues that truly need their attention, either in update meetings or on an ad hoc basis. Working for a boss who does not give you a lot of time (or hand holding) can help you to work more autonomously, even though it may be out of frustration—"I can't get an answer from Lori, so I will just go ahead and do what I think is right." If your course of action works out, all is fine and you have learned a lesson about your judgment. On the occasions where you err in your decision making (which, you should hope, are rare), do not use your boss's inaccessibility as an excuse. It was your decision, so analyze what went wrong, learn the sometimes painful lesson from this episode, and move on. One more important note: Bosses *do not* like to be surprised. If there is an issue in progress that your boss should know about, as she or he may be questioned on it, be sure to tell her about it early. Handwritten notes or a message through your boss's secretary are sufficient. If your boss wants more information than a brief message conveys, he or she will give you the time to expand on the issue. Never use the fact that your boss is not available or traveling (there are always faxes) to leave him or her without notice of a tempest brewing.

Rx _____

If your boss, like Lori, leaves you waiting and then shortchanges you on time, learn to manage your time with them better. Here's how:

1. *Acknowledge that your boss may be late.*
   - Call your boss's secretary before leaving for the meeting to see if he or she is on schedule. If not, ask the secretary to call when your boss is ready for you. This, obviously, works only when your boss's office is reasonably near yours.
   - Bring other work with you so that, if you have to wait, the time is not wasted. It is best if you can find a desk or office to work at, but if not, bring reading materials with you so you can make use of idle time.
   - If the meeting is to be just a few minutes late, use the time to establish rapport with your boss's secretary, who can be a great ally to help your interactions with your boss. Recognize, though, that you are taking time away from his or her work day if you stand there and kibitz for 10 or 15 minutes.

2. *Use your time well.*
   - Bring a prioritized list of ideas with you.
   - Be ready to discuss the issues in a concise way.
   - Differentiate for yourself between issues you need your boss's opinion or guidance, versus their approval, versus something you need to give as an update. Discuss the update issues last.
   - If your boss travels a lot or is otherwise not available, send them

update memos of issues they need to know about and/or of your projects and their status. That gives you continuous visibility and will make your boss confident that the projects are moving ahead. Just don't wear out your boss's eyes or mailbox by overdoing these with volume or frequency.

- For those times you need to give your boss information or absolutely need an approval, use a handwritten note left on his or her desk or with his secretary (noting that it is "priority"), or use electronic mail if that is how your office communicates. You can also leave word with his or her secretary that "XYZ is happening and the contract won't fly unless we have Lori's go-ahead." The trick is to not cry wolf and make everything an emergency—that would mean you are not doing your job. If you use your priority "help" messages judiciously, you should be able to get your boss's attention when you need it most.

WHEN YOU AND YOUR BOSS MIX LIKE OIL AND WATER

Six months ago, Nick was moved from sales and marketing to product development. His new boss Lenore is a tough, no-nonsense manager who demands extremely high levels of performance from her subordinates. Last week she blasted Nick for writing what she called a "sloppy" report. The week before she called him on the carpet for not keeping her informed about what he saw as insignificant findings about one of the company's products. Today she called him into her office and berated him for being too casual about his deadlines—he was one day late with a major report.

Nick is beside himself. Until he worked for Lenore, he felt he was doing a good job. He was well liked by his old boss and got along great with the other sales and marketing employees. Moreover, he got the job done. One of the reasons he is now working for Lenore in product development is to give him broader experience in other parts of the company. Up until now, Nick has been considered on the fast track. In the past, his laid-back work style worked. It seemed to fit with how work got done. People met their deadlines and produced the numbers, but they didn't try to run the place like an army boot camp.

Compared to his last boss, Lenore is a menacing martinet. She lurks at every corner waiting to catch him doing something wrong. No matter what he does, she finds fault with it. Lately it is beginning to get to him. Nick feels his motivation dropping off. He wants to cut and run, but he knows it would be "careericidal" if he tried to leave before he puts his time in. He knows he can do the job, but he is having one heck of a time adjusting to Lenore's management style.

DIAGNOSIS

Lenore is a tough manager who has a very structured approach to running her department. Her actions are like the military way to getting things done. Nick prefers a much more casual style when he works. He has always enjoyed having close working relationships with his boss, including going out for a few beers after work. Lenore distances herself from her subordinates. For Nick, that's tough to adapt to. He misses the camaraderie, the feeling that he and the boss are working more like partners.

In turn, Nick's style grates on Lenore. She gets disgusted with his seemingly "ho-hum" response to problems. He sees her as a control freak; she sees him as a good ol' boy who misses his country club buddies from marketing and sales.

When oil meets water, there is bound to be a problem. But if oil is the boss, then it's water that has to learn how to fit. There are many variations on this theme in terms of different styles of working and communicating with each other. Unless you own the company, chances are you are going to work for people who have a very different operating style from yours.

Make no mistake. You are the one who has to make it work. The first step is to observe what your boss appears to value. If it's numbers of details, become the expert on minutiae. If he or she likes the big picture, develop a "helicopter" view of the operation. Some bosses like to discuss problems at length, other prefer short meetings and quick decisions.

We are not suggesting you become a clone and imitate your boss's every move. What we do suggest, however, is that you become very smart about this issue of style, so smart that you can slip easily into different styles, depending on the situations. You might think of it as a mirroring. If the boss likes to lean back in his or her chair, you lean back. If the boss talks, walks, and works fast, you gun your engine a little. If small talk is a no-no, get right to the point. In short, it isn't that you have to change who you are, but you have to become the emulsifying agent that allows the oil and water to mix.

Rx

Nick needs to make significant adjustments if he is to succeed in this assignment.

For starters, he needs to meet Lenore's deadlines and keep her apprised of his activities. The things that are important to Lenore may not seem important to Nick, but he needs to identify her priorities and work to meet them. He also needs to convince her that he can do the job, regardless of style. Nick might do well to have a heart to heart with Lenore and describe how he works and why his style works for him. He needs to assure her that he wants to meet her goals and to that end, draw up an agreement as to what he must change if he is to work successfully with her. This may seem as if Nick has to eat crow if he is to survive Lenore, but in fact, it's using common sense. We all make adjustments to live and work more harmoniously with people. By speaking openly with Lenore, Nick will be able to discuss with her the previously ignored but basic critical issue here—how their respective operating styles clash.

MISPLACED LOYALTY:
It Can Cost a Lot

Loyalty plays a large role in the workplace. Usually there is not enough of it. Sometimes there's a great deal, but only for very specific people. Many employees struggle with conflicting loyalties. It's the last situation that often causes the most difficulty.

Take Russ. Russ's boss, Todd, had been his mentor since Russ joined the company some 15 years ago. Todd was very powerful in his position as vice president of operations. Everyone knew that where Todd went, Russ would be right beside him. When Todd was given a promotion, Russ's promotion followed in two days. Todd valued Russ—he could trust him. Russ provided Todd with the type of information he couldn't always get at his level. Furthermore, what Todd said, Russ did. It was a perfect relationship, until Todd was abruptly terminated for reasons that no one would discuss. That left Russ without his boss and mentor; many people speculated that he would be next. But nothing happened to Russ; he kept his same job and when the new vice president was appointed, Russ picked up right where he left off with Todd. It appeared to be a seamless transition.

However, there was a small problem. Russ still kept up with Todd. They had lunch, they played golf, and their wives were still friends.

From time to time Todd called one of his old employees in the department, and it soon became clear that Todd knew a great deal more about what was going on inside than was appropriate. In fact, Todd had information that, if shared with the wrong people, could hurt the company or some of the people in the department. It was the kind of information that could be useful to the competitors as well as possible ammunition against the new vice president of operations. Clearly someone was telling tales out of school. When the new vice president was convinced that someone was feeding Todd information, he confronted the most likely source. He called in Russ and asked him point blank if he had given Todd information. The new vice president even ticked off the specific areas where there had been breaches of confidence. Russ's face grew red and he said he didn't remember discussing those issues with Todd.

The vice president was not satisfied, so he asked for a meeting with Todd. He told Todd exactly what he was hearing—that Todd had information that he had no business having and that he had heard it from Russ. Todd played it very cool. He told the vice president that he, Todd, had many sources, and it would be difficult for the vice president to put a muzzle on all the employees who formerly reported to him. Moreover, Todd said, "You know, a lot of people were pretty unhappy when I was let go. Maybe this is the price the company is paying for making that decision." At that point, the new vice president had heard enough. He thanked Todd for the meeting and he stormed back to his office.

He was very angry and he was determined to do something about what he saw as a possible conspiracy against him personally. He called Russ into his office and confronted him. Russ started to deny any wrongdoing. The vice president looked at Russ for a long moment and then he said, "You know, Russ, we can do this the hard way and it can really get outrageous because I am prepared to go to our lawyers right now and ask them to investigate how Todd knows what he knows. As far as I am concerned, you have violated our policies and given Todd information about our company that was strictly confidential."

Russ looked shaken. Then he said, "I really have blown it. I never thought of all of this as being illegal. I've made a big mistake. Is there anything I can do to undo the damage?" The vice president paused, then answered, "I don't know. You are right. You really blew it. As for the damage, while it may not be irreparable, it's going to affect your career. For starters, I'd advise you to drop your relationship with Todd. Right now I'm still too angry to discuss the situation with you further." With that, Russ wisely made his exit.

DIAGNOSIS

Russ was caught in a classic case of conflicting loyalties. On the one hand, he owed a lot to his old boss and mentor, Todd. On the other hand, he reported to a new person who expected professional behavior, particularly as it related to inside information. Todd had made it difficult for Russ by pushing him to share information just as in the old days. Russ was so naive that he didn't think through all the consequences of what he was doing. He also didn't think that Todd would brag to some of his former employees what he knew about what was going on. Russ was caught in the middle, a position that proved to be costly.

RX

The boundaries defining how you should deal with conflicting loyalties are not always clear. However, there are some basic principles. Number one, once your old boss leaves for whatever reason, you no longer have any business sharing sensitive information. Period. You are going to feel tempted to spill what you know and the person who has left wants very badly to hear about the old place. But you must draw the line on what you share. Gossip is one thing. Confidential information is another. You can be fired if you divulge confidential information; that is part of your work contract. Be wary of those who would try to use the old relationship to pry information from you. Even if you would trust them with your wallet, credit cards, and new car, don't give in and cross that line. It's not only dangerous, it is illegal. More likely than not, you'll be the one who ends up paying the price.

WHEN THE BOSS PUTS ALL THE BLAME ON YOU

Marty's boss, Gordon, couldn't make up his mind about how to put together a marketing campaign to generate the sales needed for summer programs. The discussions began in March, dragged through April, and died in May. When June came around, no marketing letters had gone out because Gordon still couldn't decide on a strategy. As a result, the company missed an entire selling season.

Now Gordon blames Marty. He claims that if Marty had developed a good strategy, he, Gordon, would have signed off on it. The truth of the matter is that Gordon never even asked Marty to develop a strategy. Gordon had always been the strategizer. His problem, however, was that he was also a procrastinator. So when it came time to put together a plan, Gordon could not make the decisions. Hence, the collapse and eventual demise of any marketing campaign. Marty's first response to Gordon's putting the blame on him was to explain what the real story was. He showed Gordon the calendar for all the meetings that were scheduled by Marty to move the marketing campaign forward. Gordon simply waved him aside and told him that he was trying to escape the responsibility that was his.

Now Marty is depressed. When the senior management committee met last week, Gordon explained why the summer marketing campaign had never materialized. Marty learned from one of the secretaries who took notes that Gordon had identified Marty as the culprit. Marty is in a dilemma. If he goes to the senior department executive, he will not only earn the ever-lasting enmity of Gordon, but the executive may not believe him. If he stays quiet, Gordon may owe him one, but it may not matter in the long run because now Marty has been fingered as incompetent.

DIAGNOSIS _____

Getting blamed for something you did not do can be very painful and potentially damaging to your career. It is a no-win situation. In this case, Marty had a record of the meetings, but he had no other documents other than his notes to support his position that it was Gordon who scuttled the marketing opportunity. He can probably get some of his coworkers to verify his story, but they will be at risk if they take Marty's side in this, and Marty is reluctant to ask them to do that. He can look for another position, but he likes his job, even though Gordon is difficult to work with.

Rx

If you get caught in a situation like this, you need to think through very carefully how you will respond. If you decide to keep quiet and take the hit for your boss, he or she may repay you some day if for no other reason than to assuage his or her conscience. You can try telling the truth, but you may not be believed, and you surely will alienate your boss. On the other hand, if you fail to say anything, you could be challenged for lacking the courage to stand up for yourself.

If your boss's mistake is so serious that it can do or has done irreparable damage to the company, you may have no choice but to bring the issue to senior management. The company needs to know about the risk this person poses for the company. If you manage to survive the first hit, you must start developing a paper trail of all your future dealings with the boss. Then if he or she tries it again, you will be prepared to fight the charge. In the meantime, keep your colleagues informed about your efforts and work so that if they are ever asked about your role, they can verify your story.

This scenario has the potential to damage you in many ways, so use your best judgment in handling it.

WHEN YOUR BOSS IS IN TROUBLE AND YOU NEED TO DISTANCE YOURSELF

Herb has been Barry's protege since he joined the company some five years ago. Herb started out in data processing where he soon became the project leader for his team. Barry plucked him from that division and brought him into his department to help him develop the new information systems. They made a good team. Herb was a good listener and could implement. Barry was the idea person who found Herb a ready supporter. During the ensuing years, they became known in the company as Frick and Frack. Where Barry went, Herb followed.

Recently, Barry got himself in trouble. Someone higher up called for an investigation of Barry's expense accounts. The investigation was concluded without any public announcement, but Herb now knows that Barry is in deep trouble. Management thinks Barry had taken advantage of the company's lax accounting systems and pocketed a significant amount of money he claimed to have used for company expenses. While no one is talking about firing Barry—they haven't documented the theft yet—his career is probably over.

Herb was not involved with Barry's financial affairs. He had wondered at times about Barry's bookkeeping, but he kept his doubts to himself. However, now Herb is afraid he will be associated with Barry, maybe even as an accomplice. Herb had a long talk with Barry's boss and expressed his regrets that Barry had gotten into trouble. But he is not sure what that talk meant. Does he need to plead his innocence: Should he offer to have his expense accounts reviewed just to convince everyone he's on the up and up? Should he still hang around with Barry? And what about his career? How does he establish himself as an independent player who can work without Barry's support?

DIAGNOSIS

Herb's situation is not all that unfamiliar. In this case, his boss was caught with his hand in the cookie jar. But there are other situations where you may need to distance yourself from your boss. For example, if your boss has pulled a real political boner or unwisely taken on upper management, you may need to analyze the consequences of being too closely associated with this period. Herb allowed himself to get into a comfortable and cozy position with Barry even though he suspected Barry fooled around with his expense reports. Now he will need to find a way to create an identity for himself that doesn't depend on Barry.

RX

Herb's best course of action is to continue to do his usual good job while he looks for a new opportunity in the company so that he can establish himself as someone who stands on his own two feet. He needs to build his network to find those opportunities. He needs to be seen as competent in his own right. He also needs to distance himself from Barry without being disloyal. After all, Barry took good care of him for many years. But the time has come for Herb to fly on his own. To do that, he will need to earn visibility for who he is, not for whom he knows.

Last, Herb needs to keep his mouth shut about Barry's difficulties. He should play dumb, avoid gossip, and refuse to be drawn into any discussions about Barry's difficulties.

WHEN YOU'RE RIGHT AND YOUR BOSS IS WRONG

Saletta works for a small but very successful company that develops and markets products that other companies can use to promote themselves. For example, her company has developed a very slick, but inexpensive, datebook that organizations buy by the thousands to use as giveaways to their customers. Another very successful line of products is the small ballpoint pens with the company or individual's name engraved on them. Saletta has been with the company for over ten years. Before that, she worked as the assistant marketing director for a large retail firm.

Saletta is afraid that the company is about to become a victim of its own success. The woman who runs the sales and marketing department wants to launch a new line of gifts. She has decided to go upscale and put out a new catalogue that sells high quality gift items such as gold engraved clocks and leaded glass vases. Saletta has argued against the move. She knows from her experience about the market for those types of gifts. She is also concerned since this new line of products departs from the company's niche to market attractive, but inexpensive, products. Saletta has offered to develop new research data on the potential for the high-scale gift items, but the marketing director says no, that she had been in business long enough to know what sells, and this was the direction the company was going.

Saletta is deeply worried. For one thing, the company has always made its money in part by manufacturing its own products. Its expertise in high-volume manufacturing is state-of-the-art. The upscale items, however, will have to be bought from other vendors. This little company has no experience in buying finished products. Saletta remains convinced that there are solid and good reasons for not going into another line of business.

Saletta is frustrated; she firmly believes that she is right and her boss is wrong. The problem is, she can't seem to get her boss to reconsider her decision. At this point, Saletta does not know what to do next. Her own livelihood is tied to this company's fortunes. If the company goes under, she goes under. She can't walk away from the situation. And she doesn't want to. Last week she had dinner with the marketing director and tried to show her the figures—where the sales were and where the losses could be. She told the marketing director she was headed for disaster. Her boss was very annoyed and told Saletta that she was "irritating" her.

DIAGNOSIS

Saletta is caught in a tough spot. She has the expertise and experience to know what she is talking about. What may be driving the marketing director to make this poor business decision and to cling to it even though it is wrong is not the issue. Since Saletta's future is tied to this company, at least in the short term, she needs to do anything she can to change her boss's mind and decision. Saletta has never been strong on influencing. She has always depended on her ability to run the numbers to make her arguments. Now she needs to go beyond the numbers since that strategy is not working.

RX

Saletta can begin again by sitting down with her boss, but this time her focus should be on listening to every thought and argument the marketing director has on this business strategy. She needs to find out as much as she can about how her boss sees the market and her reasons for wanting to go ahead with the new product line.

Saletta's goal should be to build a common understanding as to what the marketing director feels and thinks. The idea behind this strategy is not to prove her wrong, but to get a dialogue going that allows her to think aloud and share her reasons for going ahead. Saletta needs to back off from telling her boss she is wrong. Instead, she needs to help her rethink the problem with a view to solving the business crisis. Saletta also needs to share her deep concerns with her boss, including how she feels about this business (to which she is deeply committed). If that doesn't work, she may need to consider telling the owner of the business about her concern. But she will need to alert the marketing director that she is going over her head.

Telling the boss that he or she is wrong is usually not productive. It tends to get their back up and put them in a position of getting defensive about their decisions. Instead, the approach should be to sound them out, using your best listening skills so that you really understand where this person is coming from. You may not be able to change their minds, but you have at least taken them through a problem-solving process that may yield a better result.

Six Steps to Take When Your Boss Is Wrong

It is a difficult and challenging time for you when you need to deal with a boss who disagrees with you about a significant issue. Tread carefully! Here's how:

1. First, listen; learn as much as you can to understand why your boss believes as he or she does.
2. Document your facts to shore up your position. Then use rational persuasion to make your points.
3. Present alternatives in the hope that the boss will like one of your options enough to take ownership.
4. Develop a strategy. If you decide to do battle, then choose the battlefields carefully. Prepare by building up alliances and support for your position. Go to external experts if necessary. Then make your case.
5 If that doesn't work, you might confront your boss—but be aware of the stakes. Make sure it is worth the risk for what might follow.
6. Go over your boss's head, but only after you have notified your boss that you are going to do that. Because this is an extreme and dangerous step, make sure the problem has the potential to do serious damage to the company. This is not the occasion to complain about management style (unless, of course, it is affecting bottom-line profits and you can show the relationship). Be ready to forgo your own job because that is a real potential consequence.

BROWN-NOSING THE BOSS?
Beware, It Can Backfire

Barbara had her boss's number and she knew it. He loved it when people agreed with him and told him how smart he was. She did both—often. He liked it when he got compliments on how he handled something. She sang his praises. He liked to hear the latest gossip. She kept him very informed. He liked inside information—a spy, if you will, who looked out for his interests. She fed him every tidbit she uncovered.

She took good care of him. However, when her boss was sent on an extended overseas assignment, Barbara was left hanging. Her behavior had earned her the disdain of her colleagues. They didn't trust her, and they certainly weren't going to support her.

When Barbara met with the new boss, she tried to use the same tactics. She told the new boss that he was the best-dressed man in the company—a comment that he ignored. Next she told him that she had some important information that she thought he ought to know and that the meeting would have to be strictly off the record. He told her that he was uncomfortable with those kinds of meetings and asked her to tell him what it was that she felt he ought to know. Barbara's "important" news was the latest hall talk about who might be moving into the vacancy in the executive suite. The boss listened politely and then suggested that they both get back to work.

Barbara didn't give up that easily. She wanted badly to create the relationship she had with the former boss, so she tried another tactic. She suggested that they meet periodically to give each other feedback on how things were going. As Barbara put it, "That way I can learn from you, which would be so helpful, and you would have a sense of where things are with the rest of the staff on the Q-T." The boss shook his head. "I don't think we need to do that," he said. "We've got the performance appraisal process in place; I will use it to give you feedback on a regular basis. As for what's going on with the other members of the team, I hope to stay on top of that by working very closely with each one of them." He then looked at Barbara a minute and said, "Barbara, maybe I need to describe again the type of organization I am trying to develop. We need to work as a team if we are going to meet our objectives. That means we all need to be open and above board with one another. The last thing we need is meeting with one person or other members of the team to discuss them or me. I need you to be a part of the team. Right now I see you standing apart from the rest. I don't see you as having good working relationships with the other people on the team. I don't know what your relationship was in the past in this department, but I am looking for team players. While I want your support, I want it because I have earned it. I see that as reciprocal—I will support you, but you have to earn that support."

Barbara was quiet for a moment. Then she said thoughtfully, "I think I get your drift." There was another long pause, then she said, "I need to think about what you have just said. Maybe we can continue this discussion when I have had time to digest it." With that she left the room.

DIAGNOSIS

Barbara's blatant brown-nosing worked with her old boss, but it is not flying with her new one. She was very effective in her role as the court flatterer, but that role is no longer available to her. Now she must learn how to trust and to earn the trust of others. She also has to move from a position of advancing herself at the expense of the rest of the team to a position where her self-interests are in alignment with the team's interests. For the present, she is not trusted by her colleagues because of her manipulative behavior.

Rx

Few people, including most bosses, like a "kiss-up," "brown-noser," or whatever else you call someone who plays up to the boss. Brown-nosers have zero credibility with their peers and peers are always possible future bosses. People see this relationship for what it is—a raw neediness on the part of the employee who dishes it out and unbridled narcissism on the part of the supervisor who eats it up. Barbara needs to learn to build open and honest relationships with everyone she works with. She also needs to earn her Brownie points by being competent and trustworthy, not by playing the role of a sycophant.

A corollary to the brown-noser is someone who becomes too dependent on the boss. Often this becomes a close relationship where the boss is the mentor supreme and the employee is seen as an appendage of the manager. They can be viewed as an excellent team, but the danger arises when each loses their identity to the duet and others begin to assume that individually, there is insufficient strength. If the team is separated—the boss transfers, leaves, and so on—the employee can lose that reflected light and not appear to shine as before. The employee usually cannot get beyond being "Joe's minion" and will not be trusted by the new boss. It is not healthy to be too close to the boss; everyone will know "Tim protects her" or "he's Kathy's favorite," and you as the hapless employee will have lost your chance to establish a separate identity and credibility.

YOU AND YOUR BOSS—
Till Death Do You Part

Five years ago, George worked for one of the most difficult managers in the company. Jay was so abusive that grown men would weep at their performance reviews. Employees outside the department measured their happiness in terms of Jay. As bad as their own situations were, working for Jay would be worse. Being transferred to Jay's department was seen as a trip into the inferno. Most of Jay's employees suffered in pain and silence, awaiting the day they could escape or be rescued.

George managed to endure three years of this corporate water torture and then one day he blew. He stomped into Jay's office and proceeded to tell him off. George had three years to rehearse what he said, and it was quite a performance. He called him names even Jay hadn't heard of. It was a blast, literally and figuratively.

Interestingly, Jay did not say much. He stared at George rather intently, made a few notes on a pad, and quietly advised George to think about where else in the company he would prefer to work. A few months later, George was transferred to a new department and that was the happy ending of the story. Except that last month, Jay was reassigned to George's new division. And George is now faced with working for the very person he wiped up the floor with three years ago. And as you might guess, George is deeply worried.

DIAGNOSIS

A boss can make your life and career progress wonderfully or be a living nightmare with every gradation of pain and ecstasy in between. Therefore, among the most important relationships you develop is the one with the person to whom you report, your boss.

A common misconception for people new to the job is that once a boss—or you—leaves, you are free of him or her forever. *This is a fallacy.* In all probability, each boss you have had can and probably will affect you all your working life. In many companies, you may work for that person again. One company calls this its "Company Legend"—you will work for the same boss more than once, but in a different capacity (yours or theirs). They even go one step farther by saying the ultimate definition of the "Company Legend" is when your former boss works for you. As people progress within organizations, these types of occurrences become fairly common. In other words, always assume that you may work again for or with a particular boss. Therefore, treat that relationship with the long-term care and consideration it needs and deserves.

Even if you or your boss leaves the company, he or she may always be the source of a future reference check, so it's important to keep your bridges intact. Often these references are informal—"Say, did you know _____?" or "She worked for you? Well, then. . . ." It really is a small world, and the chances of your crossing paths with former colleagues or bosses are more probable than people want to believe.

One more note on George and his dragon boss. You may need to stand up to abusive bosses, but not by being abusive yourself. One tactic is to set up a meeting with your boss for the specific purpose of building a better working relationship with him or her. As difficult as it may be, try to get into the person's shoes to understand the reason for all the abuse. (Insecurity and fear lie behind much abuse.) You must also let your boss know how the abuse affects you. "When you yell at me, it makes it difficult for me to concentrate on doing the work. I get very angry, and it gets in the way of my doing a good job for you." Remember, part of your job is to build and maintain a good relationship with all your bosses. If you're savvy, you'll realize it's till death do you part.

Rx

George will now have to deal with Jay in his new role. Most likely George will try to get out of this department to avoid the abusive environment Jay creates, but until that is possible, George needs to take immediate action to try to mend the broken relationship.

He can start by dealing openly with the issue. George could do a "mea culpa," saying he regrets the way he acted several years ago and that he has learned much since then about how to handle conflict. Jay may or may not accept this, but their common goal is to accomplish the department's objectives, and they both need to work toward that agenda.

TWELVE WAYS TO BUILD A GOOD WORKING RELATIONSHIP WITH YOUR BOSS

1. Assess your boss's strengths and weaknesses. Accept the weaknesses as part of the whole package and get on with the job of learning to work with him or her.
2. Identify the obvious as well as the not so obvious pressures your boss faces. Most bosses face a very complex set of demands and expectations that they must integrate with their own hopes and dreams.
3. Figure out the basis on which your boss is being measured—what he or she has to do to succeed. Then help him or her make it happen.
4. Develop a sensitivity to his or her work style. A stickler for details? Lets things fall between the cracks? Can't operate until she has had coffee? Loses it when his boss gets on his case? Analyze it and then go with the flow.
5. If you need to have it out with your boss, get into his or her shoes before you confront him or her. Tell him or her you understand their world; then describe how their actions or decisions have affected your ability to perform.
6. Learn to defuse your boss's anger by listening to the feelings behind the words and reflecting them back. "You are really getting a lot of heat on this one, aren't you?"
7. Don't walk in with a problem without some solutions.
8. Give your boss sincere positive feedback when he or she does something good. Most bosses get a lot of hammering from the rest of the company.
9. Use your strengths to compensate for your boss's weaknesses—create a partnership.
10. Make friends with your boss's support staff. You all need each other.
11. Talk with your boss when you need his or her power to help you get your job done.
12. Support your boss even when he or she is off base. Save your criticism for a more private moment when you are alone with your boss

HOW NOT TO DRIVE YOUR BOSS CRAZY

Clare is driving her boss right up the wall. She stops by her office daily and asks her boss a million questions about the projects she has underway. Then Clare gives detailed accounts about whom she's met, what they've said, and where each of the projects stands at that very moment. Her boss has told Clare, "Just give me the highlights," but Clare doesn't get it.

Louis also is driving his boss nuts, but in a different way. Louis provides his boss with only sketchy details about his project status, saying, "Don't worry, everything is under control." His boss tries to ask for details, "Did you talk to Ralph today? What did he say? Where is the vendor statement?" Although Louis can answer all the questions, he only gives his boss the bare basics, which makes his boss crazy.

Two bosses—two different styles. A secret to success with your boss is to identify his or her style. One way to keep your boss satisfied with your work is to figure out what they want, when they want it, how they want it, then to deliver it. This is often called "managing up."

Every person has some idiosyncrasies as well as broad operating styles. Some micromanage, some work at arm's-length distance. Some like every gory detail, others are annoyed at anyone who cannot tell it in 25 words or less. To succeed, analyze the following about your boss.

- How does he or she process information—hearing it (your verbal reports or explanations)? seeing it (reports)? details (ten-page analysis) or broad brush—just give me the bottom line (two-paragraph executive summary)?

- How often does he or she want to meet with you—scheduled weekly updates? or the door is open and drop in anytime or the door is open, but "This better be an emergency"?

- How much of an imprint does he or she want on your work or, in other words, how much autonomy should you exercise? Clear everything before going forward? or "Tell me about it when it's done"?

- How much advance notice does he or she like—or how flexible are they? Some like a plan to be carried forward without deviation, others like to fly by the seat of their pants, making up the strategy as they go along.

- What is his or her prime time—morning, afternoon, midday, late? Some crabs at morning coffee can be very relaxed and open at 5:00 P.M.; others make the most of their early hours and want out at the end of the day. Tuning into your boss's clock can help you strategize the best time to approach them.

- How do they think—structured, methodically, creatively? Do they talk numbers or feelings? Adapting your presentation to fit with your boss's style will help you make your case and resolve issues to everyone's satisfaction.

HOT BUTTONS (WHAT REALLY TICKS BOSSES OFF)

- Missed deadlines with no previous warning that the dates will not be met.
- "Surprises"—you knew of some problem, but failed to warn your boss.
- Blaming others for your mistakes.
- Errors in work to go out under your signature—or worse, theirs.
- Being constantly late for meetings.
- Turning every call into a 20-minute chat—regardless of its significance.
- Changing something you and your boss agreed to, without discussing it first.
- Having a private agenda that is not in alignment with the group's objectives.
- Breaking your promises.
- Discussing your beefs about the boss with everyone but the boss.
- Making the same mistakes again and again.
- Cost overruns without forewarnings.
- Not keeping confidential information confidential.

WHAT TO DO WHEN YOU'VE GOT A GREAT BOSS

Enjoy!!!!!!

PROMOTING YOUR CAREER HEALTH—
Managing Your Boss

Your ability to "manage up" will solidify your career. The tenuous relationship between boss and employee can run the gamut from great mentor, ally, sponsor, promoter, and good friend to terrorist, dictator, and career-destroyer. You cannot often choose your boss, but you can maximize the relationship and find ways to effectively interact. The result will have a significant effect on your career.

What You Need to Master

- How to adapt to changes in management
- How to create good working relationships with all of your bosses, even those you hate
- How your boss can affect you—now and later
- How to adapt your communication style to mesh best with your boss's
- How to negotiate for what you want from your boss

Barriers to Success

- Stubbornness, inability to understand the implications that the boss is always right
- Sabotage from peers
- Not reading the organization well enough to understand how your boss is perceived
- Inflexibility (yours)
- Ineffective management skills (yours)

Payoff for You and Your Career

- Closer to the power center when your boss is in the "in" crowd
- Improved management skills—you have seen the good and the bad and incorporate the positive management skills into your own style (the boss as a role model)
- Increased responsibility as your boss gives you more latitude
- Endorsement from your boss will help you win the key assignments and job opportunities

Chapter 5 AVOIDING THE LAND MINES

Recognizing the Traps That Can Explode Your Career

HANDLING DISAPPOINTMENT WITH APLOMB

An important aspect of corporate savvy is handling disappointment. Take Louise. Her calm outward appearance hid a fierce drive to get ahead. She had been with her company several years, worked as hard as anyone else she knew, and felt she was due a promotion. When someone else was promoted to a job she wanted, Louise let loose with all four barrels. She had a royal scene with her manager that included crying, swearing at his secretary, and finally slamming the door as she left his office. Her manager, a mild-mannered individual, was beside himself. He didn't know how to handle her rage and asked personnel to intervene. Louise was asked to come to the personnel office and discuss the situation with one of the human resources representatives.

Louise poured out a tale of woe that ranged from lack of management training and opportunity to shine, to accusing her manager of playing favorites. It went on and on, and it was all the manager's fault. She not only dumped on her boss with the h.r. rep, but she told the same story to anyone who would listen. She wept in the ladies room and pouted at staff meetings. She wore her pain and suffering like a neon sign on her forehead for three weeks after the announcement. Everyone knew Louise had been wronged.

DIAGNOSIS

Louise has sabotaged her own career in a way that no one else could ever have done to her. Not only did the entire company learn she had not been promoted, but her behavior insured that none of the other managers would ever want her to work for them—period—regardless of her expertise.

Disappointment will test even the most stalwart of the get-aheaders, and like the bad boss, it is fairly inevitable. You are not going to get everything you want or deserve. And when that hits home, it is going to hurt. How you handle that hurt and disappointment is as important as how you handle your job. The key to managing your image when you are disappointed is to hide it from the public domain and keep it outside of the workplace. That doesn't mean that you should not discuss such issues with your boss; rather, the key is to keep that conversation private and manage your emotions.

RX

Louise has a lot of growing up to do and a lot of image building as well. She needs to apologize to those whom she dumped directly to—her boss and the personnel rep. She also needs to put on a positive face, even if it is not representative of how she really feels. The only way she will be able to shake off the reputation of being immature and unable to handle bad news is to prove that she can take the good and the bad and not let it throw her so publicly.

If the reasons are personal, take them to heart and do what you need to do to change and succeed. If they are more job-related, work to identify what you need and develop strategies for overcoming them.

WHAT TO DO WHEN YOU ARE DISAPPOINTED

1. Keep your feelings to yourself. Don't discuss how you feel with anyone but your most trusted friends and then preferably friends who do not work for your company.
2. Find out why you weren't promoted or didn't get what you wanted. This information is critical to your career advancement.
3. If corrections are in order, make them. The reasons could be as impersonal as your lack of experience in a particular area or as personal as you are too rigid or that you are not perceived as management material.

BUILDING BRIDGES, NOT BOOBY-TRAPPING YOUR COLLEAGUES

Some people look at managing their careers as picking their way through a field of land mines. Sometimes the dangers are obvious; other times they are well concealed. Some people hit a mine early in the game. For others, the land mines don't go off until they are far along, when they have a long record of accomplishments. Then everything blows up. Employees who let the ends justify the means don't usually set off their own land mines until they have accumulated a record of successes. The land mine goes off when the cost in human casualties becomes so counterproductive that the organization decides the price is too high and calls a halt to it.

This was the case for Walter who, after 3 years of "success" was put on probation and subsequently fired. By that time, sadly, he had set a company record both for the speed with which he moved his company's products to the market and the number of people he alienated and enraged in the process.

Walter was brought into his organization because he understood how to maneuver products to the market. His assignment was to speed up the process of getting to product launch, and he did. But the way he did it finally destroyed his career. To begin with, Walter was arrogant; he let everyone know he was twice as bright as anyone he was working with (and he was, IQ-wise). Second, he used his mandate to speed up the process to bulldoze, insult, and generally abuse the people involved in the process.

The company allowed it to go on for a long time because Walter was producing results. He was shaking up the system and making things happen, and his efforts were closely related to increasing the company's profits. So for about three years, Walter was a hero—at least to senior management. But as Walter's successes grew, so did his arrogance and abuse. He became more demanding and insulting and even staged full-blown temper-tantrums over issues as minor as the location of his parking space. Eventually, people stopped cooperating with him and even began to sabotage his projects. Walter retaliated by running to the president with the names of all those employees who were making it "difficult" for him to do his job.

The day of reckoning came when a new company president decided that as much as he wanted quick results, he could no longer afford Walter. The cost to the company in human bodies was too high. So Walter got the word and was put on probation to see if he could cool down his approach.

His reaction was to include the president and his immediate boss in his publicly stated evaluation of their intelligence, and that, of course, ended Walter. He was called in and given his walking papers.

DIAGNOSIS

Notice the way Walter had sabotaged his own career. He had all the knowledge and drive he needed to do the job, but he had little regard for the means he used to get results. He actually believed it was his "right" to do whatever was needed to get the job done. Even after he left the company, Walter remained largely ignorant of how he had ruined an otherwise promising career.

Rx

Walter needs to understand that it was his treatment of others that tanked his career. He is smart enough and focused enough to be able to change his behavior (if not his thinking) and treat others with dignity, respect, and professionalism. What could stand in his way is his superiority attitude. Walter needs to get beyond that and recognize that excellent management skills include the ability to influence and lead others.

Interpersonal Skills: The Key to Your Success

Of all the skills needed to be successful in your career, interpersonal skills are the most important. Walter didn't get fired because he lacked technical expertise or didn't understand how the system worked. He failed because of the way he interacted with people.

Building Relationships

Interpersonal skills are critical, and you will further your career as you develop and strengthen yours. Here's how:

- Take a personal interest in people. Getting to know others may not be a priority for you; in fact you may see it as wasting time. But it is the personal relationships that will help you to get your job done. Get to know everyone you come in contact with or who works with your department in any way.
- Take the time to learn about the interests and concerns of your colleagues, including those at levels different from yours. Bosses and secretaries are human beings. You need to treat them as people, not in terms of their functions.
- Become invested in the success of those around you. Your interest in their careers will surprise and delight them. In turn, they will be more likely to care about you and work on your behalf.
- Become more approachable. Quiet, reserved people often give off signals they never intend. Remember that if people don't know you, they will draw their own conclusions about the kind of person you are. More often than not, their conclusion will be that you are unfriendly or don't like them or are snobbish. Whatever their conclusion, it is seldom favorable. People need to know that you think they are "okay." For them, no news is bad news.

Handling Conflict

Conflict among colleagues is like rain. You need it to have a healthy organization, but no one really likes getting wet. However, conflict is as inevitable as precipitation from the sky and must be effectively dealt with. People with poor interpersonal skills often fail to handle conflict well. They may dismiss a colleague out of hand: "He doesn't know what he's talking about, I can't work with him" or "Why won't she listen to me? I explained how to do it, but she just has to do it her own way." Or worse, "They don't know what they are doing, and they are refusing to cooperate with me. Therefore, I cannot do my job because they are deliberately trying to sabotage me." As you can guess, the underlying problem for people with this type of poor interpersonal skills is their lack of respect for anyone's ideas but their own. Their disdain for others, coupled with their inflated ideas of their own correctness, is a sure formula for a disastrous working relationship.

You must respect others and communicate that respect, even if you don't agree with them. Nothing builds barriers as fast as treating people as numbers or "know nothings." If you convey a message that you devalue them, they will set up a defense against you that will seriously inhibit, if not destroy, your ability to get that close to them again. And for you, that translates into a nonworking relationship.

Working with Your Colleagues

- Think of yourself as part of a team rather than a lone performer who has to get the work done in spite of the rest of the team. Show your team approach by taking an interest in the team's work problems and pitching in when possible to help them. Because many workplaces are very competitive, your coworkers may not expect to get anything from anyone else except a hard time. Your collaborative attitude may surprise them, and you may find that you will be repaid in kind.

- If you are having difficulty getting along with a peer, analyze the causes and make a determination about what you can do to improve the relationship. You might even want to discuss the issue with him or her, emphasizing that you would like to develop a better working relationship and asking for help in doing that. You can check your progress by noting the degree with which they do such things as share information with you, discuss ideas and problems with you, and work with you rather than against you. Even if you just can't stand someone, try to structure a workable relationship about your areas of commonality—how your jobs or objectives overlap, what you need from each other to get the job done, and so on.

Developing Diplomacy

The inability to communicate gracefully and tactfully is another factor that torpedoes many careers. Poor communicators are often insensitive to the feelings of others. For example, when they disagree with someone, they rarely give the opposition any credit for their ideas. Instead, they rush to put the other person's ideas down and argue for their own. As a result, the person they are trying to persuade becomes defensive and the would-be persuader is left standing making an enemy rather than making a "sell."

Diplomacy also includes knowing when and how to give feedback. People who are unusually forthright often blunder because they criticize another person's actions or ideas without considering how the other person will take it. While there are some individuals who can handle a high degree of forthright behavior, most people are not so constructed. If they must hear bad news, it needs to be communicated in such a way that their self-esteem is not damaged. Forthright people forget that their so-called honesty is sometimes communicated in a brutal fashion and hurts others. As a result, people avoid the forthright person even though they may be right about what they have to communicate. You must think through what you want as the end result when you disagree or have to give bad news. If you have no interest in maintaining the relationship, then you can drop your bomb, "Jenny, your idea really reflects poor thinking." But if you are going to have to work with this person in the future and need his or her cooperation to get your job done, you need to be much more diplomatic: "Jenny, tell me more about how you arrived at your conclusions so I can really understand where you are coming from." If Jenny's thinking is second rate, then use the occasion to help her by offering some new way of approaching the issue. She will learn something, and you will have a colleague who will work cooperatively in the future.

Getting Information

When you want information, don't come on like a police detective with your questions, especially if you want to check out their story against what you know. People become very defensive when they feel they are getting pushed against the wall with that style of inquiry. They wonder if you have a different agenda, or if you are trying to trip them up, or if you want to see if they have as clear a recollection of facts as you do. Whatever their fears, there will be a noticeable decrease in how much they communicate or even deal with you in the future. Instead of asking for information KGB style, begin the inquiry by saying something like, "I'm still trying to put together a history of how we got to this point, and I need help in understanding what happened when and to whom. Here's my understanding to this point. . . ." By asking for help rather than playing "gotcha," the person will be much more inclined to share what he or she knows with you and help you with your problem.

A variation on this theme is the individual who has the ability to remember not only the sequence of events, but the precise conversations that accompanied them. While this is a valuable talent, if it is used to entrap people or show off the superior ability to recollect, you set up the potential for adversarial relationships. Your colleagues will begin taking notes of every meeting and conversation to defend against your ability to broadside them with your memory for details.

Final words of wisdom:

Be sensitive to the feelings of others.
Never cause others to lose face.
Get conflicts on the table for discussion.
Show value and respect for everyone—each person and their perspective.

THE POOR-LITTLE-OLD-ME GAME AND WHY IT WON'T WORK

In contrast to piling up the bodies to achieve your goals, the "poor-little-old-me" people adopt a strategy of being very, very nice to everyone under all circumstances. This type doesn't fight, confront, argue, or make demands. Instead, they comply, bend over backward to do little favors, are disarmingly self-effacing, and never, but never, have any purpose in life other than to serve the needs of others. And to cover all the bases, they have heart-rending stories about their personal trials and sorrows that they are willing and eager to describe.

If it's hard to imagine that being too nice can actually sabotage a career, take a look at Helen. Helen has achieved one of her career goals—to work in the customer service department. She chose customer service because it fit her background and she saw it as a way to get into sales and marketing.

Helen soon established a close working relationship with the office manager. She saw to it that he had coffee when he walked in, she always checked to see if he needed a snack. "It is no trouble, I'm going that direction on my way." She dropped in at his office during the day to see if there was any way she could help out. She volunteered to go with him to important meetings in case he needed anything.

In fact, Helen made the office manager her best customer. The boss wasn't the only recipient of all these favors. She was the department saint when it came to remembering birthdays, calling to inquire about an illness, going to family wakes. You name it, Helen was there. She even worked overtime to help others meet their deadlines.

Helen didn't show her colors until five to six months after she was into the job. Then the purpose became more clear. Helen began to identify a number of special favors she needed from people and she asked for them. With one colleague, it was that Helen needed help in writing a major report. The colleague felt he couldn't say no because Helen had given his twin boys a birthday present last month. The report was a difficult one and would mean he would have to work that weekend to get it in shape. But after all the favors, Helen had done for him, how could he refuse?

For others, it was a variation on the theme. "Would you do me a favor, I'm really in a tight spot. I need someone to copy this by 3:30 this afternoon. I know it is a lot to ask, but if you could just make 150 copies I would be eternally grateful." "I know it is a lot to ask, but I must get my car into the garage for repairs. Would you be so kind as to pick me up tomorrow morning? I know it means leaving a half hour early, but it would be such a favor to me. And I would be so grateful."

Another theme that Helen played often was the poor-little-old-me song. She let it be known how badly off she was financially, how stressed she was from her marriage, how bad was the health of her aging parents, how difficult her childhood had been, and on and on. If people didn't feel obliged to Helen, she made sure they felt sorry for her.

When a vacancy occurred in customer accounts department, Helen asked her boss out for lunch. Then she put it to him ever so demurely, but plainly. "You know, life is hard for me, Otto, but I have really worked to make you successful. There wasn't and isn't anything I wouldn't do to see that you achieve your goals. Now I need your help in return." And then she laid out her plan. She wanted him to move the current supervisor to the customer accounts department and give her the position. She recounted how she had worked with the boss in the past, even mentioning that as always she would "be there" for him.

Otto was nonplused. He had never been comfortable with Helen's style. He felt disarmed by her intense thoughtfulness, and her tales of woe overwhelmed him at times. Now she wanted him to move a good supervisor to another department and give her the position. He did feel sorry for her and he felt that he owed her something, but he had no immediate plans to make her a supervisor.

He wanted to buy some time to think about it, so he responded by telling her that he would try to do what he could, although it might not be as soon as she wanted. When Otto left the meeting, he felt he was in a no-win situation. If he didn't find a way to repay her for all her favors, he would feel like a heel. If he gave her the promotion, it would be from a sense of guilt rather than because he felt she was ready.

His problem was solved for him two weeks later when he was asked to take another position in the distribution department. So Otto walked away from the problem and left his successor to deal with Helen.

His successor had heard about Helen from some of the people in customer service. She was something of a company legend when it came to being poor-little-old-me—Miss-Nice-Nice. So when Helen began her same "What-can-I-do-for-you?" routine, he played it very differently than his predecessor. He said thank you but no thank you. Helen doubled her efforts, but they fell on deaf ears. In the meantime, her behavior with her colleagues was beginning to wear thin. Now when Helen ran through her "This-is-just-a-little-something-to-let-you-know-I'm-thinking-of-you" routine, they were wary. They knew that at a later point Helen would be asking for something in return and that they would find it awkward to refuse her. Like the new manager, their response was to disassociate themselves from Helen and to avoid getting themselves into "debt" with her.

Now Helen is confused. She can't understand why people are pulling away from her. She also feels she is losing ground in terms of making supervisor. She doesn't think she has the support of the new manager. Worse, she really doesn't know what to do about it.

DIAGNOSIS

Helen has tried to work on people by using favors and her tales of woe to force them to be obligated or sorry for her. This technique worked for a while, but eventually her boss and her coworkers realized what the game was all about and they turned away from her. For

Helen to achieve her goals, she will need to be open about her agenda.

The poor-little-old-me syndrome smacks of immaturity. Fully operational adults have and exhibit the full range of emotions. To pose as totally unselfish, as someone whose own career is secondary to everyone else's and whose only quest in life is to see others happy is dishonest. One of the problems for many people is that they were taught as children that if they were "nice" or "good," they would be rewarded. As a coping behavior, it may have even worked in childhood or adolescence. But when people continue that behavior into adulthood, it backfires. First, if people always put the needs of others before their own, they are going to lead a very unhappy life. Others will begin to take them at their word, and they become the company doormat. Second, other people will suspect that no one can possibly be that "nice" to everyone 365 days of the year, and they will distrust them because they will suspect that there is another agenda. Third, while people do special favors for people they feel sorry for, they will resent it if they are taken advantage of.

Rx

For starters, Helen needs to be honest about her agenda. She wants to get ahead. She needs to stop playing "poor-little-old-me" and pretending that she is less competent or ambitious than she is. Above all, she must become more honest in her relationships with people. It's okay to be nice, but if the only reason you're nice is to get something from others, then it will eventually backfire because people will feel used. They will know that you didn't care about them, but acted nice to get something you wanted from them by using the old guilt trip game.

Helen needs to understand that she can get what she wants without manipulating people. She can build her reputation based on competence and good working relationships rather than through manipulation of her coworkers and boss.

JOINED AT THE HIP
When a Mentor Does More Harm than Good

They were quite a pair. Donna was senior vice president of a large real estate firm; Cheryl was the office manager. Wherever Donna went, Cheryl went. Whatever Donna suggested, Cheryl endorsed. Whatever Donna ate, Cheryl ordered. Whatever Donna wore, Cheryl copied. Donna started each day meeting with Cheryl. They had frequent meetings together throughout the day. They left work at the same time and met for drinks after the office closed. In short, they looked and acted like corporate Bobbsey Twins or as the rest of the staff wryly observed as if they were "joined at the hip."

Now there is nothing wrong with two colleagues working very closely together. In Cheryl's case, it meant that when Donna was promoted to the corporate office, Cheryl was made senior vice president and took over Donna's job. So being joined at the hip has its rewards.

But with Donna gone, Cheryl was faced with something she had not trained for. She was completely on her own. And now she had to deal with a staff that had become increasingly alienated as a result of the preferential treatment given to her.

As Donna's buddy and sidekick, Cheryl had not earned the trust of the rest of the staff. In fact, she reputedly acted as Donna's spy and reported the comings and goings of the other members of the staff. The staff had even begun to play a bad game that included feeding false stories to Cheryl to see how long it took before Donna reacted. As the new senior vice president, Cheryl soon realized she had problems. So she called Donna and asked for help. Donna's solution was to show up at the next staff meeting and "order" people to cooperate with Cheryl. Then Donna began spending one or two days at the office to make sure people were doing as they were told.

As you might guess, this type of thing just doesn't work. Cheryl never even got out of the starting gate before Donna (her good friend) came back to take over. And, of course, best friends can't fight, so Cheryl had no alternative but to stand aside and let her "best friend" run the show. When the senior management of the company discovered that Donna was still doing Cheryl's job, they pulled the plug on—you guessed it—Cheryl. Who did not try to rescue Cheryl? You guess right again—Donna. Cheryl finally found a position in another company, but not at the level she had been before.

DIAGNOSIS

Now what's the moral of the story? For Cheryl, the moral is beware of people who, in the name of friendship, use you. Donna needed what Cheryl had to offer—loyalty, a confidante, a pipeline, an errand person. It was great for Donna. It met her needs, and as a manager, she thrived in the type of unswerving support and adulation that she got from Cheryl. In turn, Cheryl got recognition, visibility, and the top assignments.

But Cheryl became absorbed by Donna. She ceased being her own person, she stopped learning and experiencing and growing. She did master "clonemanship," which fortunately has a limited application in most organizations.

Rx

Cheryl was put in a tough position by Donna's demands on her. She took the most expedient route, which was to become what Donna wanted and needed. Donna was a very dominating person and Cheryl found it easier to go along than fight.

But the price was high. Cheryl lost not only the respect and cooperation of the rest of the staff, but ultimately her job as well.

If dominating people appear to overwhelm you, avoid them. If you can't avoid them, resist their efforts to take you over and make you one of their own. Tell them that you are uncomfortable with the lopsided attention you are getting and that it is making it more difficult for you to work with the other members of the staff.

It's one thing to have the boss as a mentor and a champion. It's another thing to become so psychologically and emotionally attached that you start to lose your sense of identity. Even the best of friends do better when they have their own growing space.

HAVING AN "ATTITUDE"
Whether It's Yours or Someone Else's, It's Bad News

One of the most frustrating situations for supervisors and managers is subordinates who have an "attitude." The "attitude" varies. Sometimes it's an "everyone-here-is-out-to-get-me" attitude or "the-deck-is-stacked" attitude. For some, it's a "they-hope-I'll/we'll-fail" or "they-owe-me-something" attitude. For others, it's "I do just what I'm told and no more" or "they always pick on me." Whatever the attitude, it's usually a negative one and includes seeing the "system" as the enemy. The system, which can be the whole company or a group of individuals, is viewed with great suspicion and each event is further evidence of the validity of the "attitude."

An even greater danger occurs when these attitudes begin to infect other people.

The story of Rita and Gail illustrates how negative attitudes can become addictive and even self-destructive. Rita and Gail were in charge of different aspects of the office operations of a small manufacturing company. Their work was good. Gail had mastered the computer and had figured out how to integrate all the business systems on one data base. Rita handled payroll, benefits, and office correspondence.

However, serious problems around morale and turnover plagued the front office operation. Most of the difficulty stemmed from the way that Rita and Gail related to the rest of the organization and the other members of the office staff. Rita and Gail saw themselves as victims of a terrible and unfeeling system. They had a litany of complaints that they trotted out at every occasion. These included their feeling that they were overworked and underpaid, that everyone else could make mistakes, but they had to clean up after everybody, that other departments got little perks while they were treated like second-class citizens, and that they carried the company and did more work than anyone else.

Those who had to work with Rita and Gail told quite another story. They described how the two women would gang up on new employees and force them to choose their side (which was anticompany) or risk being frozen out in the office relationships. Frozen out meant that Rita and Gail would not speak to that person, would not help that person, and would go out of their way to make life miserable for the newcomer. Most of the new office workers quit after a few months.

Other people in the company received the same treatment. Rita and Gail ran campaigns designed to punish anyone who did not fawn over them or who took issue with how they had done something. They refused to even speak to those employees who didn't treat them "right." They bullied and humiliated people until many simply stopped dealing with them.

Finally, the head of administration had it with the behavior of these two. He confronted them and told them they had to act like professionals. He told them to clean up their act or leave. The women took his criticism as one more proof of how horrible the company was, and by spring both of them had resigned. But that was a bad solution to a problem. The women were valued and experienced workers. The company wanted them to stay, but not at the cost of the morale and productivity of the rest of the company.

DIAGNOSIS

This was a perfect illustration of how an attitude can become addictive. In this case, Rita and Gail became addicted to bashing the company. It was like a daily fix: each day they needed more evidence to support their negativity. This type of addiction is characterized by a constant search for new evidence to support a grievance or attitude about things. At its extreme and most dangerous level, it is the stuff that feeds many of the fanatics of the world and justifies in their eyes the destruction they wreak on their "enemy."

RX

When managers encounter employees with a negative attitude, they need to confront the problem even as this manager did when he confronted Gail and Rita. However, he needed to more than just tell them to cease and desist or get out. Gail and Rita are too removed from reality at this point to manage the addiction. From the company's point of view, the manager has a responsibility to save valuable employees when possible. The manager saw the effect their attitude was having on the company, so he confronted them. However, if he wanted to save Rita and Gail, he needed to give them more coaching. For example, he could have sat down with Rita and Gail and described what was working (what they did well) and what wasn't working (what behaviors were counterproductive). He could have then asked Gail and Rita separately to draw up development plans for changing their behaviors. He would need to give them a time line and describe how he would measure the change. One way to measure attitude change is to do a survey of the coworkers. While this may seem drastic, it will take this type of action if employees like Rita and Gail are to understand how their behavior affects the rest of the company. They also need to understand that such behavior is not acceptable.

If you see any of yourself in this description of Rita and Gail, you must face the possibility that you have developed a negative attitude that has become addictive and that you need to get over it. Try writing down every thought you have about your work situation for a week. If most of your comments are negative, beware. It may be time for you to examine yourself and ask if you have succumbed to "a negative attitude."

Feeling negative can begin with the observation as simple as "it's not fair." That's a statement that reflects reality. The bottom line is that work is not always fair, companies are not always fair, people are not always fair, and in fact, life is not always fair. But as a statement, it can become a self-fulfilling prophecy. And, then, it becomes the beginning of the end.

LEAVING FOOTPRINTS ON THE BACKS OF OTHERS

Joe was a fellow who lived by his own agenda. In meetings when others suggested new ideas, he would attack with "why do we need that" or "we already tried that" or "that will never work" or "how could you be so blind/stupid/naive, and so on?" He would bring attention to others' mistakes—always in a public forum—and if an apology were required, he would offer it only in private. Joe was no dummy, however. He was smart, and he worked hard. His track record was impressive. But he left behind a trail of bruised people as he climbed over them to get to where he wanted.

Bruised people notwithstanding, Joe moved up the ladder (or maybe because of it—he seemed to "profit" when he made others look bad). When he reached the senior level, he used similar tactics on his new peer group, now the executive management group. He knocked down their ideas. He pointed out their errors. He even tried to create dissension by recruiting "spies" from other departments to keep him informed about his fellow executive group members. This group was more savvy in dealing with Joe. They knew they needed to be a team and Joe was not a team player. After a year of enduring his behavior, the group confronted Joe at an off-site team-building event. The CEO finally saw how detrimental Joe's behavior was to the team, and he sent Joe back down the ladder. Joe had no support at any level; people were almost glad to see him fail since they felt he deserved it.

DIAGNOSIS

By failing to cultivate allies, Joe had developed detractors and no one was willing to stand up for him or even help him. Instead, they felt he had brought his downfall upon himself. "Who you step on on the way up, you'll pass on the way back down" was a comment often made about Joe.

Rx

Joe needs allies to be effective, and if he works hard at it, he may be able to repair some of the damage. First, he needs to be more supportive of others, publicly and privately. He can begin by offering encouragement and positive comments to others at meetings. Even when he disagrees with the ideas presented by others, he can mention his opposition in a positive way such as "perhaps we can also consider..." or "another thought would be...," so that he's not seen as attacking the person voicing the idea.

He also needs to work with people individually to cultivate relationships. He can meet with them individually regarding specific issues or ideas and then follow up consistently at meetings so others can see his intention is to be an ally. People will forgive someone like Joe, but they won't forget, so he needs to be consistent in his new behavior to show he has changed.

Employees who make themselves look good at others' expense will usually be caught at some time by the people they have stepped on earlier. People's memories about others who treated them shabbily go a long way. The best way to avoid that trap is to show some sensitivity to others. That golden rule about treating others as you would like to be treated still stands as the world's best guide on living and working with others successfully.

WHAT TO DO WHEN YOU'RE CAUGHT IN THE CROSS-FIRE OF COMPANY POLITICS

About a year and a half ago Sean's boss, Amy, decided she needed more help. She persuaded the president of her division to fund another position for her department. The new manager would pick up much of the work from the other six departments currently reporting to Amy, including Sean's area. Sean was a little surprised to learn of the new position. Amy strongly subscribed to the old management style, sometimes called theory X, where the boss commands and the employees obey. He wondered how Amy would be able to let someone else take over some of her responsibilities or share power with her.

So it was with great interest that Sean and the rest of the crew watched the interview and recruitment process. When Amy selected an experienced professional from one of the company's competitors, Sean was pleased. It meant at least he would be working for a pro. He also hoped that the new person would act as a buffer between him and what he privately called "the dragon lady." The new manager, Joel, seemed like a good person. He was friendly and appeared confident.

That was 12 months ago. Since then, life in Sean's division has become like a war zone. Joel has worked hard at establishing his territory. Amy has worked just as hard at keeping it all to herself. Joel issues one set of directives, Amy countermands them or ignores them and sends out her own directives.

Amy openly criticizes Joel, and she has no hesitation in going around him to work directly with the rest of the groups thereby cutting Joel out of the loop. Joel is no pushover. He is fighting hard to gain the respect and loyalty he needs from his people to do his job. Amy appears to be working to undermine everything Joel does.

A few weeks ago, Amy and Joel had an argument. Joel stood his ground. Finally Amy gave him an unusually withering look and said, "You're beginning to annoy me." Sean overheard the remark and was shocked. This week he was caught between writing a report the way Joel wanted it, which was different from the way he had always written it for Amy. He chose to do it the old way. When Joel read it, he called Sean to his office and told him that if he ever again failed to follow his instructions, he would see that Sean was fired. Sean left the office, head swimming, realizing he was in a no-win situation.

The relationship between Amy and Joel is so bad that the only time they talk with each other is when Amy wants to hammer on Joel. Sean suspects that Joel will be gone once he has put in his time, which doesn't seem very far off. In the meantime, Sean is dodging the bullets and hanging on the best he can. He is very afraid that he will become an innocent victim in this game of managerial warfare.

DIAGNOSIS

Sean is caught in a dilemma that is all too familiar in the workplace. He's in the middle of a fight that isn't his but one that may get him shot anyway. Clearly, Amy has no intention of yielding any power in spite of the fact it was she who requested adding another layer to her organization. Joel is trying to hold his own, but he cannot win this one. Whatever the motives of Amy, they do not include the support and development of the new manager. Her secret agenda may include making this guy look bad so she can look good. It may be that she really needs help, but cannot let go of the power. Sean would like to support Joel, but to do so risks the displeasure of his ultimate boss, Amy, who can be very vindictive when crossed.

Rx

For Sean to survive this situation, he will need to keep a very cool head. He might try talking with Joel to discuss the position that he is in. Joel needs to know that Sean is not after his job or that he wants to join Amy in the pot shots. The two of them may be able to work out an understanding on how Sean can work with Joel to get his job done without getting into trouble with Amy. He could have the same conversation with Amy, pointing out that he and the rest of the staff are getting conflicting messages and that it is impacting their ability to get the work done. Such a discussion will probably not change the situation, but it would give Joel some support while putting Amy on notice that the war games are affecting productivity.

If Sean thinks that a discussion with Amy would be counterproductive, he might try approaching a friendly face in human resources to get a new perspective as well as let human resources know about the difficulty. At a minimum, he needs to try to ride this one out until the two of them fight it out to the finish. Since Amy looks like the one with more bullets, Sean should stay clear of her. Whatever he does, he should not take sides. This is a battle that has to be resolved by the two players. If productivity deteriorates to the point that someone at the senior level takes notice, the relief troops might be sent in. It all depends on what the company values and tolerates.

Some companies will take results any way they can get them. Other companies may have operating principles regarding what is acceptable behavior and what is not. Up until now, Amy has been able to get the results. If her department continues to produce, the company may leave her alone, regardless of the toll she takes on the people who work for her. If the problems with her style affect productivity, only then may there be executive intervention.

If you find yourself in the middle of a potential fight, your best bet is to negotiate one day at a time until the players self-destruct or you can escape to more peaceful surroundings. In the meantime, keep a very low profile. If necessary, take very tentative positions until you know where the bullets may come from. Only after you have determined it's safe should you show your face.

Surviving Office Politics

Regardless of level or job, you cannot escape office politics. Of all the problems facing companies, politics are the most pervasive and perhaps the most insidious of the maladies that affect work life in the corporation. Politics are like living in a house full of fleas. You can spray and fumigate, even burn the place, but politics will return to bite you. The biting is not only indiscriminate and random, but inevitable. No one, but no one escapes corporate life without running into and being affected by politics. Politics is how we manage the relationships in the corporation. We barter through politics. We use politics to get information, to gain favor, to sell our ideas, to bring pressure on others, to punish, to create, to frighten, to start rumors, to embellish rumors, to plant land mines. In short, politics are how we get things done our way. It's humanity's way of working together. We get our early training in politics in our families of origin. In fact, depending on the family system, some children become superb political players. It's the way we learned to cope in a system with an uneven distribution of power.

It's hard to avoid politics. Some people disdain the games. Others try to ignore what's going on. There are even short-lived crusades to destroy them. But, like fleas, we can't get rid of them. Politics are another fact of life.

That brings us to the "so what?" question. Well, you can save yourself a great deal of anguish, hand wringing, and misplaced righteousness if you simply accept politics as a reality. Even if you don't want to play, politics are here to stay. They comes with the territory, part of being human and working with other similar beings. Once you have accepted politics as a fact of life, you can decide how you want to respond. But that's another subject. For now, make peace with the fleas.

WHAT TO DO WHEN YOU HATE YOUR JOB

Ruth detests her job. She has found lately that as she approaches the hour she has to leave for work, she prays that something will happen so that she doesn't have to go that day. Once she is there, she settles down, but by 3:00 in the afternoon she finds the feelings coming over her again. By 5:00 P.M. she is ready to bolt out the door. If there is even the smallest delay, she becomes very irritated and can barely remain civil to those around her.

When she first got this job, it seemed like a good opportunity The company was hiring many young people to train for the expanding customer relations department. Ruth liked people. She had her PC skills. The company was solid and making money. So the job met many of her requirements. However, what she didn't consider was the repetitive nature of the work. Once she learned what she had to do, she could do it in her sleep. Each day was like the one before. Her tasks didn't change or challenge her; she wasn't learning new skills. What she did was exactly what the other people in her department did; only the names and faces were different.

Last week Ruth's supervisor called her in and asked her to sit down for a little chat. The supervisor told Ruth that her performance was slipping. She said she didn't see the old sparkle she used to when Ruth first began three years ago. More important, she said the customers' feedback on her performance had been essentially negative for the past months. Ruth was a little surprised. She told the supervisor she didn't think her feelings about the job were so noticeable. The supervisor told her that she would have to do something about her attitude. "Otherwise" she said, "you may find yourself without a job."

DIAGNOSIS _____

Ruth has slipped into a funk around her career, and it's showing in her work. She has allowed her lack of enthusiasm for the job to show, which in today's competitive marketplace can be lethal. Her boss is right in demanding 100 percent from Ruth, regardless of how Ruth feels. The supervisor's job is to see that her subordinates meet or exceed the standards the company has set forth. This company values good employees and rewards them, but it doesn't feel it is responsible for each employee's job satisfaction. People like Ruth are a dime a dozen. If there is to be any relief for Ruth, it will have to come from her, not the company.

Rx

For now, Ruth needs to work with her boss by asking for her help in bringing her performance up to snuff. They need to develop a plan that specifically describes what Ruth needs to improve upon and a timetable for achieving the necessary changes.

Ruth also needs to decide what she wants from her job and career and how she can best attain it. Poor performance will not help her cause.

Ruth's situation could be the story of many workers. They hate their jobs, their work shows it, and then the boss gets on their case. If you are among those who hate their job, you must realize that unless you do something about it, nothing will change. The tragedy in not liking what you do is that you are spending so much of your life doing something that is deeply unsatisfying. Given that you only have one life to live, you must act on the problem if you are not to get caught in a career that is basically unrewarding.

No one can rescue you from this situation but *you*. The pain you feel from doing a job you dislike can be the energy source that fuels your determination to change your circumstances. If the pain isn't great enough, you may settle. If the pain becomes so debilitating that you dread going to work, it is a sign that the time has come for you to address the problem.

The secret to a satisfying career is to identify what you enjoy doing. You can begin the process by making a list of all the times you felt a keen sense of joy in what you were doing. By analyzing the components of those peak experiences, you can begin to identify what types of activities you enjoy. Look at the skills you were using, examine the circumstances surrounding the experiences, look at the role you were playing, and finally ask yourself why you found these activities so satisfying.

For example, if as a kid you really enjoyed being in the spotlight, you will probably enjoy a job that includes making presentations or being in a sales or training function. If you loved those activities where you could see tangible results, you need that dimension in your work. A job that involves doing work that has no tangible end product will frustrate you. Some people like the role of coach, others that of leader. Many prefer to support the troops through back office administrative work. The point is, you must initiate the change if you are to avoid a work life of quiet desperation. The starting place is to know yourself. Then go to the library and more fully research career development concepts. Put together a plan to change your direction, then actively work to implement it. Take control of your own life. Don't give that control over to your company—you may not always like what they do to or for you. By giving yourself direction and control, you will set yourself on a course toward career and life satisfaction.

DON'T LET THE MALCONTENTS DRAG YOU DOWN

Most people start out their career feeling pretty good about themselves and their career opportunities. The real test comes when they hit a snag and how they handle the situation.

Take Richard. At a young age, he was seen as having the potential to move into top-level management. By 30, he had been promoted to senior technologist, and by age 32 he was district manager of his division.

Then the company went through a period of retrenchment, and Richard, like many others, had to stay where he was until business picked up again. When business didn't pick up, the company instituted even more drastic measures to control costs. This included removing some levels of middle management through layoffs and demotions and putting a cap on the salaries. Richard, along with many other district managers, was downgraded and put on a two-year wage freeze.

Although it is now three years later and the business is back on its feet, Richard is still bitter. For the last two years, he has been hanging out with the "grousing committee." The group, made up of other disgruntled employees, meets every morning in the cafeteria for coffee and then trades the latest "ain't-it-awful" stories about how the company is mistreating its employees. Richard is supposed to be at his desk by 8:30, but at 8:45 he is starting his second cup of coffee. He is just daring his manager to come by and say something to him about it. What Richard doesn't realize is that he is no longer considered promotable because of the way he is handling the situation. He is still seen as a competent employee, but no one wants him in their department given the people he hangs out with and what they talk about.

DIAGNOSIS

Where did Richard go wrong?

First, he took the demotion and salary freeze personally. He saw it as a statement about who he was in spite of the crisis his company was going through. In other words, when the going got tough, he didn't hunker down and do what needed to be done to get the company through the hard times.

His second mistake was to "act out." He let everyone who would listen know that he was angry. He nurtured his anger and eventually made it a part of his daily ritual.

Rx

This is another case of shooting oneself in the foot. For Richard to retrieve his reputation and his career, he will need to go back to his boss and discuss with him how he felt about the demotion and how it affected his behavior.

He could also ask his boss for help in developing a strategy for getting back on the track careerwise. He also has to stop hanging out with the malcontents. This will be hard for him because they have been his support group and have reinforced his anger and resentment. It will take time and real effort for him to rebuild relationships with the type of people who feel more positive about the organization, and it will take some period of time before they come to believe that he is no longer a professional sorehead.

Handling your emotions can be as important as doing a good job. For most people, the crisis comes when they face deep disappointment and are overcome with anger and hurt. Unless you handle the emotional crisis by acting as a professional (taking your lumps and moving on), you may unwittingly sabotage your chances for promotion. Worse, you may hang onto your hurt and anger and spend the rest of your career trying to get back at the organization. Getting mad and getting even is not a mark of leadership or maturity. Learning how to handle your emotions constructively is critical to succeeding in the corporation.

HOW TO DEFEND AGAINST THE DESTRUCTIVE ACHIEVER

Beverly is in the much-envied position of having been selected as a dean at a prestigious university—she is a leading authority on higher education, and she has been recognized for her leadership and scholarship.

When people first meet Beverly, they are usually bowled over by her. She has a way of making whoever she meets believe that they are the most wonderful and important person in the room and maybe in the country, depending on who it is. She has a smile that lights up when she meets people—she radiates charm.

The story behind the lovely smile and gracious manners is not quite as becoming. Beverly got to where she is today by being what is sometimes called a destructive achiever, defined as someone who has the charisma of a leader, but who lacks values or ethics. Beverly's struggle began 20 years ago when she needed to find a position in a university. Armed with her doctorate in education, she set her sights on finding a setting where she could build a career that would take her to the highest levels of academia. She chose a small, but highly competitive, college to begin her climb.

She made a great first impression on the president when she interviewed for her position, and from there on, Beverly never looked back. She did her homework, balancing the role of professor with that of researcher and scholar. She was granted tenure in record time and quickly moved to being head of the education department. From there she built her network that resulted in her being offered another position in one of the Ivy League schools. And from there she moved to developing a national presence that netted her this appointment.

Behind the scenes is another story. Even as she presented a facade of charm and warmth to outsiders, those who work closely with her see another side. She is very hard on her staff. Those who disagree with her are branded disloyal. She has misrepresented her research.

She has used the studies of other scholars without attributing the work. She has made promises to her graduate students concerning sharing the recognition on education projects only to hog the whole show when the honors are awarded. She appears to cooperate with the other members of the department, but in private, she dismisses their work and worth as so much nonsense.

She has systematically destroyed anyone who opposed her ideas or her way of doing things. Students who do not meet her demands find themselves unfunded the next year. She publicly ridicules faculty members who try to introduce new ideas. And she has been known to push some of her students to the point of having nervous breakdowns over writing their dissertations.

There appears to be no sense of decency or honesty when it comes to Beverly getting what Beverly wants. At this point, she appears invincible. She is too powerful for anyone who knows her to take her on. The president who hired her was so charmed that he called a meeting with the rest of the faculty. He announced his decision and asked them to support her in every way they could, which was shorthand for give-this-lady-a-hard-time-and-you'll-hear-from-me.

DIAGNOSIS

Destructive achievers can be more dangerous for your career than simple despots because their charismatic leadership style is so seductive. Furthermore, they often have the edge when it comes to presenting a professional appearance. They look good, they speak well and convincingly. They are usually highly energetic and competitive, and they will work around the clock to make things happen. Few people can match them when it comes to achievement.

RX

You have your work cut out for you if you work with or for a destructive achiever. You not only have to watch out for your back, but for your front, sides, and top. Destructive achievers can come at you from all directions. Your first task is to diagnose the situation correctly. The key difference between destructive achievers and other leaders is the formers' lack of principles and ethics. What makes them dangerous for you is that you will be sucked in by their charm only to discover their dark side later.

If you believe you are working with a destructive achiever, you need to be very careful believing in their promises or being seduced into giving your life to their cause. If the destructive achiever is your boss, keep your distance. Do not develop a close relationship, however tempting.

Because destructive achievers cannot be trusted, you need to protect your work and your reputation by developing good solid relationships with other people in the organization. If you are asked to do something illegal or unethical, you must refuse. You can expect to be punished for your response, but the alternative is to compromise your own principles, or worse, become involved in something that has the potential to ruin your career and possibly your life.

In short, try to limit the damage to yourself and the company by remaining coldly realistic about the type of person you are dealing with and act accordingly.

TRACKING THE DESTRUCTIVE ACHIEVER

Characteristics of the destructive achiever include

Seductively charming
Using people for personal gain
Arrogance
Self-aggrandizement
Rigidity
Punishing those perceived as disloyal
Self-protectiveness
Pursuing self-serving goals
Using power to destroy trust and commitment
Suppressing innovation
Turning organizations into "survival of the fittest" bureaucracies

DEFLECTING THE SNIPER'S ATTACK

Marybeth has worked seven long and difficult years to get where she is today. Her job includes supervising ten employees in a small manufacturing company. She came up through the ranks, first as a glorified clerk (in spite of a college degree), then to office administrator, and now finally to manager. She is excited about her career. Although the company doesn't have a sophisticated training program, Marybeth reads everything she can on how to be a good supervisor. Even her boss is impressed with her management savvy.

Everything is working just the way she planned except for one thing—Connie, another manager in the company, is taking shots at Marybeth. When it first began about a year ago, Marybeth didn't attach great significance to it. She knew Connie could be difficult, but she ignored the early signals. However, now it is becoming clear that Connie is out to unseat her. Two months ago, the managers had a one-day meeting to discuss the company's business strategy. Every time Marybeth opened her mouth, Connie was there to put her down. Connie has mounted a running campaign called "Look at what Marybeth has done lately." The sniping is subtle, but powerful. Other employees have asked Marybeth what is going on between the two of them. Now Marybeth has become superalert to everything she does in anticipation of how Connie might use it against her. She fears that one of the employees who works for her is a secret agent for Connie, acting as a pipeline feeding Connie material.

The insidious nature of the sniping is getting to Marybeth. She sees Connie at every corner, lurking, ready to get her. The job is beginning to lose its luster. She's noticed that she is having trouble concentrating on her work.

She would like to speak to her boss about it, but she doesn't think he will believe her or he will tell her to take care of it. She also feels it would be unprofessional for her to go to him about something as personal as this.

The last straw came this week when Connie passed her in the hall and said, "I hear you're having a little trouble in your inventory check. Too bad, That's something that gets taken very seriously in this company. Good luck." For Marybeth this was a signal that her current struggle around the integrity of the inventory controls was going to be Connie's latest salvo.

Marybeth whirled around and asked Connie to stop at her office. When both of the women were in the office, Marybeth closed the door; then she began. She told Connie that she had had it with her and that she had better get off her back or else. Connie only smiled, opened the door, and left. Ten minutes later, Marybeth got a call from the department head asking her to come to his office. He asked Marybeth what was going on between the two of them. Marybeth said it was personal and she would rather not talk about it. The department head then said, "All right, but I don't want to have any more of this, whatever it is about."

Now Marybeth is fuming and very frustrated. She doesn't know what to do about Connie, and she is concerned about the unprofessional impression she made on the department head. She is beginning to wonder if she is cut out for management after all.

DIAGNOSIS

Snipers like to target their anger toward people who will play their game. The game goes like this: I keep taking little shots at you until I get you riled; then I keep on taking shots until you get so frustrated and angry that you do something foolish. Marybeth has hooked into Connie's sniping game. It not only has cost her a piece of her reputation, but Connie's game has undermined Marybeth's self-confidence as well.

RX

If you have someone sniping at you, the first thing to do is to ignore the attacker. Snipers enjoy getting under other people's skin. So the worst thing you can do in their eyes is to ignore them. Even if they up the ante, ignore them. It will soon become obvious to your coworkers that there is a bad game going on and that it's not one in which you are playing. To put it another way, the best way to expose snipers is to ignore them. If the sniping begins to erode your belief in yourself, find a trusted friend you can talk to about what is happening. Ask that friend to be your sanity check so that the damage to you personally and professionally can be contained.

Remember, the sniper wants and needs you to hook in. Your best defense is the I-didn't-hear, you-don't-exist-defense. Then let your work speak for itself.

STOPPING A "GO-GETTER" WHO WANTS WHAT'S YOURS

Marita is two months into a new project and she is ready to tear her hair out. She was asked by the president of the company to organize a three-day off-site meeting for the 100 top executives in the company. Her responsibilities include finding a place, making the arrangements, and working with outside consultants on the schedule and entertainment. The president is very picky; he likes to have the best, whether it is cars, office furniture, or hotels.

The problem is not in the assignment. It is the other person she is having to work with on the project. Greg is fairly new to the company. He has shown a lot of enthusiasm and energy. But Greg wants to take over the project. He is so eager to get the visibility that goes with this assignment that he is trying to run over Marita. She doesn't mind sharing the glory, but Greg knows nothing about this type of meeting and even less about the president's tastes. However, ignorance and inexperience don't stop Greg. He continually bugs Marita to let him take over the project with her acting as an "advisor" as he puts it. He drops in at her office at the slightest excuse to "see how things are going." Because this project is only one of the many things she is working on, she resents Greg's visits. He asks her all types of questions about her other work, much of which is not information she can share or even wants to.

Last week she got a call from the president to stop in a minute. Greg was in her office when she got the call. He started to walk with her to the meeting. When she asked him where he was headed, he said, "With you." Marita told him that the president asked to see her, not the two of them. Greg was undaunted. "Well," he said, "I think it would be okay if I came along." Marita didn't know what to do. She knew the president well enough to know that Greg's showing up at the meeting would not go over well. She told Greg that this had to be her alone because she didn't know what the president wanted to see her about. Greg kept right on walking. Finally, when they reached the president's office, Marita turned to him and told him that he was not attending the meeting with her. Greg looked at her for a long moment and then said airily, "Well, I'll wait for you in your office. Have fun." Sure enough, when she came back to her office an hour later, there he was, looking through some papers on her desk. Marita was incensed. She said, "Greg, some of that material is very sensitive. I would appreciate it if you put it all back." Again, Greg was nonplused, "No big deal," he said. "Just trying to learn the job." With that he walked out.

Marita doesn't know how to handle the situation. If she voices her objections about Greg working with her, she may look like a cranky employee who cannot work with others. He is too new for others to understand what her objections might be about him. Yet if she tries to work with him, she knows he will push her to the limit and she will blow up. It has gotten so bad that she doesn't even want to be in the same room with him. He, in turn, appears totally oblivious to her discomfort.

DIAGNOSIS

Marita is working with someone who plays by another set of rules. Greg wants to get ahead. He is determined to use any opportunity or person to make that happen. His insensitivity may catch up with him, but for now, he is the new kid on the block and he is being given the benefit of the doubt.

The issue for Marita is how to handle Greg. She is more senior than he is in terms of experience, but he does not report to her. The boss hired him because he was impressed with his "go-get-em" style. Marita is having difficulty thinking through the problem rationally because she can no longer bear working with Greg.

One of the problems here is that Greg's role was never clearly defined. Greg is unusually aggressive: he continually pushes into what Marita considers her territory. Moreover, he does not appear to be interested in building a relationship with her that works. He has one thought, to get ahead—however he can.

RX

The best time to nip this type of problem is at the beginning, when you sense that you may have a problem with someone. Greg gave out lots of signals, but Marita didn't know how to respond because she had never run into Greg's type before.

Now that it has gone on so long, she will have to face it head on. The first person she needs to talk to about this is her boss. Marita needs to be sure she is clear about Greg's role and what her boss is expecting from him. She also needs to clarify how her boss sees Marita's and Greg's roles interacting. She can do this in a nonconfrontational manner without indicting Greg. This conversation should result in an understanding of her boss' expectations, which she can draw upon when talking to Greg.

Next she needs to speak openly (but carefully) with Greg. She needs to describe the difficulty she is having in working with him and, if possible, arrive at an understanding about boundaries and responsibilities. He could use a little advice on how to work with others, but she may be too angry with him to be that helpful.

Marita must be firm with Greg if she wants to make this work. She may be uncomfortable with that role, but she needs to learn how to handle a bulldozer.

If you are faced with a situation like this, your red flags need to go up very quickly. Bulldozers tend to run over people, so you must try to diagnose what is going on. If you are forced to work with a bulldozer, you need to get the undiscussable on the table and develop an understanding as to how the two of you will work together.

Pushy types always surprise us because of their audacity and sheer gall. Many people retreat when faced with a bulldozer type. A better answer is to face your discomfort and work out an understanding. If you can't make it work, then there is time enough to consider other strategies. The advice for this situation is friendly, but firm.

PROMOTING YOUR CAREER HEALTH—
Avoiding the Landmines

Knowing what can blow up in front of you will help you to be prepared for the explosions. Corporate landmines come in many different forms. Often they are in the form of a coworker; sometimes they are in the form of your own boss or another key executive. Sometimes it is the politics of the situation or the politics of your unit. There are even times when you might inadvertently wire yourself for destruction.

The key to your success in handling these potential disasters is the ability to see them (preferably in advance) for what they are and then work to defuse them quickly, minimizing the damage they can do to your career potential.

Things you need to master

- How to assess and work with difficult people
- How your actions and reactions will impact the business
- How to size up the politics of the situation—what is each person's own agenda? Who is backing or directing them? What is the possible

outcome if one resolution is reached versus another? How might it affect relationships?

- How your responses will be seen by management
- How to portray a positive attitude about the situation you are in

Barriers to Success

- Surrounding yourself with negative types
- Not portraying yourself as a team player, company person
- Choosing the wrong battles
- Out of touch with reality; thinking you are omniscient or indispensable
- Power goes to your head
- Winning the battle but losing the war

Payoff for you and your career

- Being seen as a problem solver, not creator
- Having a positive impact on the business
- Heading off the problems before they become too big
- Enhanced political skills
- Increased knowledge of what makes your organization tick

CORPORATE STREET SMARTS

How to Get Where You Want to Go

WHAT IT TAKES TO MAKE IT

Getting your first promotion into management is usually a heady experience. You've been spotted as a "comer" and the world is your oyster. However, this can be a major "make-or-break" situation. The difference between those who make it and those who don't is usually a matter of omission rather than commission.

Consider Katherine, who works for one of the nation's largest organizations. Her company is deeply committed to developing women. As a result, she has had a great deal of support and encouragement from her organization in her climb up the management ladder.

However, about two years ago, she hit a block. She has worked hard for the next promotion; thus when a spot opened up in one of the divisions, she expected to get it. To her great surprise, the position went to another woman. Katherine was stupefied. She knew her work was good and that she had exceeded expectations in her job as department manager. So what did it take to get promoted and what did this woman do that Katherine didn't?

Once Katherine had recovered from her shock, she was determined to be totally professional. In spite of her deep disappointment, she wanted to find out where she had gone wrong. She decided to ask the woman who got the promotion for advice. She didn't know her well, but she felt she would have a perspective that might be helpful to Katherine. The other woman was willing to talk to Katherine, and told Katherine that she was seen as spending too much time working with her subordinates and not enough time building relationships with the other key people in the organization.

DIAGNOSIS

Most employees begin their career in highly task-oriented positions. How hard they work and how well they do their jobs are the criteria on which they are evaluated. But as employees move up the ladder and take on supervisory responsibilities, being highly task oriented is not enough. Who you know becomes as important as what you know. It is vital for ambitious employees to cultivate a wide range of relationships, particularly with those people who have the power to promote and reward. Some people see this strategy as politics, and for them, that's a dirty word. They are right about it being politics, but it's not dirty or destructive to be political if it increases your ability to get the job done and to get the recognition you want and deserve for your work.

The higher one goes in the organization, the more that gets done through relationships. People get to know you and begin to trust you. They find out that you are a person they like to work with and that you can get the job done. It only follows that they will support you at promotion time. But if you are buried under your work all day and never build relationships, you can expect to be left out of things.

Rx

Katherine understood immediately and proceeded to reorganize her workday so that she could spend more time outside her office getting to know the people who had the power to make decisions. She scheduled lunch appointments, joined task forces, attended all the company functions, and volunteered for the company's annual char-

ARE YOU MANAGEMENT MATERIAL?

Management Profile Inventory	*High Medium Low*
Rate yourself on the degree to which you	
1. Prefer to delegate versus personally finish a task	10 9 8 7 6 5 4 3 2 1
2. Are ambitious, competitive, a self-starter	10 9 8 7 6 5 4 3 2 1
3. Set very high standards for yourself and others	10 9 8 7 6 5 4 3 2 1
4. Need to control, be in charge, have the last word	10 9 8 7 6 5 4 3 2 1
5. Are very energetic, enthusiastic, on-the-go	10 9 8 7 6 5 4 3 2 1
6. Are outgoing and enjoy attention	10 9 8 7 6 5 4 3 2 1
7. Feel confident and enjoy being with people	10 9 8 7 6 5 4 3 2 1
8. Enjoy joining groups and teams	10 9 8 7 6 5 4 3 2 1
9. Feel comfortable with and can initiate change	10 9 8 7 6 5 4 3 2 1
10. Are in touch with what you are feeling and can express your emotions appropriately	10 9 8 7 6 5 4 3 2 1
11. Can express your views assertively and handle confrontation and conflict	10 9 8 7 6 5 4 3 2 1
12. Can be loyal to your company, but not unduly deferential or defiant	10 9 8 7 6 5 4 3 2 1
13. Can work without having everything spelled out for you	10 9 8 7 6 5 4 3 2 1
14. See yourself as a leader	10 9 8 7 6 5 4 3 2 1
15. Enjoy delegating and working through people	10 9 8 7 6 5 4 3 2 1
16. Can build and maintain relationships with large and diverse group of people	10 9 8 7 6 5 4 3 2 1
17. Can see the big picture and avoid handling or getting immersed in detail	10 9 8 7 6 5 4 3 2 1
18. Feel comfortable working with and making decisions based on incomplete or fuzzy data	10 9 8 7 6 5 4 3 2 1
19. Make decisions in a confident and timely manner	10 9 8 7 6 5 4 3 2 1
20. Understand the system and how to make it work for you	10 9 8 7 6 5 4 3 2 1

Assess your degree of fit by rating yourself on the Management Profile Inventory.

Total Scores

Scores 200–140   High potential for management

Scores 140–80   Take a careful look before you commit yourself

Scores 80–below   Chances of success are limited—reexamine strengths, interests, and goals and identify where you have a better fit.

ity drive. She was able to give her staff more autonomy and discovered that they flourished, so her "bridge building" did not create any negative effects on her department's work. In fact, the other relationships she developed actually helped her staff to get things done more easily. The payoff came quickly. By the end of the first year of her campaign, she got her promotion.

Promotions are made on a subjective as well as an objective basis. Smart employees like Katherine learn how that system works and then figure out how to make the system work for them.

WHEN YOU BECOME NUMERO UNO

Bob was very excited and proud when he was appointed to manager of finance in his division. He was also very nervous—it was a big move up, his first supervisory position. He was pleased with the vote of confidence from management but knew he would be carefully watched to see how he performed at this new level of responsibility.

Bob knew many of the issues facing the department—he had seen them as a member of the group and often had discussed his point of view with his peers. However, when he was promoted, he realized that his perspective was one-sided and that he needed more information before deciding what his priorities and tactics for managing the department should be.

For starters, Bob set up meetings with the key people that his department supported and with the headquarters financial management staff. He asked each a series of questions:"What had this department done well?" "Not so well?" "What do you see to be important issues related to my new group?" "What type of interactions has your department had with mine?" "How could they be improved?" He asked similar questions of his new boss and the people he now supervised. He also asked his staff about his new role versus theirs and what they expected or wanted from him.

Based on these meetings, Bob set up a strategy and developed plans to make it happen. He discovered some weak links in communication with the manufacturing department and saw the importance of interacting more closely with the headquarters group. He uncovered some interpersonal conflicts that could have hurt him later and handled them before they became more destructive.

By doing his homework before simply plunging ahead, Bob demonstrated four critical behaviors: he was a good strategist, he was analytical, he was service oriented, and he was a team player. By reducing the likelihood of unpleasant surprises, he was able clearly to move his department—and his career—ahead.

HOW ARE YOU PERCEIVED BY OTHERS?

Ask people who work or have worked for you to rate you on the following items. Directions to rater: Circle the number that best describes the degree to which the statement fits this person.

1-Never 2-Sometimes 3-Often 4-Always

	Never	Sometimes	Often	Always
1. Listens actively	1	2	3	4
2. Sensitive to how other people feel	1	2	3	4
3. Admits personal mistakes	1	2	3	4
4. Knows his or her weaknesses	1	2	3	4
5. Confronts effectively	1	2	3	4
6. Can handle pressure	1	2	3	4
7. Is enthusiastic	1	2	3	4
8. Champions other people	1	2	3	4
9. Acts decisively	1	2	3	4
10. Can be counted upon	1	2	3	4
11. Is diplomatic	1	2	3	4
12. Works hard	1	2	3	4
13. Shares credit	1	2	3	4
14. Inspires others	1	2	3	4
15. Acts fairly	1	2	3	4
16. Does his or her homework	1	2	3	4
17. Uses good timing	1	2	3	4
18. Not afraid to speak up	1	2	3	4
19. Avoids becoming cynical	1	2	3	4
20. Asks the right questions	1	2	3	4

Scoring: Identify your top three strengths, as indicated by scores of 3 or 4, and your top three developmental needs (scores of 1 or 2). If in doubt about the meaning of any of the issues, go back to your raters for more input. Then work to capitalize on your strengths and develop action plans to correct your deficiencies. Ask your raters to reevaluate you six months later to see where progress has been made.

DIAGNOSIS _____

Often, new managers who feel that they are expected to have all the answers and act accordingly will end up proving just the opposite. New managers do much better asking for input—from peers, boss, and staff. It not only provides them with valuable information, but it helps build relationships and credibility. Within three to six months, though, the boss should be in charge and judicious about where he or she goes for help. Later, peers at other companies or divisions may be better sources for information and advice, rather than others within the same organization.

Rx

Bob's attack of his new job was clearly well thought out. He recognized that he needed allies but that he also had to establish himself as being "in charge." By asking others for their input—before he told them or showed them what he would do—he bought support that would be critical to his success, especially since he had come up from the ranks. The "interview" mode also gave him an entree to dealing effectively with his former peers as he made the transition in his new role.

WARHOL REDUX
Your 15 Seconds of Fame

Carl was proposed to senior management as the project leader for a key assignment. Carl's boss had offered his name in an executive review meeting. The vice president of the department stumbled through his memory to try to place who Carl was—and finally hit upon it—"the guy whose shirttail is always hanging out the back? I rode up with him on the elevator the other day and he looked like he'd slept in his clothes."

Joan was asked to make a presentation to senior management in the unexpected absence of her boss. She had only 30 minutes to prepare for the meeting, but was fairly confident about her knowledge of the subject matter, since she had done most of the backup work for her boss's presentation. Nonetheless, she spent the five minutes right before going "on stage" composing herself and repeating over and over the attributes of a good presenter.

Her presentation only lasted 10 minutes, but Joan made the most of each second. She was polished in her delivery and precise in the points she made. As she left the conference room, the senior vice president said to her department director, "That was a darn good presentation. How is the quality of her work?" Joan had capitalized on her brief window of exposure.

DIAGNOSIS

Some people don't understand how important it is to make a good impression, even on an elevator at the end of a day. Recognize that executives may see an individual employee for a few brief moments and that they often make snap judgments about the individual based on that brief exposure. The reality is that management may often make up their minds about people based on inaccurate or incomplete or subjective information.

Rx

Smart individuals will capitalize on each opportunity to present themselves the way they want to be viewed and be consciously aware of the impressions they are making. This doesn't mean gushing or rattling on about activities in the presence of senior management. It does mean acting as if you are in or belong in a role one, two, or three steps above where you are. Savvy employees will also seek out those opportunities at office social events and other times when management mixes with the masses. The trick to doing this is to appear natural, not manipulative, and to do some homework beforehand to give you an icebreaker. Following up on a boss's interest in baseball can give you a nice segue to a brief conversation. However, don't corner a boss or expect him or her to stay with you for any length of time, since there are others with whom your boss likely wants to spend time. Don't ever, ever forget that your behavior at a social event is being evaluated and taken as seriously as your behavior in the office.

YOUR REPORT CARD—
The Performance Appraisal

Judy had been in her job for three years. Now it was time for the annual ritual—the performance appraisal. She was not particularly looking forward to it, because she was unsure about how she was viewed by her boss this time around. She did prepare for the meeting, however. Over the past year, she had kept a list of the major projects she worked on. She also kept the "score" on her results—good and not so good. In addition, she kept her "atta girl" file—the one with the complimentary letters regarding her work.

Before her review, Judy read through her accomplishment list and analyzed what she had learned (either the easy or the hard way), what she had contributed, and where she needed to continue her development. She knew that her career interests might also come up as an issue, so she did some critical thinking on what she wanted and how she thought she could get there. On the day of her performance review, Judy's boss started his conversation with "Judy, it has been a good year for you—many challenges, many successes, and a lot of learning. I would like to hear your perspective, then I will give you mine." Because Judy was ready for this, she was able to lay the groundwork for a fruitful discussion of her performance and development issues.

DIAGNOSIS

Each of us is like a balance sheet complete with individual assets and liabilities. Only the overall perspective will determine if the bottom line is in the black (fits well in the job/organization) or in the red (an overall liability to the group). If you remember that, it will help you handle your performance review more productively.

In the ideal world, managers provide continual feedback and input to their employees and help them achieve higher levels of performance. In the real world, many managers, when writing up the annual performance appraisal, surprise their employees with comments, recollections of past "performance deficiencies" (heretofore not mentioned), or kudos for previously unrecognized successes.

Rx

Your ability as the employee to "handle" performance appraisals is another one of those subtle nuances that can affect success. There are some general guidelines that you should bear in mind. First and foremost, you should realize that each appraisal given to you is the "tip of the iceberg," the distillation of the boss's perception of your work, attitude, and overall performance of the past year. There will be many things not said in the review, but you should assume that the boss has culled out the elements he or she thinks are most applicable or important. Second, you should know that most bosses hate to give performance reviews, even when it's mostly good news. Because many managers find it difficult to tell employees how they're doing, smart employees help their bosses through the process.

The Initial Performance Session: In the initial days of a new job, it is natural for you to wonder how your boss likes your work. In some organizations, an initial review will be required after some short period, say, one month or one quarter. If such a review does not automatically occur, it may be beneficial for you to initiate an open conversation with your boss. An informal discussion to review your progress can help you be sure you're on the right track and provide you with an opportunity to find out how your boss sees your work. Such a request is completely appropriate. If your boss doesn't typically conduct these discussions or makes no overtures about such a review, you should initiate the meeting by requesting a specific time to review your progress (don't just hit your boss cold in the middle of discussing last night's football game). Then, prepare an informal list of things you'd like your boss to cover, in case he or she doesn't discuss all the issues you want. Overall, you should discuss what your boss thinks about the quality of your work, your integration into the department, and the areas on which you need to concentrate. You also should discuss how you feel about the department, your boss's communications with you, and any job-related concerns you have.

For this conversation to be productive, you should be positive and sincere. This isn't the time for cuteness or whining. To get the important feedback you need at this time, you need to set the right tone for the discussion. If things are not good, or elements of the job are less than satisfactory, you should address them now with an underlying theme that you are willing to work within the rules and mores of the department and want to make it work.

Your Annual Performance Appraisal: The annual (or periodic) performance appraisal process varies from company to company and can range from a very formal MBO (management-by-objectives) format to an informal "Ed Koch—'How am I doing' " discussion. The best way to handle any performance review is to not be defensive (remind yourself of this as you are entering the room for the discussion and keep repeating it). Unfortunately, most people do get defensive when hearing negative things about themselves. However, the input you get from a manager who gives you honest feedback will be invaluable (even if you don't want to know it). You can make it easier for your boss to tell you things that are often tough to relay by requesting both negative and positive feedback. If you don't act defensively, your boss will be more able and more open to giving you this type of information.

During your review, take notes. Many companies have a system that gives the employee a written document covering the main points, but your boss may impart some "tidbits" beyond the written verbiage. You should note where your work was seen as positive, and where you need to concentrate your efforts for improvement. That way you can reflect on your review afterward, when you're more relaxed. You should review these data monthly so you can see if you're making progress (at least from your own perspective) and if you're concentrating on the most appropriate elements of your performance.

One last word about performance reviews. People die from hunger, disease, gunshot wounds, and drug overdoses. But *no one* has ever died from a performance review. So as tough as it may seem to be to get some negative feedback from the boss, you will survive. Even more important, you may learn what you really need to do to get ahead. If that's what you get out of a poor performance review, consider yourself a very lucky employee—because now you can make the changes you need to move on and up.

HOW TO GET ON THE FAST TRACK

Choosing who is selected to be on the fast track is usually a mysterious process. At some point when you least expect it, someone may tap you on the shoulder and whisper in your ear, "You are now one of our Hi Po's." Or you may get the sense that you are on the "A List" through the attention or assignments you are getting. It isn't clear how or why you were chosen, but now that it's happened, you know you're on the track.

If you were to sit in on the meetings where high potentials are identified, you would find that the process is a fairly rigorous one, although it can be quite subjective. The executives look at stated or unstated criteria and ask for evidence of these behaviors. That's why any extraordinary action on your part has the possibility of becoming a topic at these discussions. While it's the nuances in corporate life that may torpedo your career, it's the results of your work that brings you to someone's attention. Therefore, regardless of your level, if you perform in some outstanding way, it will not go unnoticed.

Elaine worked as a scientist for a small company. Her job interested her because she loved research and she believed in what the company was trying to do. Her particular department was developing a product that would compete in a very lucrative market. The work was exceedingly demanding, not only because of the standards and creativity needed to create a cutting edge product, but because the time frame in which the team had to develop it was very narrow. The company to get the product to market first has the potential for the largest payoff. If the company does not come in first, then four years of work and many dollars may very well go down the drain.

As the project completion grew nearer, the work intensified. Elaine and her colleagues found themselves working 12- to 14-hour days, often straight through the weekend. As the holidays neared, the group began to droop. Two weeks into December, one of her coworkers was hospitalized for exhaustion. Three people came down with the flu. Another broke his wrist when he fell on ice in his driveway.

Everyone on the team found themselves growing increasingly depressed, and of course, fatigue was exacting a terrible toll on the group's ability to function, let alone remain creative. Elaine's boss, Chuck, saw the group falling apart before his eyes, and he did what he could to cheer them on, but he worked even longer hours than the team. No one had spent a Saturday or Sunday at home in over three months. The situation was very serious.

Elaine watched what was going on for her and her colleagues and decided something had to be done. She understood that the project schedule had to be met, so getting some relief was not a possibility. The company had strained itself to provide the team with as many resources as possible to help with the work load, but no outsiders could substitute for the scientists. Because she was so concerned, Elaine went to Chuck. Chuck shared Elaine's concerns and offered his support in any way, shape, or form that would be helpful, but he had no specific ideas or suggestions.

Finally, Elaine realized that the only people who could save the group would be the group members themselves. She asked the group to meet with her for bagels and coffee before they started their day. Elaine explained why she had brought the group together: she told them that it looked to her that if the group was going to survive the next three months and make the deadline, they would have to find ways as a group to make survival possible. She asked the group to describe what they were going through in their jobs and at home so that at least they could express some of their feelings about it. It wasn't difficult for the team members to talk about the effect that the job was having on their lives. A number of people expressed concern about long-term effects on their health. Yet they all agreed that some way or other they would make the project deadline.

Elaine asked them to brainstorm for ways to help one another. As the group threw out ideas, Elaine saw even talking about it was helpful. By the end of the meeting, the group had come up with a number of specific ways to reduce stress, including bringing in healthful food for people working through the dinner hours, scheduling break times for brief walks and exercise, and taking time to celebrate even the smallest accomplishment on the project schedule. One woman suggested they develop what she called support partners; that is, each person would be paired with someone they felt comfortable with and the two of them would set aside at least 30 minutes a week to act as each other's listener, much as Elaine had done at the beginning of the meeting when she asked the group to describe how they were feeling. The group also decided to meet every Monday morning to discuss how things were going and to discuss other ways to support one another in the weeks ahead.

The change in the group's attitude and productivity was immediate. Elaine's boss stopped by her desk at the end of that first week and said, "What happened in the meeting? This is like a new group." Elaine described what had gone on, including how the group had come up with its own strategies to rescue themselves. Chuck was delighted. Elaine now had a champion. When the project was finished, Chuck was moved into another division and Elaine was named his successor.

DIAGNOSIS

It was not that Elaine had better skills or was more creative than the other members of the team. What she did, however, was to take the

EIGHT ACTIONS THAT LEAD TO SUCCESS

1. Always try to look and sound good when near a senior executive.
2. Keep tied into the grapevine, but don't feed it.
3. Always try to be gracious to others.
4. Be sensitive to what your boss wants and needs, not what you think he or she needs.
5. Always make your boss look good in front of his or her boss.
6. Don't criticize anyone, especially your staff, in front of others.
7. If you have an important idea to sell at a meeting, solicit support from individual attendees before the presentation.
8. Don't develop intense intimate relationships with your boss or your subordinates. Keep it professional and job focused.

initiative, and that set her apart from the rest of the scientists. She saw a need and she figured out a way to respond to it.

Rx

Wanting to be selected for the fast track is not enough to get you on the short list. You must demonstrate that you have something to offer that is valued by the organization and in short supply. In Elaine's situation, the organization needed grass-roots leadership in a situation that someone at Elaine's level could give more effectively than even her boss (Chuck might have tried this, but he was not as strong on people processes as he was on technical processes; therefore, this might have been hard for him to accomplish.)

You must see the "big picture" if you are to be seen as a high potential. And remember, opportunity knocks, but it doesn't linger.

What You Can Do to Get on the "A List"

Getting on the fast track takes a great deal of know-how. But the prize can make it all worthwhile. What follows are some suggestions for making it to the big time.

- Be seen as your own person—too much dependency on the group and its attitudes positions you as a follower, not a leader.
- Identify the skills needed to be a leader in your organization and learn them. For example, if presentations are the road to fame and fortune, take a course in making presentations.

- Ask for feedback from your boss and select clients and colleagues who will be honest with you. Draw up a development plan based on that feedback
- Own up to your mistakes, but make sure you are taking enough risks to make some mistakes. Consider all mistakes as invaluable learning experiences.
- Walk your talk.
- Develop personal and professional goals and work to achieve them. Don't let yourself off the hook. Keep the contract you made with yourself.
- Do something outstanding whether it's making an extraordinary effort, developing a superior analysis, taking the initiative where you see a need, or performing unfailingly at a very high standard.
- Bring out the best in others. Do not succumb to the back-stabbing and negativity that grows so robustly in many workplaces.
- Develop a possible solution for every problem you are dealing with. Never go to the boss empty-handed. Remember, if you're not part of the solution, you're part of the problem.
- Reward yourself for your personal victories, and don't neglect smelling the roses. Fast tracking should include "getting a life," not just getting ahead.

THE AMBIGUITY TEST

Kevin has had a very successful career so far: one of the top sales reps in his company, then a district manager, and then sales manager in a key region. He has recently been brought into the headquarters office to run the sales operations area as part of his development plan.

Kevin is not very happy about this move. He has no interest in a staff role within the headquarters and thinks that it will not be a challenging job, being away from the line of fire and in a more bureaucratic environment. Kevin is used to being measured on his results, and the idea of doing work that does not show directly on the bottom line holds no interest for him. His new responsibilities are to run the sales analysis group that pulls together all the sales results for the field reps; to run the sales training group; and to prepare for major sales meetings by coordinating with the vendors who do the logistics backup. All these jobs are thankless, headache-producing tasks that bring with them complaints from all factions of the sales units; Kevin knows, since he used to be one of the loudest complainers about the services this group provided.

When Kevin was presented with this job opportunity, he told his boss he was not really interested in moving to the headquarters. He realized that he really did not have a choice since it was presented to him as critical to his development. Now that he has been in this job for several months, he is struggling with his own evaluation of what he has accomplished. He has made some adjustments to the sales training department's focus and gotten through one sales quarter without any major problems in the sales analysis area. He also has dragged himself through negotiating the deadly details of a sales meeting, such as how many rooms are needed to accommodate the reps. All in all, he has not enjoyed this job nearly as much as his previous assignments. He finds the crazy structure of the headquarters group to be without focus; it seems that every day there is a new priority. It is also very frustrating to be without the weekly sales figures that used to tell him how he was doing in his job. At this point, he is debating if he should have a discussion with his boss about how unhappy he is in this role.

DIAGNOSIS

Research suggests that the ability to deal with ambiguity is a strong predictor for management success. In the corporate world, there are not always black and white answers to the problems and issues that managers confront, and there is the constantly changing tableau within which we work. Effective managers are those who can tolerate and thrive in an environment that often leaves us feeling that there are more questions than answers.

In this case, Kevin is seen as a high-potential employee. Management has been keeping an eye on him for an executive slot but recognizes that he needs to prove himself in a role different from one in the field. The higher-ups want to see what breadth and depth he has: Can he still be strategic in a different job? And how will he operate in a headquarters environment? They also think this is a good job for him, since he has been at the top of the lists of the sales managers who have complaints about the sales operations area. This should give him some experience to see the other side of the picture.

RX

Kevin is operating in a whole new world. He thinks this assignment is penance for something he's done or not done. He is sure that if he

AMBIGUITY INVENTORY

To assess your preference for structure versus your tolerance for ambiguity scale, read each statement carefully and circle True (T) if the statement describes you and False (F) if it does not.

1. When I go on vacation, I like to go without detailed plans. T F
2. I prefer to live day to day without always trying to fit my ac- T F
tivities into a plan or set pattern.
3. I feel comfortable even when I have questions in my mind for T F
which I have no answers.
4. I often start working on something when I have only a very T F
hazy idea of what the end result will be.
5. I rarely consider the weather report when thinking about what T F
to wear.
6. I prefer a life that is unplanned, one without a regular schedule T F
or hours.
7. For most important questions, there are no simple black and T F
white answers.
8. While I admire people who have a plan for everything, I have a T F
difficult time being that organized.
9. I don't get particularly upset when someone interrupts my T F
daily routine.
10. I seldom base my arguments on so-called matters of principle. T F
11. I tend to moderate my statements with words like "probably," T F
"approximately," or "perhaps."
12. I tend to start in on a new task without thinking about the T F
best way to do it.

Total number of True (T) scores____

How to Interpret Your Scores: Count the total number of True (T) scores.

> Scores 1–4 Suggests that you do not like ambiguity or uncertainty in information, that you want all questions answered completely and that you like to know ahead of time what will be happening. You prefer to make decisions based on definite knowledge, rather than on probabilities or theories or guesses. In short, you like and need structure in your life. People might describe you as precise, exacting, perfectionist, rigorous, literal, rigid. You will be more satisfied if your job involves using data or measurements that are precise. Your contribution to a company will be your ability to work carefully with details. The type of company you work for may not be as important as the type of work you do in that company. You need to be involved with work where your sense of order and the need for precision is valued. Possible places for your talents would be the finance department or in information systems. Stay away from areas like human resources unless you are involved in the information systems connected with human resources.

Scores 5-8   Suggests that you are comfortable in situations that are somewhat disorganized or unstructured, but that you need a certain amount of order in your life. While you think life is not black or white, neither is it without some answers or principles. People might describe you as careful, but not perfectionistic, as flexible, reasonable, somewhat organized, a little restrained, temperate, middle-of-the-roader. You will be able to work in a number of areas and be successful. While you are not as flexible as someone with scores from 9-12, you can move toward structure or away from it, depending on the situation. Most companies will provide an appropriate work environment for you. People will perceive you as bringing a stabilizing force to the workplace.

Scores 9-12   Suggests that you are a highly flexible person, one who prefers an informal environment or work setting. You don't need or want a lot of rules and procedures. You are open to trying new things even if there are doubts about the possibility of succeeding at them. While you are aware of tradition, you are seldom inhibited by it. People might describe you as disorganized, adventurous, impulsive, open, imprecise, creative, tolerant. You will need to pick your spots and your career carefully. While you are badly needed because of your tolerance for ambiguity, your tendency toward trying new things can be unnerving to people who are less flexible than you. You will thrive in entrepreneurial environments. However you may become isolated in companies where change is not welcome. You can take some consolation in the fact that research on what factors predict effective leaders suggests that a high tolerance for ambiguity is a major predictor of success.

gets out and back to the field, his life and career will be on a better track. In reality, though, if he is not able to master this job and perform as well as he has in other positions, his career potential will be limited to jobs in the field only.

Since Kevin is an ambitious fellow, he needs to get a handle on the goals and roles of his new group. By tying these to the goals of the organization, he will feel better about the value this department has to the big picture. He needs to change his thinking about the glamour of the field and concentrate on making his department successful. This is a great opportunity to correct some of the things Kevin complained about when he was in the field and to make his mark on the headquarters functions. He can also show that he is capable of thinking strategically by aligning his own goals (and his department's) with the corporate goals, rather than just the sales and marketing goals. If he is able to understand that the report card may not always be based on bottom line numbers but instead on less definitive or tangible results, he will prove he is capable of moving up.

CORPORATE SMOKE AND MIRRORS:
Marketing Yourself

Part of learning how to play the game includes learning how to market yourself. It's not enough to be very effective or productive. The right people need to learn about it; that's where marketing yourself comes in. Some people seem to have a real flair for marketing themselves. They often are motivated by their own need for attention. For others, marketing becomes one of the skills; it must be learned and then carried out.

Linda had to learn the hard way. Three years ago she was appointed to a task force to develop a quality program for her division. Her company president had read the literature and talked to other CEOs who had initiated quality programs in their corporations. So with the blessing of the top executive, the task force succeeded in putting together a program and implementing it. So far, so good. The division was happy, the CEO was happy, and the task force was happy. The company made long-range plans to introduce the quality approach to the other divisions as soon as it was feasible. The task force disbanded, and Linda returned to her regular duties. However, six months into the new year, she caught wind of a presentation on the company's new quality program. Upon inquiry, she discovered that three of the members of the task force had developed a very slick presentation on the company's quality program and were making the rounds of the various professional societies plugging the work and themselves. Moreover, they had convinced the president to fund a video production with themselves as the star performers. The president was part of the video; his part was to praise the program and the people who developed it. Linda was surprised and chagrined. Not only had they not included the rest of the members of the task force in the production, but they had represented the program as being their product. It was their faces that commanded the screen.

Linda was angry enough to confront one of the men who had taken the show on the road. His response to her objection was that there was no law that said anyone had to do any of this and that he and his colleagues had taken the initiative and used their own time to produce the road show. He pointed out that Linda could have done the same thing.

Linda never was able to get any mileage out of the project, although she was given recognition by her boss. But the people who really "made out" were the three individuals who took the project to the next step and developed a show around the program. Linda felt betrayed. Now she understood all too well that she had lost the chance to market herself.

Diagnosis

Part of your job is to advertise yourself. If you don't, someone with less talent or fewer competencies may get what you deserve and there will be nothing you can do about it. While it was not fair that all the members of the task force were not given credit for their efforts, it was appropriate that the effort be recognized and advertised. Linda has learned a hard lesson on the art of self-promotion. She had always assumed that if you worked hard enough and did a good job, you would get recognized and rewarded. Sometimes it does work that way, but more often than not, the prize goes to the person who can put the best spin on his or her work and who knows how to get attention.

Rx

Promoting yourself is a must. You may not be comfortable doing it, but the alternative is to depend on the goodwill of others to reward or promote you. Some first steps include

1. Become visible. Attend all meetings. Speak up and make certain you say enough so that people notice you.
2. Attend those odd-hours affairs like the annual picnic or the coffee-and-danish going-away party. Volunteer to help run one of these affairs and make sure you confer with the higher-ups on the plans. Visibility!!!

3. Make presentations and do an outstanding job. Presentations are *the* way to get ahead in many organizations. You get to go on stage. Make the most of it.

4. Be ready at the drop of a hat and in a concise form to talk about what you do and what you have accomplished. You may need to work on this, but the material needs to become so familiar to you that you can recite it in your sleep. Then look for the right situations and let people know what you are all about. Learn to talk about your successes without seeming to brag. "When I took over that project, I realized we were in deep trouble. But I talked with some of the people from finance and then I moved in and began to take the pieces apart and put them back together. And it's working!"

5. Look for ways to get your name in front of the right people. There is nothing more deadly than to have no one know you. Most of the decisions get made by a small group of key people who tend to promote people they know. No matter how good you are, if they don't know you, it's the same as if you didn't exist.

6. Promote yourself in your professional group. That means getting active and then taking some responsibility that puts you in the limelight. Then make certain that the decision makers learn about your efforts. Better yet, ask them to appear as speakers. You get visibility, they get visibility, everyone wins.

COMPETITION:
Play the Game, Avoid the Mud

When Marianne finished her MBA from a top business school, she had already decided on her career path. She wanted to go to the top. She wasn't sure what that would mean, but she knew she wanted to be involved in running an organization. She wanted to be at the center of power. She had understood from her work in graduate school that finance and marketing could provide a clear shot at top-level positions. She also realized that the top team was still dominated by the old boys' network. However, Marianne had already developed the wrestling skills. She had done her boot training in a male-dominated graduate school and had her battle scars to prove it. She was not about to be stopped by a clique that ran a corporation. She was determined to get what she wanted.

So when one of the country's leading companies offered her a position on its MBA track, she was impressed. The deal was this: In many companies, sales reps are expected to spend two to three years in the field before coming to corporate headquarters. Coming inside was the ticket to the marketing manager jobs, and was offered only to candidates who had paid their dues in the field. This company wanted to break out of the mold and attract people like Marianne. However, since few MBAs were willing to play second banana for such a long time period, the rules were changed. Now it was one year in the field as a sales rep and then upward and onward to corporate as a product manager.

Marianne got her "sales" ticket punched and moved inside as a product assistant. She loved it. It was just the kind of thing she was looking for. She pulled out all the stops. She curried favor with purchasing. She wooed the advertising manager. She sweet-talked the design group. And when her honeyed approach didn't get her what she needed, she did not hesitate to pull the corporate scream-and-yell act. In fact, she became so effective with her tirades that some people didn't even fight her. They simply complied to avoid a scene.

The war escalated when Marianne was made product manager of a breakthrough product. It was a coveted position and one that some of the more senior product managers thought should have been theirs. Before, they had ignored Marianne. Now she became the target of their resentment. She had come in through the MBA door, and she had won a prize. Thus began a subtle campaign of sabotage. Marianne gave no quarter. She gathered her team around her and told them this was an "us-versus-them" fight. The "them" were the other product managers. She ordered her staff to clear correspondence through her. She told them that they were not even to talk to people who worked for other managers and that if she heard of any socializing after work, she would find that most "displeasing."

Marianne moved from being a street fighter to being paranoid. She saw the enemy every place. The service groups became dens of conspiracy. Even the vice president could not be trusted. But it was only when she began to press the sales reps in the field to promote her product at the expense of other products they were selling that people finally took notice. The vice president called her in and asked her to explain her actions. Marianne went on the defensive and accused him and her other male colleagues of setting her up. The vice president became very quiet. Then he said, "I think you have forgotten who the real enemy is. If we are in a fight, it's a fight against our competition. The battle is not here." He then gave her a choice—look for another position internally or take a severance package. Her marketing career in this company was over.

Marianne was stunned. She had played the game. In fact, it was their game. It was the vice president who had set up a system that pitted product managers against one another. Now the system was turning on her. For Marianne, it was a confirmation of her suspicions that the game was rigged. And that she had been set up for failure.

DIAGNOSIS

Marianne was right about the path to fame and glory. Finance and marketing are often the fast track. In addition, she read the culture accurately. The competition inside was as fierce as it was outside. What she lost track of was why she was there. Once she moved from rough games to a siege mentality, she moved beyond what the culture sanctioned. She began to feed the monster instead of managing it. The fine line was crossed. And a system that had supported her now moved against her once that line was violated.

It's one thing to get into the rough-and-tumble and to give as good as you get. But when she moved into a "we-versus-they" approach, she went too far. As rough as the game was, it was still a game. Marianne would have been better served if she had put the game in its proper perspective. If the sabotage became too difficult, she needed to get some help. It was critical that she develop a decent working relationship with the vice president. Instead, she had avoided him and made him an enemy.

Marianne's greatest error was not building relationships within the department, regardless of the bias against MBAs or the resentment some of the product managers felt about her easy entry. Rather than become the dirtiest player, the challenge should have been to create alliances and relationships in a culture that didn't understand its own destructive dynamics. Marianne had the skills to go either way. She chose a lose-lose strategy.

RX

Her best bet now is to capitalize on her marketing experience, but she will probably need to find another company where her past does not label her. But most important, she needs to fine-tune her war games. It's easy to get hooked into a "we-against-they" attitude. The internal politics usually create a fertile growing ground for company war games. However, most seasoned warriors differentiate between the games (which are played passionately and with bloody relish) and all-out war that is reserved for competitors. While not everyone likes to mix it up as much as this group did, the competitive drive can take on a kind of corporate madness that distorts purpose and objectives. The danger is greatest for those who love to be king of the hill, the best, the greatest, who want to win the brass ring. For those people, the prize becomes the goal; they tend to lose track of what the game is all about. Their competitive spirit can become a destructive force that hurts them as well as the organization. So if you have begun to love the internal games and find yourself laying awake at night developing strategy, beware. You may have succumbed to mud wrestling madness—a virus that is both contagious and deadly.

Recognizing this within yourself is the most important first step. Until you understand who the real enemy is, you may put all your energy into fighting the wrong foe. Next, you need to take a cold, hard look at what type of relationships you are creating and how they are affecting the organization. Play the scene through to its end in your head. Where can this lead? Is it to an end that has negative consequences for you? You need—no matter what you think about this—you truly need support from others around you to succeed. That includes your boss, your peers, and your staff. Naivete or pride or an overblown self-image may blind you to this need, but you must not succumb to this distorted view. The ability to create alliances and be a team player (at least to give the appearance of being one) is critical if you are to be successful in your career.

The Do's and Don'ts of Company Politics

Political savvy will serve you well throughout your career. Here's how to get it:

The Do's

Do make time to get acquainted personally not only with your peer and support groups, but with the key people in management and executive positions. They need to know enough about you to trust you, feel that you are competent, and care about what happens to you.

Do learn how to persuade and influence people. You need to be able to sell your ideas and build support and alliances for your strategies and vision.

Do make a conscious effort to fit in the organization. If being a maverick or a "free spirit" is your "thing," keep it low-key. Unusual habits or attire only distract the very people you hope to impress or influence.

Do market yourself internally. Let people know what you've done and how you have helped the organization. If your boss has grabbed the credit for something you did, find a way to let key people know about your part in the achievement without making comments or accusations about your boss.

Do learn to be assertive without alienating people. But if you have to choose between being liked and being respected, go for respect. State your views and defend them. Remind your adversary that your position is not personal and has nothing to do with your working relationship. Make sure your own behavior reinforces what you have said about working together.

Do recognize that other people have their own agendas and that you must accommodate them if you are to gain their support and cooperation. For some, the agenda may be to get ahead; for others, it may be to gain power and control or to be recognized as the expert. Those agendas that appear to be self-serving should not be dismissed lightly or scoffed at. They are a reflection of deeply felt psychic needs and are powerful motivators of behavior. They cannot be wished away in the name of brotherhood, teamwork, or company mission.

Do take responsibility for your own mistakes. You give out three signals with such positive behavior: (1) I can make a mistake and still believe in myself, (2) you can make a mistake and it isn't fatal, and (3) we can survive our mistakes and continue to work together toward our goals.

Do identify the power centers in the organization by asking yourself whose opinion really matters. Find out what is going on, who is part of which formal and informal group, who is whispering in whose ear, and who knows important information that is not available through regular communication channels. This includes getting to know the support people who more often than not "know the score."

The Don'ts

Don't badmouth your boss or others in the workplace. The grapevine is one of the most powerful forms of communication. Unfortunately, it is often a source of gross distortion and misrepresentation. You can't control how you will be quoted, so keep your observations and feelings to yourself.

Don't let the whole world know when you are disappointed or when you feel the system or the boss has been unfair. How you handle disappointment is one of the yardsticks of maturity. Don't pout or start taking pot shots at management, seek revenge, or carry out minor sabotage. Ventilate somewhere (alone or with a trusted friend) and then get back to work and do the job—with dignity and with your mouth shut.

Don't hang around the company malcontents. They are looking for recruits to bolster their semisuicidal position, and it always reinforces their perception of reality if they can rope in new people. The danger is twofold for you: you will get labeled by the rest of the organization (and essentially cut out of the loop), and you may acquire their siege (us against them) mentality that can only end unhappily for all parties concerned.

Don't underestimate the power of coalitions or informal networks. And don't confront them on the basis of dearly held principles. You may be right, but if you are outnumbered, there goes the war. Instead, find out the common interests or ties of the group. Is this an "old boy" network? Do they have a common enemy and are they getting ready to overthrow someone? Are they taking care of each other's interests along with a lot of back scratching? You need to understand why they are getting together and what their common need is. And you have to find a way to help them meet their needs, or at least not threaten their interests. You might not like what they are all about, but unless you can enlist their support, you will probably be thwarted or effectively neutralized, or both.

Don't carry around your intellectual prowess as if it's a crown jewel that demands obeisance. If you're bright, it's a gift. Use it and enjoy your good fortune. But don't use your superior intelligence as a weapon to beat up on other people or to show your superiority. Remember that we all need to feel good about ourselves and that a

humiliated coworker or boss is a powerful force that may come back
to bite you.

WHEN YOUR GREATEST STRENGTH BECOMES YOUR GREATEST LIABILITY

Diana is an aggressive engineer who makes sure her projects are
done on time, on budget, and nothing and no one will get in the way.
Her diligence and persistence have always been cited as her
strengths; whenever there was a key project, she was made the
project leader to be sure it was done right. Her performance reviews
sang praises of her tenacity and commanding style.

Lately, however, her boss has been making some unusual comments. "Calm down, take it easy, be sure to take time to get the customer on board with your projects," he has warned. Finally, Diana
decided it was time to take the bull by the horns and find out what
was really going on.

In an intense meeting with her boss on the issue, Diana was
shocked to hear what he had to say. He told her that she is starting to
be a liability to the department because of the reputation she is
getting. The project engineers don't want to work with her due to
her argumentative style; she will lambast anyone who stands in the
way of what she wants to get done. Even the clients are losing sight
of the results, good as they are, because getting them is so painful
when working with Diana.

Shaking her head in disbelief, Diana said to her boss, "I don't get
it. My ability to get things done and push through the tough projects
has always been my greatest strength. You know what it takes to get
things done around here. I have been able to move mountains. Management has always known how I have dealt with tough clients and
coworkers who need to be pushed to be sure we make our deadlines.
How could this be coming back to me now?"

DIAGNOSIS

What has happened to Diana has derailed many careers. She has built
upon her strength and yet it has become her greatest weakness. What
was her shining glory is now haunting her and her department. Believe it or not, this is one of the most common causes for people to

fall off the track. The greatest irony is that management often creates these "monsters"—encouraging people to capitalize on a specific attribute. The problem is that it goes too far or the time comes when that mode of operating is no longer appropriate. This type of problem is most often related to interpersonal skills, although there are other areas in which your greatest strength exposes your greatest developmental need. When it is an interpersonal skill issue, the results of not being able to get along with others or effectively build a team will eventually have a negative effect on the department and its reputation. At that point, individuals become liabilities rather than the strong contributors they once were. Sometimes, as in Diana's case, it seems to occur almost overnight, but it usually is something that has been bubbling around and is now hitting the surface.

Rx _____

Diana is a bright woman and can recover from this, but she needs to turn around her behavior if she is to continue to progress in her company. If she doesn't, this is such a severe problem that it could lead to her demise. She needs to understand the effect her behavior is having on her coworkers and clients. *How* she obtains results has become as important as what the results are. This may be very difficult for her to buy into, but if she resists it and her manager's efforts to help her change, she will be missing an important opportunity for personal growth and development.

She might ask her boss for help in understanding how others perceive her. There are many ways to solicit that type of information, including using a third party to interview clients and coworkers, then feeding back the results to Diana. There are also feedback instruments and methodologies, where raters—including Diana's boss, peers, and staff—complete forms to evaluate her skills and competencies. She would get back the results in a summarized, confidential report. By collecting this information and putting her energies into working to improve her relationships with others, Diana should be able to put herself back on track. She will not only have to do some fence mending, but she will have to sustain her new behavior; the very tenacity that has moved her along this far should serve her well as she meets this new challenge.

Rules 1, 2, and 3:
The Customer Is the King

Art is a business analyst who provides support to one of his company's major marketing and sales regions. His responsibilities are to prepare monthly profit reports, analyze business expenses, and give advice on expenses to the marketing and sales management team. He has been in this job for two years and has established himself as reliable and accurate in the work he produces.

Lately, he is feeling uneasy. He had always been considered one of the top analysts, but Bruce, a newcomer to the department, seems to be getting glowing reports. Bruce had recently transferred from another group and now all Art seems to hear is that Bruce's clients adore him.

Art decides that competing against the new kid on the block will not get him anywhere—anyway, he is a known, and liked commodity, so why should he be nervous? Art does decide, though, that he will see if he can learn anything about the way Bruce works that could potentially be good for himself. He devises a strategy that will have him quietly take note of Bruce and his clients.

Bruce is hard to scrutinize—he is rarely in his office; he is usually down in his clients' area, meeting with them on their turf. On a ruse about some information Art keeps from Bruce, Art goes to find Bruce in the marketing bullpen. He finds Bruce working on a PC that he has been loaned by a product manager. Bruce is using the PC to run some of the customized reports he has developed for each of his major clients. He designed them to meet the clients' needs that are not met by the standard department reports.

Art takes note of Bruce's client interactions. His demeanor is friendly, helpful, and service-oriented. He spends a lot of time figuring out how the product managers use the information from the financial system, what decisions are affected by the data, and what are their wish lists. He has proposed several changes, and even if only one product manager was interested, he uses them as a pilot to see if there is value to the idea.

Diagnosis _____

Art sees that Bruce's key attribute is his client orientation. Bruce's approach to his work is to understand the clients' needs and build on those opportunities. In today's environment, your greatest contributions can come from stepping into your client's or customer's shoes and learning what will help them support the business better, faster, easier.

Your client is the person whom your job serves. It can be people inside the company or outside, depending on the focus of your role. Since client satisfaction will help determine if you are performing your job appropriately, it is to your advantage to find ways to improve the service you give your clients on an ongoing basis.

Rx

Art has always thought that if he upheld the financial integrity of his work, he would be performing at a high level. Given that he has a strong base to build on, if he changes his focus to more of a client orientation, he could greatly improve his effectiveness.

Art needs to spend more time with his clients, including doing an informal survey of their needs and wants. He should go to more meetings with them to understand their roles and how his job can best support their requirements. He also needs to get over the idea in his mind that, after two years, it will be difficult to change the relationships and expectations of his clients. To his surprise, he will find his clients very receptive to his new-found focus. Moreover, he will be able to enhance his relationships with the marketing and sales groups. Last, he won't need to keep looking over his shoulder at Bruce.

LEADERSHIP—
Walking Your Talk

Alicia is on her way to a team meeting to discuss how to position a product her company is going to market. The group that she represents, product promotion, will need to support the marketing efforts by deciding where and how the advertising will be placed to reach the audiences for this product. The members of the team represent all of the major functions.

Although the product manager who is leading this team has already sent out an agenda, Alicia is hoping that some key decisions will be made today because she has to meet printing and journal deadlines for advertising the new product. However, she didn't spend a lot of time preparing for the meeting since she figured most of the decisions would be made by the project team. During the meeting, there is lots of banter back and forth as the group runs through the agenda in rapid-fire manner. The team leader makes sure that his points are addressed and asks everyone if they think the project is on schedule; are there any glitches that anyone sees? Alicia mentions that if they don't resolve the positioning issue soon, and don't finalize the targeted audience, she will be in jeopardy of missing some key due dates. The product manager assures her that at the next meeting in two weeks, they will cover this issue, and she will be able to meet her deadlines—then he ends the meeting. As she walks out of the meeting, Alicia shudders to herself; she knows her boss will flip out when she tells him that the issue is not resolved yet because it means that the pressure on their department to meet their goals and deadlines will only get worse.

DIAGNOSIS

Alicia does not see that her job includes taking a leadership role around getting her project out on time. She did not do her homework and prepare effectively for the meeting. She missed a leadership opportunity because she did not set her own agenda in advance. If she had, she would have been able to strategize about how to be sure that her needs—and her department's—would be met. For starters, she needed to get her items on the agenda. Then she had to press for a decision. Instead, she took a passive role and let the opportunity to resolve the issues pass.

Unfortunately, most meeting participants go into a meeting with only a vague idea of what the meeting will cover. They assume that the group will come to some resolution of the issues through a discussion. Where you are willing to go along with the decisions of the group, that is not a problem. However, if you do not walk in with your own idea of what you want to get out of the meeting, you may get lost in the shuffle. Taking a leadership role includes taking an active role in meetings. Leadership means planning what you want—a decision or course of action—with specific ideas about which decision or course you want to achieve. Leadership may include working with a group to convince them to take your course of action. However, it is also appropriate to defer to the group's input, which, of course, may mean that the end result will be different. The trick is to not be dogmatic about your issues—unless it is absolutely critical to the success of the company. In that case, you will need to use all your influencing skills, regardless of your role or responsibilities. You should never walk into any meeting without a plan for what you want the results to be.

Rx

Alicia can take several actions if she wants to take on a leadership role to get what she needs from the next meeting. For starters, she should sit down with the product manager and be sure he understands the deadlines she is under and the negative effect it will have on the project if they don't get into the advertising cycle by the right date. From that discussion, she can build the product manager into the process, since he will now have a better understanding and even a vested interest in Alicia's deadlines. Leadership is a two-way street.

Alicia can also help move the discussions along by coming to the meeting with some of her own ideas about the product positioning. By adding to the discussion in an area that she has knowledge, she will be seen as a contributor with a broader sense of the project than just her own small piece of it. The ability to "bring something to the table" rather than care about only what you can take away will serve you well in your interactions within your organization. It is also a mark of leadership.

SELLING YOUR IDEAS

Gretchen is a bit of a maverick in her company. It is not that her organization is stodgy or wedded to how things got done in the good old days, but it is a conservative group. New ideas are measured against the "if-it-ain't-broke, don't-fix-it" theory. The company is meeting its financial goals and in general, things are stable. Gretchen always seems to be the one who is stirring things up. Two years ago she identified that there was a need for flex time and on-site day care. When she brought up the ideas at the division quarterly meeting, her idea was met with cold silence. Finally, one of the senior executives asked her where she obtained her data. That question cut off the discussion because as soon as Gretchen said it was anecdotal, he dismissed it out of hand. Anecdotal information doesn't cut it with this group.

Last year she tried another one. She had gone to a conference on career development and came back full of ideas about how such a program could be helpful to the company. Once again, she was shot down before she even got to explain the idea. "What makes you think we need it?" Boom. End of discussion.

This year she wanted to sell the company on using feedback reviews in all the first- and second-level management development programs. Now, however, she is going about it in a very different manner. She began by reading all the literature on the subject, including some of the early research on the technique that in this case supports the efficacy of using a review to improve managerial effectiveness.

One she felt confident about the development and use of feedback reviews, she identified some of the companies who were using it as a tool in their management development programs. She then interviewed them to find out how the process was working and what value it added.

Encouraged by what she heard, she then contacted some of the vendors who sold the review process to evaluate their effectiveness. Finally, she persuaded two managers to try using a feedback review with their subordinates to find out how they came across, what was working and what was not. The managers were surprised and supportive. Both told her they got information that they could not have gotten any other way. They heartily endorsed using feedback reviews in their management development program.

Armed with her information and hands-on experience, Gretchen began making the rounds. She met with every key person who would be in on the decision about whether to incorporate the new technique. Many were skeptical, although most agreed that the idea might have merit. Her last stop was at the office of the head of operations. Although this person did not have any more formal power than the other office heads, he had excellent relationships with the top brass. Once he blessed something, it was a go. Gretchen made her pitch and he bought in. She asked for a spot on the next quarterly management

What to Do When Making the Pitch

- Before presenting an idea, run it by someone who is in the know. Ask for their feedback. Get their help on developing a strategy for moving the idea forward.
- When you want to sell an idea or start a project, figure out who the key people are and involve them when the time is right.
- Keep your objectives aligned with the company's objectives. Better yet, tie your ideas to the bottom line.

  Learn when to fight and when to back off. Analyze your agenda in terms of "can drop," "nice to have," and "must have." Now you have a basis for negotiation.

- Ask people for their input and then listen. Don't focus on what you are going to say to argue back or rebut their ideas. But listen carefully to their needs, endorsements, objectives. Explore with them until you find common ground.
- When faced with resistance, get help from key people, including your manager.
- Make sure that your "win" isn't at the expense of others who will hold it against you.
- Never criticize people personally in public.
- If you must criticize, criticize ideas, not people and do it tactfully. Avoid making others lose face.
- Identify those who may, for whatever reason, try to sabotage your efforts. If possible, change the nature of your relationship with them. If they insist on remaining negative, neutralize them by surrounding yourself with supporters.
- Don't seek revenge when you have been done in. Stay on the high ground. What goes around, comes around.

meeting to present the idea. It went exactly as she hoped and planned. Everyone at the meeting already understood what she was trying to sell. The group entered into a lively discussion about the pros and cons, and in the end, they gave her the go-ahead to start the project.

Diagnosis

Gretchen at long last has learned what organization savvy means. After running into the brick wall a couple of times, she got smart and did her homework before she introduced a new idea. She also built the support she needed before she asked for a decision. The group was impressed with her knowledge. They particularly liked it that she had identified the best practices in other companies. That some of their competitors were using the review process made them sit up and take notice, a cue to Gretchen as to what to include in her strategy the next time she wanted to sell an idea.

Rx _____

If you want to be an agent of change, you need to lay the groundwork for your ideas. This means becoming an expert about the subject and being able to make your case with the key people before you ask them to make a decision about it. Gretchen's success lay in becoming savvy about how the process really worked and then discussing the idea ahead of time. Call it politics, if you will, but if you want to get your ideas accepted, you must do your homework that includes identifying where the power is in the decision-making process. Sometimes it includes knowing the hot buttons. In this case, the hot button was what the competition was doing. Gretchen was able to use that knowledge to gain a win for her project and herself.

THE PRIZES AND THE PRICES

Deborah had her sights set on a job in a high-tech industry. She had done her undergraduate work in a technical field; then she decided that marketing and sales was where the action was, so she took off another two years to get her MBA in marketing at one of the country's top business schools. Job offers were plentiful the year she graduated. She finally settled on a position at one of the nation's largest software manufacturers because she was attracted to its youthful spirit. Deborah was immediately drawn'into the excitement of the work. It was challenging, results were measurable, and the group she worked with were real go-getters. It was also a party crowd. After hours the group would consort into the wee hours of the morning. Three or four hours of sleep and everyone was back in the office bright-eyed and bushy-tailed, ready for another go at it.

It was more than Deborah had hoped for. What's more, she discovered she was one of the outstanding players. Her ideas worked. She was able to influence how things got done. People liked working with her. Two years into the job, she was offered a project of her own to run. Her boss told her that if she kept going the way she was, she would be on the high-potential list.

A year later, she was given another promotion. This time she was transferred to another division to head up the product promotion for an important product line. The market was very competitive, which Deborah liked. Now she could really make an impact. She met with her new team and went through the customary team-building vision exercises. People seemed to respond. There were a few nay-sayers in the group who didn't seem to want to get on board with her style of management, who didn't like her direct, aggressive style. Deborah worked with them continually to try to enlist their participation, but their levels of drive and motivation frustrated her.

She noted that as she moved up in the organization, she became more isolated from her staff. They would sometimes invite her out for drinks after work, but she knew from office talk that the group often partied after work and she wasn't invited. As a result, she sometimes missed the old days.

Deborah was very successful and her group's results brought with them accolades and public recognition. She got used to the congratulations, but once in a while she would pick up signals that told her some of the compliments were not authentic, especially from several of her peers from the early days. Six months ago the president of the company called her into his office and asked Deborah to head up a special task force focused on cleaning up how the company did business overseas. He felt there was a lot of waste and that people were not pulling their weight. He wanted her to assess the situation and give him recommendations.

Suddenly, Deborah's power increased exponentially. This time she would be reporting directly to the president. What an opportunity! But again, she saw people pulling back from her. They didn't treat her like one of the crowd. Conversation was more guarded. She wasn't invited to the informal beer parties after work on Fridays anymore.

Three days ago she overhead a conversation in the rest room. At first she ignored what the two women were talking about. But suddenly she heard her name mentioned and realized they were talking about her. The conversation was wicked. She heard herself described as someone who would do anything to get ahead, including stabbing her friends in the back. She also heard herself described as a real "buster" in terms of how she gave performance reviews. Now Deborah understands the price she is paying for her success. She knows the gossip about her is probably sour grapes, but it hurts just the same.

DIAGNOSIS

Success always has its price. Many people not only envy Deborah, but they now fear her. She is very talented. She is headed for the big time, and she has the president's ear. She has worked to get to where she is. But that doesn't mean that everyone in her company wishes her well. In fact, she has in all probability made a few enemies along the way, wittingly or unwittingly.

Deborah feels hurt that her successes have isolated her from the rest of her old buddies. She always thought that people understood what competition was all about. If she chose to work very hard and to give up a great deal of her personal life to get ahead, that was her business. But she is puzzled over the cold shoulder treatment.

Rx

Deborah is learning one of the great truths of company life. The higher you go, the lonelier it gets. The road to riches and glory is traveled by many, but only a few actually get the prize. It is human nature for the "wanna-be's" to feel envy. Deborah has no doubt stepped on a few toes along the way. Although she has tried to build good working relationships, there is no way she has been able to make everyone happy or even like her.

If she has created enemies, her best bet is to first consider the source. If someone is envious of her success, there is little she can do about it. If she has hurt someone's career in her role as manager, she will need to assess the situation. Is this person likely to be vengeful? Does this person carry a grudge? Is there any way this person can get to her?

She also needs to be sensitive to those coworkers who competed for the prize. She needs to do what she can to maintain those relationships—including taking an interest in their careers if appropriate.

In the end, however, she will have to accept the fact that not everyone loves a winner. She may lose old friends along the way. That is part of the price. She may even have made enemies that is also part of the price. It is important that she doesn't take responsibility for other people's failure to attain their goals. She has played the game as well as she could and she is winning. Her best bet is to stay focused on her work, do the best she can in handling the disappointed also-rans and get on with her success.

BUSINESS ACUMEN:
How to Get It, How to Use It

Kendall has a great track record in her career. She has advanced up the line fairly quickly and is now the head of administration in her company. One of her greatest strengths has always been her ability to understand the business, the competition, and how her departments can contribute to the bottom line.

From the beginning of her life in this company, Kendall has been a student of the organization. She studies the industry carefully—she even sat in on several sales training programs to help her understand the issues at the front line and to find out what's important to know about the competition. She voraciously reads her *Wall Street Journal* and *Business Week,* looking for articles about her company and its competitors. She always starts conversations with managers from other units with "What's happening in your area this week?" Because she can intelligently ask questions and discuss issues with a strong base of knowledge, she is able to elicit valuable information from others.

The real key to Kendall's success is the way she integrates her business knowledge with her department's goals and activities. When she knows there is an important management meeting in marketing, she sends in her top graphics specialist to help with the executive presentation. When the product oversight committee meeting is one week away, she meets with the research staff to see if they need any more support for their proposals. When she read of a new computer modeling capability, she met with the head of the finance group to see if there would be a need for the system's capability.

Each of her clients values Kendall's knowledge because she translates it to make her group contribute to the company's success. If it's not in line with a current management or organizational priority, Kendall does not waste her time—or her staff's—putting energy into activities that don't support the business.

DIAGNOSIS _____

The ability to understand the organization's priorities and how your work fits with them is critical to your success. In this difficult world of too much work to do and not enough resources (time, staff, money) to get it done, you will be getting (and giving) more "bang for the buck" if your activities are tied to the organization's needs.

Every successful employee sees himself or herself as a business-oriented person. The more you understand your company's business environment and competition, the integration of your work and value that it adds will be enhanced.

RX _____

You can strengthen your knowledge thorough networking, reading, and studying. Here's how:

- Learn your company's history; then extend that learning to include the history of its competitors.
- Hone in on the events that changed the course of these histories. Who did what when? What events caused what? Which projects advanced the cause? What actions were brilliant and which ones were disastrous?
- Examine the organization chart to find who is doing what; then analyze it in terms of who has what kind of power. Who is tight with whom? Which departments are working well? Which are not and why? The idea is to formulate a picture of your organization that encompasses the whole scene, not just your little corner.
- Read, read, and then read more. A great deal of information you need to know about corporate life is revealed in newspapers and magazines. The daily business events as they unfold are a textbook unto themselves. Add books and conferences to that and you will begin to develop a deeper understanding of what is going on and why.
- Talk to salespeople. Listen to their experiences from the front lines. They can tell you how it is. Because they have to deal with the bottom line, you are more likely to get straight stuff without the public relations spin.
- Study finance and accounting. Learn to talk the language of the business.
- Get to know the decision makers or the smarts behind the scene.

- Get in on or organize those informal "bull" sessions that are always rich with unpublished but critical information.
- Learn everything you can about all functions. If that means having lunch with someone from information systems, do it. Be open about your objective, which is to understand as much as you can how the organization operates. Most coworkers will be glad to share their stories with you.
- Get involved. Gain access to the relationships and knowledge of the inner circles. Join task forces, sit in on meetings where your presence is not a threat, get to know the people who are moving and shaking things, volunteer for extracurricular affairs just as in the old college days. It is as good now as it was then.
- Think carefully about how your group, project, or idea impacts other groups or individuals in the organization. Find out who has a stake in the outcome. Get their input and, if possible, their support.
- Develop as wide a network as you can given where you are in the organization and the time you have available. The point is: Never let your job limit your contacts. Make it happen if it does not naturally occur as a part of your routine interactions.
- Develop a passion for how your organization can come out on top. Once you have that vision, pull out all the stops. If you are going to give so much of your precious time to this enterprise, be sure you're contributing in a way that pushes the organization forward.

PROMOTING YOUR CAREER HEALTH—
Corporate Street Smarts

The more you know about yourself, your company, and today's workplace, the greater your chances for career success. Your ability to fit into your company's culture, carry yourself as a key player, and bring something significant to the party will assure your success—today and tomorrow.

Things You Need to Master

- How to market yourself
- How to create teams and alliances
- How to interact at all levels within your organization (as well as externally)
- How to concentrate on the concerns/needs of the organization
- How to be highly competitive without stepping on others
- How to outperform your peers

- How to influence and motivate others
- How to think conceptually, how to think big
- How to function in an ambiguous environment

Barriers to Success

- Putting your agenda before the organization's
- Being too focused on tasks; not building relationships around you
- Wanting to have every little fact before making a decision
- Ineffective management skills
- Exaggerated self-assessment

Payoff for You and Your Career

- Ongoing opportunities for growth
- Rewards: status, perquisites, recognition
- Chance to impact the organization
- Being where the action is
- High levels of personal satisfaction

MASTER YOUR CAREER

How to Make the Prescription Work for You

Through reading this book, you have learned a great deal about the kinds of things people do to shoot themselves in the foot. You probably identified many, if not most, of the self-defeating behaviors in the stories. You may have even spotted people in the stories who closely resemble people you know. Certainly you recognized some of the scenarios as similar to some things you have witnessed or experienced. So far, so good. Your awareness of self-sabotaging behavior has just shot up 50 points. The big question now is *What can you do about the sabotage you may be bringing to your own career?*

THREE-STEP PRESCRIPTION FOR CHANGE

What follows is a step-by-step program for helping you change your behavior.

Step 1: Recognize that everyone who has ever lived has in some way or another sabotaged themselves. Our ancestors did. Our grand-

parents did. Our parents did. Everyone who has or is presently working in the business world, in all probability, has sabotaged themselves
at one time or another.

As human beings, we are on a continuous development curve
from the moment we are born until the day we die. Learning how to
identify and change our self-sabotaging behaviors is a critical part of
our development. Therefore, all of us have work to do on ourselves. It
is time to begin this journey.

Step 2: Identify those behaviors that have the potential to get
you in the most trouble (or already have). This is not the time to do a
total makeover on yourself. All you want and need to do is determine
the behaviors that are most critical to your career. Keep your list to
two or three, at most.

You may already have begun that process just by reading through
the different scenarios and noting which ones sound like things you
do or have done. If you were not able to relate to any of the charac-
ters, try reading through the list of self-sabotaging behaviors listed in
the appendix. Check off those behaviors that might be the ones you
need to address.

If light bulbs still have not gone off, try this: Think about a time at
work when you felt uncomfortable about your own behavior, but
didn't reflect on it afterwards.

For example, you are in a meeting. You have developed a great
idea about how to reach more customers. Your idea is a good one—it
could change how the company does business. You can't wait to tell
everyone about it. When you get your chance at the meeting, you lay
it out. Your adrenalin is pumping; you are really excited. But you
hardly get the words out of your mouth before people start attacking
you. A few mutter something about it being a really dumb idea.
George over in the corner calls out, "We tried that four years ago and
it bombed." Louise, your arch rival for the next promotion, asks very
sarcastically if you ran your idea past the boss before you presented it.
Someone else says something about how much all of this will cost.

In order to counter all the resistance, you remind the group that
their success depends on increasing sales and it behooves them to be
open to new ways of doing things. You plunge again into a lengthy
description of your idea and why it will work, but the body language
around the table tells you that no one is really supporting you. You
feel defeated and angry at the end of the meeting and you will walk
out alone. You have already identified two people who will never get

your support for anything they need. Louise and George. You also decide that it will be a cold day in July before you go out on the limb again for this company.

Now imagine that this whole scene was recorded and that you can review the video and watch yourself on the screen. What did you do that might be self sabotaging? Watch the scene carefully. You walked in full of ideas. You dumped it on a group of people who were not receptive. When you hit resistance, you came at them even harder. When you were shot down, you sulked and planned revenge. Note what didn't happen. You did not sell your idea. In fact, you have lost ground.

What went wrong? For starters, you were so full of enthusiasm that you neglected to lay the groundwork for introducing your new idea. Savvy professionals know that new ideas always meet resistance. They develop a strategy for gaining acceptance by enlisting key people ahead of time ("just want to run this past you"), by doing the homework around numbers that will impress the finance types and by building a case for their idea that is based on more than just their own intuition and enthusiasm. When they present an idea, they purposefully draw out their colleagues on what they are thinking and why they see things the way they do. If the idea doesn't fly the first time, they figure out who can help champion it and who needs to be at least neutralized. They do not take opposition personally, even when it is personal (Louise, case in point). They understand that it's all part of the game.

Let's try another one. Your manager has given you a so-so performance review. She appeared to support you in general, but you took some hits in a number of areas. She says that although you have been in this job for about a year, you have not developed the level of expertise that she thinks you should have. She also says you aren't coming across well with upper management—they are not very impressed with you. She tells you that you have to do something about the problem or your career will be limited.

You are very upset with what she is telling you and take the offensive. You ask her which executives (naturally she will not tell you) and you reel off a list of all of your accomplishments to show how much you have learned. You also challenge her on her right to judge your expertise since she is still new to the area. You leave the meeting feeling very angry.

Now you suspect every executive you meet is one of those who doesn't think much of you. Who could it be? Suddenly your world is filled with potential enemies. Even the boss seems to have turned against you. You start trying to figure out what each person's secret agenda must be that they would go after you like this. Your boss is an easy target; she "feels threatened by you." You know more than she does even if she doesn't admit it. She needs a scapegoat to cover up her deficiencies. As for the executives, what do they know? They couldn't punch their way out of a paper bag. And so it goes.

We do not have to run the video again to see what the self-sabotaging behaviors are in this scenario. However, if this were really your story, you may have a hard time spotting your own self-defeating behaviors because you are so close to it all. What's more, your boss has put you on the defensive and you are probably reacting emotionally instead of objectively. You may be blindsided by your own defensiveness.

The key is learning to identify where and why your behavior does not serve you well and how you can change that to be sure you are doing yourself—and your image—the most good.

That brings us to one other way for you to get a handle on what you may be doing that is hurting your career. *Ask for feedback.* Ideally, you will include your boss in your list of people to provide you input. At the minimum, you should include one or two of your trusted colleagues and clients. Friends and astute family members may also be helpful.

Asking for feedback takes courage. It is difficult to do, but those who can get up the gumption to ask will learn vital information about themselves. It is the kind of information that money can't buy, yet it may give you what you need in order to achieve a true breakthrough in your development.

Step 3: Now that you have identified what you may be doing that is sabotaging yourself, you need to develop a plan for fixing the problems. You can do three things about self-sabotaging behaviors:

1. Change the behavior.
2. Eliminate the behavior.
3. Learn a new behavior that is more effective.

How to Change a Behavior

Let's imagine we are watching the video again. You are on camera and you have just done "it" again. You're in your office. Someone interrupted you while you were deep into working with your computer. You looked up, said something curt and went back to your work. You might be asking, "So what?" How else do you handle it when someone is rude enough to interrupt what you are doing? Now put the video in reverse and go back to the part where you look up and said to the person who intruded on you, "You're interrupting me; it will have to wait." Note the effect your response has on the other person. Recognize that your ability to interact effectively with others is an important skill.

In this case, you can isolate the issue to see that the behavior that needs to change is how you handle interruptions. Instead of saying what you did, you could put a more user-friendly expression on your face and say "I'm really busy, can it wait?" So simple, yet so different. And so much more effective. You have just changed your behavior from being a curt, abrasive employee to that of a friendly, polite colleague.

Changing a behavior begins with identifying the exact actions and words that need to be changed. It is as simple as that. Notice that we didn't tell you to learn to love intrusions. All we suggested is that you change how you handle them when they happen.

To change a behavior, identify what you need to change and develop a better way of behaving. It will take discipline to stay with your plan, but the payoff will be worth it.

How to Eliminate a Behavior

Eliminating a behavior means that you stop doing it, period. Easier said than done, however. Let's go back to the video to see how it works. You are on camera again. The scene is your office. One of your colleagues has just come back from a conference on how to change organizations. He is bursting with ideas and wants to share everything he learned with you. You have been down this path before, so you are highly skeptical about the prospects of really making change in this place. In fact you are skeptical about most new ideas. You have been accused of being too negative, of always looking on the down side. However, for you the cup is half empty, not half full. That is how you see life and to you, it is a realistic assessment. Basically you doubt that many things will turn out well or work or succeed. You see your tasks as needing to hold the line on people by pointing out to them all the possible dangers.

Here you go again. You see yourself telling your colleague how hopeless things are and how he should not get so excited about what he learned, that no one will listen to him anyway. Did you see what happened? Did you see how negative you were? Did you see how your colleague left your office looking depressed and demoralized? Did you see how you totally ignored the effect you had on him and turned back to your desk without reflecting on what just happened?

Up to now, you may have been rationalizing to yourself your negativity based on your experience in life. But as a behavior, it is dangerously self-sabotaging. It has to go. You may not be able to turn into Ms. or Mr. Merry Sunshine, but you must stop reacting negatively to other people's ideas. If you can do no more than shut your mouth, then do it. That eliminates the behavior. It is as simple as that. You just need to work on it. It may take post-it notes, a friend cuing you, or other continual reminders, but you can do it. You can eliminate a behavior when you realize what a negative effect it will have for you if you do not.

How to Learn a New, More Effective, Behavior

We are moving up the learning curve. Modifying or eliminating a behavior is relatively easy. Learning a new one is not. Let's put some-one else on camera this time. You can act as coach while you watch an imagined colleague learn a new behavior.

We are going to watch Alex in one of his self-sabotaging scenes. Alex has just found out that he has to leave Sunday for a trip to Dallas. Weekends mean a lot to Alex. He hates giving up family time to the company. For Alex, it's just one more example of how lousy this company is run. So Alex lets loose. He walks out of his office storm-ing. The first person who gets in his range gets it with all barrels. Unfortunately for his secretary, she is in his line of fire. He yells at her for not having all of his correspondence on his desk by 8:00 a.m. Then as he heads for the rest room, he runs into Harry, whom Alex promptly pins against the wall in order to describe what a screwed-up company this is. Now Alex is working himself into a real

Next he heads for his manager's office to tell her how he feels about Sunday trips. The boss is busy with someone, so Alex has to wait. This makes him even angrier.

Do we need to go on? You can diagnose Alex's problem in the first minute of the video. Alex does not handle anger well. He does not know how to deal with it when he gets mad.

Now, you the coach need to help Alex learn a new way to deal with anger. What might you say to him, assuming that Alex admits it is a self-sabotaging behavior?

As coach, you would probably start with helping Alex to talk about his anger. You may ask him to describe what goes through his mind when he gets mad. By helping Alex watch how he builds on his own anger, you have helped him see the point in the process where he needs to change his response. You do not advise Alex not to feel angry, you teach him a way to stop his anger from becoming uncontrollable.

You suggest he try a couple of different approaches. One is to commit himself to counting to ten and then ten again and to keep counting on until he is past his crisis point. Only then will he be able to respond less emotionally to what is happening. You also suggest Alex do a little introspection about why he pops off so easily. Alex may develop some insight about what his hot buttons are.

You might even suggest that you and Alex rehearse better ways to deal with situations. You could role-play the new Alex explaining to his boss in a calm and rational manner why flying out on Sundays is so hard on his family. You role-play includes Alex negotiating with his boss on how to avoid Sunday travel unless it is vital to the company's interest. What you have just done is teach Alex how to get the results he wants without losing his temper and inflicting damage on himself.

People who lose their temper usually go through a period of building up for the big blast. Learning how to change his thinking when he is angry and how his own thought process is part of the problem may be helpful if Alex is insightful enough to understand what you are telling him.

You may not have Alex's problem, but the process is the same. You coach yourself or get help from a friend on how to develop and reinforce the new behavior you need to learn.

Step 4: It's now time to pull this all together. You have identified the two or three most important self-sabotaging behaviors. You know that you can do one of three things about a specific behavior. You can change it, eliminate it, or learn a new behavior. Now it's time to go to work on yourself.

Using the worksheets in the appendix, begin by listing the two or three behaviors you have targeted for change. Next write a brief description about what you see yourself doing in each behavior. This step is important because you need to document your sabotaging moments in order to plan your next moves.

Read through your description on how you sabotaged yourself. You may have a couple of scenes that you can review so that you begin to see patterns in your behavior. Analyze those scenes. What was going on? Who was with you? What was the significance of either the situation or the person? Examine how you behaved. Look for the moment when you began to exhibit the self-defeating behavior. Red-circle that point once you have identified it.

Now, look at the behavior you want to change and decide whether you can modify the behavior, need to eliminate it or have to learn a new behavior. You may need to talk to a trusted other on this part if you are not sure how to proceed.

Once you have decided which approach you need to take, develop a plan for changing your behavior. If you need to modify your behavior, think of how you might handle yourself differently without doing major surgery. Write down your ideas. Choose one of the approaches as a test pilot. The next time you get into a situation where you are in danger of repeating that old behavior, try out your plan. See what happens. If the world does not turn somersaults over how you've changed, do not be discouraged. Remember, you have a track record around the old behavior. It's going to take a while for people to get used to the new you.

If you need to eliminate a behavior, your plan needs to include how you might reward yourself each time you succeed. For example, if you can go one week without falling back on your old bad habit, do something for yourself, whether it be a great lunch, a gift to yourself that says you did it, etc. By rewarding yourself, you will be reinforcing the change.

Eliminating a behavior and rewarding yourself when you do is not unlike the way you may have helped a child grow up. When they were "good" they got a treat. It works for adults just as well. It may sound a little strange, but you can actually strengthen your ability to deal with sabotaging behavior through positive and negative reinforcement.

If you need to learn a new behavior, you may need to get some help from someone who is doing it right. For example, if you need to develop more effective interpersonal skills, begin by observing those people who seem to have that magic touch. How do they enter a room? What do they do? What do they say? What you will discover is that there are a number of discrete behaviors that, when put together, comprise good interpersonal skills.

You will not be ready at the beginning to do all of them at once. Learning interpersonal skills is like learning how to ride a bike or play a good game of golf. You first master the individual behaviors, then you begin to put them together. For example, people who have well-developed interpersonal skills usually greet everyone when they enter a room. They find ways to say something to each individual, looking them in the eye or at a minimum, just making eye contact. They usually have a friendly expression on their faces. If this was an area you were working on, you could begin your learning by emulating the behaviors we just described. If you can learn how to enter a room and make a friendly contact with everyone there, you are on your way.

GETTING STARTED:
Your Personal Career Prescription

We have included some worksheets in the appendix that you can use to record your plans. You will note that the worksheets take you step by step through the process we outlined for you in this chapter. We strongly encourage you to start immediately on developing a plan. It may mean just jotting down some preliminary thoughts. This is a case of you striking while your own fires are hot. If you close the book, lay it down and allow your resolve to change or weaken, you may let the golden moment of opportunity pass, which means you would miss the chance to become the master.

Think of this book as one of your coaches. We will begin by reminding you that the reason you read this book must have had something to do with you and your career. You know how difficult it is to manage a career in today's world. You may want some help with your personal issues. We all know that the race is a tough one. Our opening story about the two sailors what a metaphor for how you need to learn not only the basics, but to become a master.

Ridding yourself of self-defeating behavior is a key to that mastery. Developing mastery may not be as much fun as learning how to golf or learning a new technology. In fact, it may not be fun at all. But it is vital if you are to be successful. It will also be very satisfying. Take the plunge. Commit to identifying those behaviors which may be getting in your way and commit to doing something about them. Then honor your commitment. It is a commitment you make to yourself and your career.

Develop your own prescription for success. Become the savvy corporate player, maximize your career potential and be the master of your own future. Here's to your health!

APPENDIX

ACTION PLAN
Correcting Your Self-Sabotaging Behaviors

Behavior:

Describe in detail two incidents which demonstrate you self-sabotaging yourself:

1. _____

_____

_____

_____

_____

2. _____

_____

_____

_____

_____

Check which action is most appropriate to changing this behavior:

       _____ Modify it

       _____ Eliminate it

       _____ Learn a new behavior that is more effective

Describe how you might work on this behavior:

_____

_____

_____

Develop an action plan for modifying, eliminating this behavior, or for learning a new behavior that is more effective.

_____

_____

_____

_____

ACTION PLAN
Correcting Your Self-Sabotaging Behaviors

Behavior:

Describe in detail two incidents which demonstrate you self-sabotaging yourself:

1. _____

_____

_____

_____

_____

2. _____

_____

_____

_____

_____

Check which action is most appropriate to changing this behavior:
    _____ Modify it
    _____ Eliminate it
    _____ Learn a new behavior that is more effective

Describe how you might work on this behavior:

_____

_____

_____

_____

Develop an action plan for modifying, eliminating this behavior, or for learning a new behavior that is more effective.

_____

_____

_____

_____

_____

ACTION PLAN
Correcting Your Self-Sabotaging Behaviors

Behavior:

Describe in detail two incidents which demonstrate you self-sabotaging yourself:

1. _____

_____

_____

_____

_____

2. _____

_____

_____

_____

_____

Check which action is most appropriate to changing this behavior:

_____ Modify it

_____ Eliminate it

_____ Learn a new behavior that is more effective

Describe how you might work on this behavior:

_____

_____

_____

_____

Develop an action plan for modifying, eliminating this behavior, or for learning a new behavior that is more effective.

_____

_____

_____

_____

_____

_____

APPENDIX

IDENTIFYING SELF-SABOTAGING BEHAVIORS

Check those behaviors that may be related to difficulties you are having or have had in your job. Then use this with the ACTION PLAN section of the appendix.

_____ Being abrupt or abrasive
_____ Easily distracted, lose focus
_____ Worry about the smallest details
_____ Have problems taking orders from manager
_____ Disorganized
_____ Unable to handle frustration well
_____ Don't relate well to co-workers
_____ Collapse under pressure
_____ Do not understand or really hear what others are saying
_____ Do not feel like competing
_____ Feel like you have to compete with everyone all the time
_____ Easily bored
_____ Unable to make quick decisions
_____ Dislike technology
_____ Fascinated with technology and spend too much time on it
_____ Fear making mistakes
_____ Do not like taking responsibility
_____ Unable to see self objectively
_____ Give too much of yourself away
_____ Hardhearted
_____ Feel like a victim of the system
_____ React too quickly
_____ Too emotional
_____ Too shy
_____ Consumed by jealousy
_____ Can't keep a confidence
_____ Overly critical of others
_____ Can't stay focused for more than a few minutes
_____ Can't make small talk
_____ Can't play politics so ignore them
_____ Need instant feedback or reward
_____ Not disciplined

_____ Hate change and fight it

_____ A rebel

_____ Sarcastic with co-workers

_____ Sarcastic with boss

_____ Doubt self too much

_____ Think others are out to get you

_____ Too talkative

_____ Too quiet

_____ Overly pessimistic

_____ Short-tempered

_____ Can't forgive or forget

_____ Too submissive

_____ Avoid conflict at all costs

_____ Love conflict, try to create it for fun

_____ Take things too personally

_____ Constantly remind yourself how you have been wronged

_____ Little or no sense of humor

_____ Self-centered to the point where others see it too

_____ Touchy, lots of hot buttons

_____ Criticize others but cannot take it yourself

_____ Tense most of the time

_____ Work way too hard

_____ Are unrealistic about what you expect of yourself

_____ Too casual about physical appearance

_____ Not really motivated to work, period

_____ Sloppy

_____ Stingy

_____ Tend to take the path of least resistance

_____ Secretly a snob

_____ Question everything and everybody

_____ Too nosy about other people's business

_____ Are unaware of how you are seen by others

_____ Impatient

_____ Cannot prioritize work

_____ Poor communications skills

_____ Poor interpersonal skills

_____ Cannot make a group work as a team

_____ Not trustworthy

_____ Not reliable

_____ Rumormonger

ABOUT THE AUTHORS

Dr. Anne Lovett is President of Lovett & Associates, a firm that specializes in working with companies in human resource development. Her particular interests include corporate career development, executive counseling and coaching, and developing learning organizations.

She is a graduate of Columbia University where she was Director of Development of the R&D Center for Life Skills and Human Resources. She is a former member of the faculty of the Social, Counseling, and Organizational Department at Columbia University. Dr. Lovett is author of numerous publications and training programs. A licensed psychologist, Dr. Lovett maintains a limited practice in addition to her business consulting.

Jill Searing has significant experience with career development issues. She has managed career development programs and has worked in the areas of employee and management development, organizational development, and managing high potential employees.

Ms. Searing has held human resources positions in the insurance and electronics industry and is currently working in the healthcare industry. She teaches management courses at the undergraduate level. She is Past President of the Northern New Jersey chapter of the International Association for Personnel Women and has served on non-profit boards of directors.

FOR MORE INFORMATION

If you would like more information about career development programs or services, please contact us at Lovett and Associates, Seven Union Place, Summit, NJ 07901.

INDEX

T

U

V

W